MW01227326

A QUEER INCUBATOR OF COURAGE, RESILIENCE AND INTERIOR DESIGN LEADERSHIP

UNMASKING OF OUR

INTERIORS

MICHAEL PLASSE-TAYLOR

 FriesenPress

One Printers Way
Altona, MB R0G 0B0
Canada

www.friesenpress.com

ISBN
978-1-03-912307-6 (Hardcover)
978-1-03-912306-9 (Paperback)
978-1-03-912308-3 (eBook)

1. BIOGRAPHY & AUTOBIOGRAPHY, PERSONAL MEMOIRS

Distributed to the trade by The Ingram Book Company

"Michael and I were teaching colleagues at Ryerson's School of Interior Design for over ten years. Although I have considered him to be a dear friend for more than twenty years, I now realize that I hadn't really known much about Michael's inner self. I always admired his many strengths as a professor, including the thorough research, organization, and timely preparation of his studio projects; the richness of diversity that he brought to the students through project design, guest speakers, and mentors, particularly as it applied to the needs of the Queer population; and his demand for professionalism from the students, perfected in his years in interior design practice. Michael fostered outstanding communication skills in his students, was intolerant of students who attended his classes unprepared for the expectations of the prescribed course schedule and was dedicated to exposing his students to a rich variety of highly respected practicing interior designers. It wasn't until I read *Unmasking of Our Interiors* that I understood how an incredible life journey, from birth to retirement, moulded Michael into the person that he is. The strength and determination that he has demonstrated in the face of adversity, all the while maintaining a wicked sense of humour, are truly inspiring."

Arlene Dougall **ARIDO, NCIDQ** (three-term board member), past CIDA
team chair

"Michael was a tireless advocate for his students and identified the potential in each one of them. They were never expected to fit a mould, rather he moulded his teachings to their individual strengths. Students working with Michael felt loved and accepted from which confidence grew. His legacy is one of design excellence and empathy—and students looked no further than Michael as his example."

Annie Bergeron, **GENSLER** Design Principal/Industry Reviewer,
Toronto, Ontario

"I first met Professor Michael Plasse-Taylor in 1999 when he joined Ryerson University. He was a fresh breath of air and brought to the School of Interior Design a more progressive teaching style along with his positive persona. His unique teaching style, with an emphasis on explorations and out-of-box thinking, have influenced my design thinking process. Many teachers come and go in your lifetime, but Professor Michael's impact will live on with me.

As a guest industry reviewer to his upper-level design studios, I have witnessed Michael's passion in guiding his young students to develop critical design fundamentals into transformational creative design development. As an alumnus, he has always encouraged me to build on our existing body of knowledge and inspire design growth in professional practice and interior design leadership."

Shannon Kim, **DESIGN CITIZEN** Chief Creative Officer/Managing Principal, Toronto

"Professor Plasse-Taylor's teachings have had a profound impact on my personal journey. Over the years, I vividly recall specific lessons, conversations, and guidance that led me on my path of success. His passion for creative excellence and his ability to identify my unique strengths allowed me to flourish as a student and pursue a fulfilling career across the globe. He equipped me with the fundamental tools to achieve aesthetic success in my creations and to think empathetically—with a human centric mindset. My understanding of the critical details that make an interior remarkable are a direct credit to his influence on my strategic-thinking abilities."

Carla Conte, **BRAND CREATIVE** Founder & Creative Director, Dubai, and India

"Professor Michael was my teacher, mentor, and colleague at Ryerson University. He taught me about great design, but more importantly he instilled in me a way of thinking: *Interior design holds the power to bring about positive change, so approach it with empathy and compassion.* Michael possesses a great sense of humour, and he has never shied away from difficult topics. He speaks openly and candidly about discrimination issues and has promoted diversity, equity, and inclusion long before it became mainstream on social media. He is an advocate and an ally to visual minorities, like me. He encouraged me when I lacked confidence, and he believed in me and pushed me to do better and better. I wouldn't be where I am today without his guidance and support. Furthermore, he inspired me to pay his kindness forward to those whom I interact with in my work and in my teaching. I owe it all to my dear friend, Michael; to his generosity and to his wisdom."

Winnie Leung, **INDIGO** Manager of Store Design, Toronto

"Professor Michael Plasse-Taylor was an inspirational and constructive mentor to his students, and his teaching systems led to the success of several students, including myself. He demonstrated his passion for design education through mindful and curated teaching practices with his students. He ensured that students who participated in his studio received additional valuable feedback on their projects from top-tier industry design leaders. Michael's commitment and contribution to educating the next generation of designers has inspired me to do the same."

Eric Truong, **ELASTIC INTERIORS**, Senior Designer LEED AP ID+C, UK

"You wanted to go to university, and since I had loved those years of my life, I wanted you to have the opportunity. You and I share the capacity to focus totally on our studies and the drive to succeed so we had careers in education. You later went onto graduate studies at Pratt Institute by winning a coveted Canadian award (Joan Harland scholarship for graduate studies). You did so well, and I was delighted to hear it."

Janet Sheffield, **YOUTH MENTOR and FRIEND** from 1972 – present, Toronto, Ontario

"Michael had asked me to write a few words about his involvement with *Buddies in Bad Times Theatre* during his time as a professor at Ryerson. As a long-time employee at the theatre, I watched as he created a new and thoughtful reality for his students by introducing them to Buddies and the cutting-edge queer theatre we were producing. As well, he was trying to create a safe bubble for those amongst his students who were exploring what queer was for themselves and the world they were about to enter. Important stuff done at a pivotal time."

Patricia Wilson, **BUDDIES IN BAD TIMES THEATRE**

TABLE OF CONTENTS

ACKNOWLEDGEMENTS   ix

INTRODUCTION   xiii

1   My Unlikely Debut   1

2   Early Life on Skid Row   11

3   Fall From Grace!   31

4   Sissy-Boy   49

5   Granny's Clutch   63

6   First Love   73

7   Surviving Cabbagetown   79

8   Jarvis Collegiate   93

9   Acceptance   103

10   Out At York University   121

11   Academic Break   147

12   University of Manitoba   163

13   Pratt Institute   185

14   Swanke   201

15   Partisan Politics   223

16   Home Again In NYC!   235

17   Sponsorship   251

18   Return   263

19   Tenure-Track Sacrifice   273

20   Academy of Design   291

21   Ryerson University   299

       EPILOGUE   319
       APPENDIX   325

ACKNOWLEDGEMENTS

What can I say? I am truly grateful for my long-time friends and professional acquaintances who have encouraged me to survive and grow from my past mistakes throughout the many phases of my life thus far. I shudder to imagine if I would even be alive if it weren't for my single-minded determination and stubbornness that surfaced as a pre-schooler, like a formidable suit of armour to protect me. Somehow with all the family chaos surrounding me, I intrinsically understood that I was not destined to remain with my family for long. And the only person in my orbit that I truly loved and felt connected with would be my sister Janet, who was one year my senior. Because I spent my life moving forward and not looking back, it took me six long decades to finally acknowledge that the lessons in my life might be of some interest and value to others. I never thought of myself as a slow learner but there you go! I had plenty of weaknesses to counterbalance my personal strengths.

The catalyst for my memoir was arguably inspired by my paternal uncle's memoir that was entitled Section Two of Coming of Age, by Alpherie O. Plasse, which went far back to his Grandmother Angela Plasse (1892-1924). It was a gift that I received from my first cousin Chris, who I never knew anything about while growing up and who I recently discovered on Ancestory.com. From everything I know, my Uncle Alpherie would most likely have been my first relative to write a private and unpublished Plasse family memoir. And I hope I can honour his legacy and make his children proud as part of the next generation. I am massively privileged to take my personal memoir and move into the next level of publication. Scary as that sounds, I feel my story has compelling universal applications that are still current to the youth-at-risk. It may not be the most elegantly written story, but it has my heart and soul embedded in the pages.

Going back to my earliest source of inspiration for the memoir, I must first acknowledge my much-beloved girlfriend Lynne Phyall, whom I dated from grades seven to thirteen. And even though I came out of the closet shortly thereafter, we went our separate ways with mutual support and blessings for each other. Lynne soon got married after high school and started a family with her very devoted husband and former high school classmate, Sandy. We have remained in touch ever since and are a lifelong part of each other's family.

After coming out at age eighteen, I met my much-beloved Glucksman Twins (Judi and Helicia), who have likewise inspired me. We have stayed in contact since the day we first met at York University in 1973. We bonded over a visceral compassion for humanity, cultural oppression, and identity discrimination under a thin veil of globally accepted societal equals. They spoke to me of their family's direct relationship to the horrors of the Holocaust, and I spoke to them about my activist concerns and a global fear of queer sexual violence, long before the current rise of the recent International Women's MeToo Movement.

In the early 1980s, after completing graduate studies in New York, I shared an apartment in the West Village with a dear friend and queer activist Brad Wright (aka "Stripe") who articulated how *outrage and anger* fuelled Boomer queers like ourselves to fight for our lives when much of the world would just as soon wish that we would have disappeared and died, to be brutally candid. He was my first activist gay buddy, and I learned a lot from him in the 1980s as he participated in many of the ACT-UP protests in NYC. In addition, he supported other local groups such as Queer Nation and The Gay Men's Health Crisis (GMHC). Brad and I were on the frontlines and although we are both blessed to have survived over the decades, countless others in our personal orbit were sadly not so fortunate.

I feel compelled to share the deeply experienced historical moments and milestones that have unfolded throughout my life. My personal narrative embraces both my failures and successes that have contributed to the invisible mask and service smile that I was forced to hide behind for decades. And with the lifelong lessons and memories of my beloved queer and straight heroes, I can finally pay a tribute toward their phenomenal lives that ended far too prematurely. Their story is a significant part of my story, and I owe them a debt of lifelong gratitude.

During the last twenty years of my tenure as a professor at Ryerson University, I was blessed to have some very close and inspirational friendships with my colleagues, including: the administrative assistant to the School of Interior Design and artist extraordinaire, Mary Dykstra; my third-year studio partner-in-crime, Professor Samantha Sannella; and my bubbly and uber- smart colleague, Professor Dr. Lorella Di Cintio, who could always crack me up. However, my most enduring friendship was with my dear colleague and sessional instructor Arlene Dougall (Dee-Dee). We initially bonded over our creative passion for interior design and have come to see how faith, humanity, and humour have intersected our different life journeys and cemented our affinity for public service. When I told Dee-Dee that I was in the early stages of writing my memoir, she enthusiastically offered to proofread my preliminary manuscript, and her initial response acted as a bellwether and metric for my publication, consideration. Over the years, there have been numerous colleagues who have touched my soul, but I have to say that Dee-Dee continues to play an ongoing compass in my retirement!

I would be remiss if I did not acknowledge and honour my estranged family members who have over the years challenged me in ways that I could never have imagined as a precocious child growing up in Toronto. The pain and sacrifices that we all made have instilled in me a higher purpose in life; particularly after the tragic loss of my family anchor, Janet, who in 1973 passed away at the early age of nineteen under criminally suspicious circumstances. Subsequently, my emotions were paralyzed, and I no longer understood what it meant to be a loving brother. Janet was not only the heart of my world, but she was also my surrogate mother who happened to be only one year older than myself.

Cutting and not ever forgetting my losses was an invaluable lesson I learned early on; it was a lesson that saved my life. I possessed an innate ability to pivot from any further existential threats as I learned to deconstruct the events of my life that eventually culminated in the composition of my memoir.

For anyone who struggles to align their identity with their passion for interior design or any other professional vocation that brings joy and meaning to their life, perhaps my story will be of personal value. If that is not the case, I know it's a universal story with some jaw-dropping experiences that will surely bring some joy and a few laughs along the way. And for some, it may be a story worth sharing with others.

INTRODUCTION

I branded myself with Unmasking of Our Interiors back in 1995. At the time, I used my platform as vice-president of the Professional Interior Design Institute of Manitoba (PIDIM) to conceive and create Canada's first National Aids Fundraiser. And since that time, I have coined the expression to express my philosophical approach to my professional interior design practice and academic pedagogy. I have always worn my heart on my sleeve, and anyone who has ever known me understands that when life is good, I can be the talk of the town and the life of the party. On the other hand, when faced with a personal or situational crisis, I can readily withdraw at the drop of a hat for extended periods to process anxiety and the fear of disappointment. I have always been comfortable talking about almost everything except my feelings; this was not uncommon for boys and men who were growing up in the mid-1950s. And especially for queer boys who suffered from abuse and acute anxiety.

Ever since my premature birth in 1954, I have felt isolated and fiercely independent in fighting for my survival, against all odds. The initial opportunity to physically bond with my mother was robbed from me by the doctors and nurses who whisked me away to the neonatal intensive care unit (NICU) to save my life. For my first two months as a newborn preemie, I remained physically restricted in an incubator with no opportunity for physical bonding or the love of my mother's touch; it was a blueprint for how my life would unfold.

I was born into a dysfunctional and chaotic family of twelve kids that were struggling with poverty and a clinically depressed mother. There was simply no time for anyone to spend any significant one-on-one attention to my needs, beyond the exception of the one person who happened to be my remarkable "big sister" Janet. She was my loving anchor, surrogate mother, best friend, and my inspiration to communicate my early wants and need for attention going back to when I was four and when she taught me how to stand figuratively and physically on my own two feet by encouraging me to use my voice to express myself. She nurtured my heart and soul and gave me permission to be curious and feel safe in her presence; a gap that my other family members could not fill. She treated me with respect and equality, and I looked up to her as a surrogate figure and the beacon in my life.

When I was barely old enough to understand, my mother explained that she had been born into hard times. She was born on August 9, 1925, at the onset of the Great Depression, on my grandparent's farm. Life was tough for everyone, and especially for girls who were considered useless as farmhands. Mother grew up in a rural Irish/French Canadian farming community, moving at different places between London, Ontario, and New Liskeard. Her classmates were children of local farmers, and there were only one or two other girls her age. My mother's limited education up to grade eight took place in a one-room schoolhouse accommodating grades 1-8. The classroom was organized by a separate half row for each individual year, and the regularity of the school schedule revolved around the changing seasons and the priority needs of the local farmers. As a young female at the time, there were no opportunities for socializing, other than at the Sunday potluck dinners at the church. According to Mother, she felt trapped and isolated. She recalled the nearby tiny pockets of Amish farming communities who didn't really mingle with outsiders, and she was horrified how they lived without modern conveniences and electricity. In her mind, all she saw in her world was hardship and servitude.

Mother would say how she felt like a second-class citizen, even within her own immediate family that was governed by strict religious teachings and commonplace gender discrimination. On rare occasions, she revealed to me her sense of hopelessness from years of parental abuse and early childhood neglect. As a young adolescent when she was just thirteen, she used the first opportunity to escape to the big city of Toronto, far away from the isolating life she had experienced as a child. Her solution was to consciously get pregnant, which was then followed by a shotgun wedding to John Taylor, who she never, ever talked about. Moreover, none of my siblings had any knowledge about him, even though everyone inherited the legal use of his surname. We eventually grew into a large family of twelve kids, consisting of several half brothers and sisters and God only knows which biological father matched up with each of us kids.

Not unlike my mother, I would eventually escape for very similar reasons of abuse and neglect, shortly after my fifteenth birthday. I felt desperate for relief from my own misery, and pregnancy wasn't an option, or I may have resorted to it! The only way out of my pain was a cry out for help and a half-hearted suicide attempt as my last resort, which landed me in the hospital for forty-eight hours with one subsequent follow-up visit to see the Psychiatrist, Dr. Murray Wilson. The hospital and social workers took decisive action and filed papers for my immediate emancipation from my family chaos, and my mother was served with legal papers to authorize her consent with a risk of having all her children removed if she didn't comply. Of course, I was not worth the risk of losing her other kids and she complied. I was left homeless and without the only family I had ever known. My mother's parting words were, "You won't last long on your own and don't come crying back later." And remarkably, I was not afraid. I could finally breathe and stand exposed but unfettered by the cloud that seemed to surround me. I was finally free and felt baptised into a new life. I felt like my spiritual soul could not be dampened, and I have never regretted what I had to do to escape from the pain of my childhood.

Mother would one day see for herself that I could not only survive, but I also had bigger dreams and aspirations for myself. This was something that I needed to prove to myself and to the world. Instinctively, I believed that I could do more with my life, and I wanted to do more with my life. Regrettably, my mother took all my biological family support away from me when she did not fight to keep me. At the time, I truly didn't have much to depend on, other than my dreams and goals that sparked my imagination. However, my curiosity was piqued with an unrelenting desire to escape the confines of my humble, tenuous beginnings.

On a wing and a prayer, I knew I would somehow find the ability to survive and fulfill my dream to become the first person from my family to attend university. From my earliest recollections, I valued the importance of formal learning, thanks to the influence of my sister Janet. Instead of depending on the school of hard knocks that I experienced in my formative years, I knew deep in my soul that education would become my passport to happiness, with a sense of fulfilment and security.

And in full disclosure, during the first two decades of my life, I was convinced I was a sensitive heterosexual who happened to be a little different from most other boys throughout my early school years. But as I matured into my late teens, I knew I was growing more and more curious and scared to explore latent gay tendencies for fear of bullying and becoming an outcast. Out of confusion and respect, I decided to express my sexual confusion to my much-beloved girlfriend Lynne, and we agreed that since I was going off to university, it might be an opportunity for us to suspend our relationship until I could figure things out for myself. Come what may, we verbally agreed that we would be grateful and thankful for each other and that we would always maintain a love for one another; it was implicitly understood that we were family.

Around the same time, one of my older associated friends became my first gay mentor during my final year of high school. Janet Sheffield was a brutally frank lesbian (no surprise), who I greatly admired and respected. She offered to take me out for a drink on my eighteenth birthday—to which I happily accepted, now that I was of legal age to drink in Ontario. The next thing I knew I was standing inside a gay bar called *The Quest*. As Jan explained, it was colloquially referred to as an upscale "fern bar" and catered mainly toward an upwardly mobile professional crowd on the main level. The second floor, where we were heading, catered to a slightly younger and preppie college crowd, and it featured a small dance floor that faced onto Yonge Street. Toward the washrooms at the back there was a line of older queens sitting on the barstools and ogling the young guys while nursing their hard liquor until closing. And because I was nervous and had kidneys that were the size of a Q-tip cotton swab, I made several trips to the washroom. Without fail, I would hear some sort of lecherous comment or grunt of approval when I walked by. I must admit that it felt very intoxicating. I took note of the seated queens, who I ignored when they yelled out to me "You're not going to be young forever!"

Remarkably, I was not shocked and offended by seeing men who were dancing together. Moreover, it felt like the most natural thing that I had ever seen. I was flooded with new erotic stirrings and emotions that I never realized I had within me. Finally, I acknowledged like a hammer to the head that I was the gay man who I was meant to become, and I never looked back! Moreover, I discovered a surrogate queer family and a sense of belonging to a tribe that was ever-expanding the concept of diversity in the gay and lesbian community under the umbrella of Queer. They became the loving and mentoring family I had never experienced in my youth.

It took me a lot of failures and trials, but I had quickly established a foot-print in the queer community and discovered that my authentic self was more than ready to literally dance my way out of the closet, beginning at *The Quest* back in 1973. Immediately, my life and attitude changed for the better. And by the time I started York University, I had transformed into a gay activist and held my head high for the straight world to see. I was fearless and full of possibilities. My sexual thermostat was dialed up. I was pumped and ready to explore gay culture and my professional career options that embraced queer diversity with all my God-given gifts. Starting with the open-minded world of the theatre, I discovered myself to be a natural performer. But alas, after a short two years studying theatre performance, I discovered that acting was not meant to be my vocation.

After a forced break-year and a short respite in Montreal, I became inspired by my resurging interest in interior design. I decided to apply to the University of Manitoba's *Bachelor of Interior Design (BID) Program*. I was accepted and enrolled in the fall. In my last year of study, my ongoing thirst for knowledge led to an application for graduate school. I was inspired by Professor Grant Marshall to apply to the *Pratt Institute* in New York City, where I was accepted and eventually graduated with M.Sc., in Interior Design. Afterward, I spent a fascinating and unpredictable decade in pursuit of my professional career. Manhattan was the place where I was meant to be; I was in the highly competitive company of 10 million others, spread across all five boroughs. It was the first place I ever identified as my home and I thrived, personally and professionally—with a few bumps along the way.

By the time I left NYC, my ticket was punched after a decade of untold losses. I was truly burned out and numb. I moved back to Canada and continued to bury myself in my work as a professionally registered interior designer with the Association of Registered Interior Designers of Ontario (ARIDO). I continued to practice until I forged a new path as an academic, teaching for over twenty-five years in interior design. This new chapter and lease on life refreshed me and gave new aspirations for my future. I adored the opportunity to nourish young minds with my professional expertise, along with an opportunity to promote equality for the disenfranchised and the vulnerable. I knew if they saw me as a role model with my unconventional queer openness, it might give some of them permission to express or accept their own personal challenges. In other words, to step out from the shadow of the masks they hid behind. Diversity and representation mattered to me! From my very first year teaching at the University of Manitoba, I began integrating queer diversity and representation of marginalized groups as part of my pedagogy. I fostered community-based learning opportunities in the curriculum that allowed for a more diverse and inclusive range of experiences. I was the most knowledgeable faculty member and case study to represent queer diversity for our students, and I was welcomed and appreciated by all.

As a recently retired person, I have the luxury of time to reflect on my life and the opportunities I sought to fulfill my life goals. Several close friends have recommended that I must do three things before I became too old: "travel; plant a garden; and write a book." And now that I have accomplished these three goals, I am happy to share the story about my unconventional journey in hopes that I can inspire others not to be afraid of failure and taking risks. It can be transformational to find the courage and forge a unique path in life, and in my view, it is a God-given right and destiny worthy of consideration. It has been my lifelong mission to encourage vulnerable and marginalized individuals to live and love freely without judgement and shame. Whether you are part of a familial tribe or an independent lone wolf like me, it doesn't really matter. Happiness is what I discovered when I took time to nurture my spirit and soul.

Survival and perseverance against all odds are intrinsic to human nature. I am acutely aware of the price one pays as a survivor of abuse, poverty, and neglect. I know what it feels like to be treated as different; it's lonely at the best of times and occasionally unbearable. That is when you really need support and kindness from others most. So, don't fear sharing your challenges with someone trustworthy in a safe environment. It makes no-never-mind if it is in a therapist's office or with a stranger over a coffee at your local *Tim Horton's*. Just as unexpected tragedies can manifest in your life, so can unanticipated blessings. Trust me when I say that nothing stays the same forever, and everything changes when you find the sun in your own backyard.

I have discovered the hard way that there is always a lesson to be learned, with unanticipated rewards that outweigh the insurmountable circumstances along the way. Stepping out of the shadows requires audacity and is essential to moving forward. I have learned that humour and spirituality are tools that have served me well in my journey, underscored by years of post-secondary education and professional work experience. I am optimistic about the local and global future of queer diversity leadership and representation in society, and I aspire in my lifetime to impact at least one person's journey to never give up. The most precious voices are those we have yet to hear from ... and some of us who have been in the trenches may just be your best advocate. I know the pain of "hiding behind a mask" and understand the freedom to face the world without a mask comes at a personal price of courage, risk, and vulnerability; a luxury I could not fully afford until I retired and began the process of writing this memoir.

Unmasking of Our Interiors provides a place for creative reflection and the "unmasking" of personal self-truth. It demonstrates the importance and value of my queer representation in education and professional practice, and it reflects my ongoing growth from the 1950s to present day. The framework and linear timeline facilitate four thematic pillars: Personal growth; queer activism; interior design; and educational outreach. These four pillars are anchored in a man filled with tainted humour, calibrated by a zipper for most of his life. I have spent lifetime hiking up my pants, and I no longer care if my pants drop in public. At my mature age, who cares already!

I would love to share a part of my journey in this memoir, including the many flaws and occasional successes. I hope, if nothing more, that my memories and distant recollections will give the reader a good ride and food for thought. So, buckle up, "it's going to be a bumpy ride."

1
MY UNLIKELY DEBUT
ST. MICHAEL'S HOSPITAL - 1954

On random occasions, my mother would remind me that giving premature birth to me was like "having a fart in the shadow of Hurricane Hazel and no one would ever notice." I was the third of four kids born out of wedlock. I was born on May 31, 1954, to my father, Lucien Plasse, and my mother, Edna Lucina Taylor. On that random day, my mother believed she was experiencing early labour pains and went off by taxi to the nearby emergency room, at St. Michael's Hospital in downtown Toronto. According to her, I was an unexpected seven-month preemie, weighing in at 2.2 pounds or the equivalent 0.900 kilograms: the weight of a small bag of rice. The odds for my long-term survival were not good, and Mother commented that I could practically fit into the palm of her hand if she would have been allowed to hold me. Her small hands would one day wash me away from her household and emancipate me from my family after my fifteenth birthday, dispatching me to survive on my own.

However, back when Mother was first admitted into the emergency room with labour pains, the attending ER doctor initially told her that she was probably having a false alarm and that she was not anywhere near full-term, nor ready for my birth. Meanwhile, as she lay on her unattended

1

gurney when the doctor stepped momentarily away, my mother recalled feeling a slight pressure in her lower abdomen like she "needed to fart." Noticing that no one was in her proximity, she gave one tiny push and hoped nobody nearby would hear her passing gas. She felt instant abdominal relief but realized she might have just had an accident in her bed! When she looked down to potentially see a soiled mess between her legs, she realized she had just given birth to me! "Holy crap," she said, looking down at me. "I was right all along!" According to Mother, she believed she knew more than the ER doctors and smirked condescendingly back at their superior arrogance. Coming back to reality, she realized my birth had been too much of a breeze and sensed there would an existential fight for my life that would erase her fleeting moment of joy. She quickly slid into an elevated state of anxiety and fear. When her doctor returned in visible shock and disbelief, he rhetorically asked, "What just happened?"

My mother raised a furrowed eyebrow and responded, "He couldn't wait. I guess my baby boy just knew it was his time to come out into the world." With no time to lose, my umbilical cord was cut, and I was immediately dispatched off to the NICU before my mother had a chance to hold me in her arms and imprint myself on her. In her mind, this was an ominous sign. In the ensuing days of Mother's recuperation, she realized my life was hanging on by a thread. It appears that all the St. Michael's Hospital's doctors, nuns, and nurses gave my mother little hope for my long-term survival. And if I did survive, it wouldn't be without the risk of some sort of physical or mental deficiency. However, they admitted that the medical team was providing the best possible medical interventions with the new state-of-the-art technology available at the time.

They had placed me into one of their newly acquired state-of-the-art incubators for high-risk infants, but it had yet to be tested at St. Michael's on an infant as young and undeveloped as myself, according to my mother. So, everyone at the hospital was cautiously guarded and hesitant to speculate on how well this new technology would impact on my life. With a lack of transparency, their medical concerns were not expressed to my mother, and she found herself feeling like a lost bird flapping around in the dark, not knowing how it would all land in the end. Their advice to Mother was, "Mrs. Taylor, you are welcome to go down to the St. Michael's Hospital Chapel on the first floor and say a prayer, if this will help give you inner peace and strength." She then told them how desperate and anxious she was to know more about my life-and-death situation. She was very concerned about the physical and financial toll it would take on her family, and she told the doctors that she did not want a potential long-term burden of caring for me. She was already making sacrifices and could not possibly afford to make any more.

Steadily, she grew impatient with the arrogant doctors who were dismissive of her questions, which was not an uncommon occurrence for women at the time. She was not privy to details and was told information would be shared with her on a "need-to-know" basis, which meant she was told nothing. Mother later told me she believed if my father had been present and not out on the road working, the doctors and staff would have responded differently to her. She was convinced of that.

Mother was so afraid of losing me that she couldn't even bear to name me for the first few weeks. The best that she could do was to address me as her "Baby boy," much to the disappointment of all the medical staff. From her point of view, none of the doctors and nurses truly appreciated the extent of shock and despair she felt. She could sense her mind starting to race out of control, and she described feeling like the walls were closing in on her and making her feel speechless and awkward in front of the nurses and doctors. According to my mother, she did not have a grip on her circumstances at the time and she felt as though she was spiralling down into a pit of despair. Regrettably, she was harbouring a dark secret that started before the time of my birth. Mother was suffering from clinical depression from severe anxiety, and she was not willing to admit the source of her ill health at the time of my birth. In addition, she felt her hectic and sometimes out-of-control life worsened her fragile health and caused her personal shame. Her biggest worry was that the doctors might consider her an unfit mother, she refused to admit to the medical staff how she felt overwhelmed by my precarious birth, and she was "barely hanging on by a thread." Despite her own personal health issues, she insisted the doctors focus on saving my life.

Meanwhile, as she lay in frustration on her hospital bed with nothing to do, she realized that she had been burning the candle at both ends. She was running a large household and supplementing her income with a part-time job. In addition, she had lost confidence and patience with my dad, which she had freely shared with the family when he was out on the road. And she recalled other factors that might have contributed to her premature labour and my unanticipated early arrival, including her lifestyle choice to smoke and drink copious amounts of coffee throughout the day and night. She rarely ate and survived on yogurt to retain her girlish figure.

"And what about the pills?" she asked. Her medications for her nerves were prescribed by her family doctor. Could it be that her doctor was partially responsible for her premature labour? she wondered. Just prior to my arrival, she felt as though she was living in a three-ring circus without a ringmaster. She knew that she was juggling far too many balls to notice how her mental health and wellbeing were deteriorating. She had been through so many successful full-term pregnancies before that it never occurred to her how my birth would be any different.

Frankly, my premature birth triggered old memories that she wanted to avoid. She knew she harboured unresolved feelings of guilt and shame from her recent loss of a previous child. She had given birth to another son, who she had named "Bobby" whom she adored and expected to live. Unfortunately, she lost him shortly after his birth when he unexpectedly died from infant jaundice. At the time, Mother claimed the doctors told her that treatment was not warranted, and that if she kept her infant son well hydrated and well-nourished from her breastmilk, Bobby would naturally grow out of his jaundice. But shortly after she returned home, the jaundice worsened. Bobby lost his desire to nurse or drink from a bottle as well as his ability to poop. From past experiences, she thought it might be that he was just being a little "fussy" and constipated. He had a slight fever, but nothing out of the norm as she compared him to her other children when they were infants. She did not understand the seriousness of the combined various symptoms related to jaundice, and before she could know, he stopped breathing and died in her arms. Her guilt over his death was unbearable and contributed to a dark cloud that hung over her. She indicated to me that if she had paid more attention or had done something earlier, he would not have died.

After my initial debut on May 31, 1954, my mother recuperated from her hospital bed, tethered to her persistent guilt and shame about why she could not carry me to term. She reluctantly blamed herself for my personal misfortune and even laid blame on her stormy relationships with her men in her life. Regardless, she always felt at her best and most happy when she was

4

pregnant, and the men evidently served a momentary sense of pleasure and purpose. This was something she shared freely in the presence of our family.

Her only distraction from her emotional mental distress was to get up and periodically walk away from her hospital bed. Her walks always took her to the smoking lounge on the floor. Although, she was socially awkward with strangers, she had a reliable trick she could rely on, as a coping mechanism for her social anxieties. First, she would see if she could bum a cigarette and a light. Then she would stand back and take continuous puffs as a ruse to not talk and to listen to other visitors talk gibberish for her amusement. There was no way in hell that she would ever expose herself to the judgement of strangers. She never wanted strangers thinking she was dumb because of her lack of worldly knowledge and formal education. She knew she was very street smart, and in her view, the hospital visitors and patients were in a smoking lounge to relax and talk about one thing, and that was their babies! And with Mother's vast experience in cranking out babies, she felt confident enough to stand in a room of new parents, family, and friends, and enjoy her smoke. She felt like an old pro compared to the many first-time parents.

After a week of recuperation, she was discharged from the hospital without me. She was to bring her pumped milk into the hospital daily, which she agreed to faithfully honour. Meanwhile, upon her return home, Mother reverted to her favourite obsession of losing weight and staying thin. She was consumed with staying thin and always limited her caloric intake, which our personal family doctor had repeatedly warned her against throughout her pregnancy.

With some reservation, she allowed herself to be distracted from my absence. She needed to become physically strong and aesthetically comfortable in her own skin again, or more to the point, she needed to regain her appearance and use her natural beauty to mask her insecurities. In her postpartum mind, she needed a new hero who would come to rescue her from a life of misery and poverty. And that meant she would eventually need to get rid of my father, who she described as a no-good truck driver without ambition and someone who drank too much, in her opinion. As predicted by my older siblings, my biological father would soon be gone; and about two years later, he was unceremoniously kicked out, never to return. Subsequently, he was only referred to by my mother as an abusive drunk, which is something I never witnessed, and I resented her for saying this about my dad.

In the interim, Mother succeeded and dutifully executed what the doctors had requested. She made her daily pilgrimage to the hospital, bringing in her milk, and she found that after a few days, it became less of a burden and more of an opportunity to get away from her problems at home. I would argue that she used this opportunity to save both my life *and* her herself. Expressing milk was a temporary and painful ritual for my mother to save my life.

I believe in my heart of hearts that she was telling the truth when she talked about how the physical, psychological, and emotional toil increased for her with each additional day that I had to remain in the hospital. She had no opportunity to cradle me in her arms and bond with me, as she had done previously with all her other full-term kids. She'd said this was her favourite part about having a baby: the initial bonding and dependency on her for its life. The rearing of a child past the young age of about thirteen was something she farmed out to my older sisters. And it was no coincidence that she was the same age when she lost her innocence and was forced to grow up.

Part of her confession struck me as particularly insightful, and I could not help but feel empathy for what she had been going through back then. Her visits were confined to viewing me from the public side of the glass barrier that separated her from the nursery bassinets and incubators. She admitted there were times when she would cry, and occasions when she felt too numb to remain any longer. She refused to name me and could not come to grips with the prospect of losing me. Then, on a random day, everything changed for my mother. She came to drop off her milk and then view me through the nursery window, as usual. Initially unnoticed by my mother, a policeman stood nearby watching his own newborn baby who was soundly resting and smiling in one the bassinets in the first row behind the glass. Meanwhile, my mother quietly shed tears as she looked toward my incubator.

"Which one is yours?" The officer had realized that the mother was alone, and she was obviously in great pain. Unable to verbally speak from the shock of seeing this man who had appeared to come from out of nowhere, she studied him for a quick second. He was a tall, strong policeman, and his closeness and question made her feel safe. The best that she could do was to respond to him with two words: "*my son,*" and she then pointed nervously in the direction of my incubator, located at the back end of the NICU. She was weak and vulnerable. That much was clear.

"Lady, look at me," he said while he stared through the glass in my direction. "I was a preemie myself and now look at me! I'm strong and healthy! Your son is going to make it." The strength and authority of his voice instantly snapped my mother into a new reality with hope. But as she turned back to face him and thank him for his kindness, he was gone. She stood there confused and considered that God had sent her this human angel as a miracle. This was the moment when she decided to name me Michael as a tribute to St. Michael's Hospital.

She then ran to the closest nurse on the floor and told her, with great happiness, that she was naming me "Michael" in honour of the guardian angel Saint Michael. Finally, she felt hope and the courage to officially register my name and have it labelled outside my incubator! She explained to the nurses how the name had been inspired by an "angel-cop" who'd stood by her moments earlier. The nun then asked my mother if she was aware that St. Michael was the patron saint of both police and people afflicted with illness. Immediately, this unexpected revelation sent shivers down my mother's spine.

For a few seconds, the nurse softly held my mother's hand and congratulated her on her choice of name. "It couldn't be any more of a blessing," she said.

Almost immediately thereafter, Mother and the doctors noticed incremental improvements in my breathing and weight, along with the manifestation of fingernails and eyelashes. I was quickly starting to look like a normal baby. After two months of steady progress, I was deemed fit enough to be finally checked out to the custody and care of my mother. My legal name on my birth certificate, dated May 31, 1954, was Michael Thomas Taylor: "Michael" was chosen in honour of the hospital; "Thomas" in reference to her favourite television star, Danny Thomas, as he had a nose that resembled mine; and "Taylor" was her married name but not the name of my biological father. Anyhow, that's how Mother explained the origin of my name when I got a little older. I can't complain that she didn't spend a lot of time selecting my name after she explained how I remained nameless in my incubator for several weeks. And in retrospect, I am happy with the time she took and the thinking behind the name she chose for me.

Decades later, in my late forties, I had the most bizarre encounter regarding my birth. I had been invited to a Christmas party in December 2002, hosted by my past real-estate attorney, Peter, who lived in a large, four-storey house located two blocks from my apartment in the heart of Toronto's gay village. As one of his past clients, I really didn't know anyone at the party, outside his male receptionist. The very first person he'd introduced to me was his great-aunt, *who was a retired sister of the Catholic church.* And I was only too happy to engage with her, as I had never ever spoken to a nun before.

At first, it was just your everyday run-of-the-mill civil discourse we shared. But as we shifted into more autobiographical details, things got more personal. She told me she detected an American accent and was curious to know where I came from. When I told her that I was born just a few blocks away at St. Michael's Hospital, her eyes widened, and she asked what year I was born and the full name of both myself and my mother. When I discovered that she had just started working in the NICU and maternity ward at St. Michael's, I told her my mother's name was Edna Taylor and she seemed to look a little puzzled. I explained Mother never used her name and always went by her nickname "Betty."

The retired sister spontaneously clapped her hands together in exclamation and said, "Yes, I remember Betty Taylor very well!" She recalled Betty Taylor was one of the first patients assigned to her when she started work on the floor. She recalled how the two of them were about the same age, but she couldn't believe how young and attractive my mother was for someone who had just given birth. Her body showed little indication of ever being pregnant, and when she would dress to go out for a cigarette, she looked more like a visitor and not like a patient of her age. And I said yes, that sounded like my mother, and I explained how she famously retained her girlish figure and wore miniskirts well into her late forties. I explained that I did not inherit any of her Irish characteristics like her auburn red hair, nor her piercing blue eyes and translucent light, fair skin. Clearly, I resembled my French-Canadian father with dark brown eyes and hair.

She stated with measured certainty that when she was transferred to the maternity floor, St. Michael's hospital had just completed the renovation of the NICU with new state-of-the-art incubators. According to her, I was one of the very first high-risk preemies to be placed in the new incubators. At the time, she recalled that my distressed mother was very blessed to have this new technology to keep me alive and how fervently all the nuns' said prayers on my behalf. I thanked her for her prayers from so long ago and told her I was glad their prayers were answered. How remarkable it was that so many decades late, here we were sitting once again, together. She simply smiled and looked up toward the ceiling.

The one last detail that she recalled was how in addition to my own precarious survival, my mother had high blood pressure that was a constant challenge for the medical staff to get under control. And she remembered my mother was the very first case she saw with the appearance of postpartum depression. I underscored her comments by confirming that this detail was part of my mother's pathology throughout her life. She took medications for high blood pressure and sleeping pills at night. In addition, she had an extensive history of taking a variety of anti-depressants before she was diagnosed with Alzheimer's disease and passed away at the early age of seventy-three.

By the grace of God, I managed to avoid any issue of serious depression, unlike some of my other siblings who have suffered with lifelong clinical depression. However, when I hit age fifty-five, I was diagnosed with diabetes and my doctor maintained that since there is no history of that disease in my family, there was a good chance it was brought on by an abundance and a confluence of stress in both my professional and personal life. He told me that I wasn't getting younger, and my body did not have the resilience and tolerance it once had. And when Dr. Pomer said those truthful but shady-ass comments to my fragile Ego, I thought, *Fine! I was no longer going to accept any further dinner invitations to his home, where he liked to tap into a little of my interior design consulting on occasion!*

I think he omitted to tell me that patience also diminishes with age, and that for someone like myself, I would no longer suffer the attention of fools lightly, either at work or in my personal life.

2
EARLY LIFE ON SKID ROW
SHERBOURNE & QUEEN
STREET, 1954-1958

My recollections of early life at home began a few short blocks east of *St. Michael's Hospital* in the heart of Toronto's skid row, on Sherbourne Street, just south of Queen. We lived in a modest row house where ten of us kids and my parents were shoe-horned into very tight quarters, with limited space for any privacy other than in the bathroom; and even there, we were not allowed to lock the door. It was sometime in the fall of 1958, and I had just learned a nursery rhyme by Mother Goose from my sister Janet, who had just started kindergarten. It struck me that the four lines I memorized were not just relatable to my own mother and our family; those first memorized lines would be a lesson in my early ability to manipulate and contextualize words that make sense out of, ostensibly, nonsense.

> *"There was an old woman who lived in a shoe.*
> *She had so many children, she didn't know what to do.*
> *She gave them some broth without any bread,*
> *Then whipped them all soundly and put them to bed."*

When I was a pre-schooler and barely old enough to understand, I overheard discussions that Mother was on medications for clinical depression and anxiety, which made her incapable of trusting others, including her kids and my dad. She had an ongoing battle with prescribed medications that she stored behind the family's bathroom mirror, alongside our toothpaste and brushes. Even in my formative years, I was aware of Mother's erratic behaviour and mood swings that went up and down faster than the whore's skirts that we witnessed in the back lanes on skid row.

Ever since I was a pre-schooler, my sister Janet and I had a childhood game in guessing which sister and brother was biologically related to our dad; many of my elder siblings looked so very different. Janet and I could visibly see that only four of us resembled my dad; we all had the same dark hair and brown eyes. Our mother, on the other hand, had blue eyes and a very fair complexion, framed with bottle-red auburn hair. When we played the guessing game of who the other mystery dads were, it was like we were playing pin the tail on the donkey. We were blind to our family's history and enjoyed all the guessing, unless it came from our neighbours and kindergarten classmates, who occasionally pried into our family business and demanded to know who our father was. Fortunately, I had rehearsed with Janet that our biological dad, Lucien Plasse, was "the current head of the household."

Janet was the first and only person in my family with whom I bonded, and we had a fabulous connection and relationship from the get-go! We had many things in common that were unique to us as siblings: we were both born in the month of May (one year apart) and both our birthdays contained a three, our lucky number. She was born a year earlier, in 1953, on May 3, and I was born a year later May 31. Together, we would own the entire merry month of May, and celebrated daily for the full month in honour of each other's birthday.

No doubt our siblings grew weary and a bit nauseated at our self-centeredness, but we didn't pay it much never-mind. And depending on Mother's mood, she would bake both of us a birthday cake with a strategically placed silver dollar or plastic button as a booby-prize secreted inside. At the time, Janet thought it was a game of chance. I was not so readily impressed and assumed that since Mother had baked and iced the cake and then cut it and handed out the slices, she'd probably used the coloured candles as a reference for the baked-in surprises. She knew bloody well who would get the money or the booby prize! And *quelle surprise,* no need to guess that I was the recipient of the booby-prize, sometimes even on my actual birthday, no less! It did not really matter; we all thought the alleged "luck of the draw" was in good fun. Our birthdays ushered in the spring, and this made it even more reason for the entire family to partake of a good mood. This was the time of year when seeds were planted, sprouted, and matured in every possible sense.

Although there were numerous older siblings in school, Janet would quickly become my unofficial surrogate teacher, and I would grow happily into her doting enthusiastic student. I was in awe and fascination of where she went each day and would eagerly devour everything, she would teach me upon completing her morning kindergarten class. We nurtured one another and acted as each other's priority. Her school musings were both hypnotic and inspired. I was truly in awe of her enthusiasm and tales of the city outside of our home. She could turn a simple walk home into an adventure with her keen awareness of all her senses. Her personal stories were far more relatable and entertaining than what she read to me from her books. And I wasn't too far behind. However, I would embellish on everything she would say to me. Hypothetically, if she said the sky was blue, I would challenge her with, "What kind of blue? Is it a peacock blue or more like the Player's cigarette package?"

It was all I could do to stay out of my mother's way by sitting still and awaiting Janet's return home for lunch. Clearly, Mother had no time for my thoughts and ideas. The moment Janet came home, the two of us would spend the afternoon playing together in the front parlour and next to the kitchen where my mother was in earshot and spent most of her time. Everything that Janet had taught me the day before, I had drilled into my memory in anticipation of her testing me on it. Only after that would we then move onto the new stuff that she had freshly learned that morning. Since I was her faithful and devoted student, she would leave her valuable schoolbooks, along with school drawings and crafts, in my protection for safekeeping.

Mother had no time for her "school junk" messing up the house. I promised Janet that I would be responsible for hiding and guarding her schoolwork in the three lucky places she pointed out in our shared middle bedroom on the second floor:

(1) under our pillows

(2) in our dresser drawers

(3) inside the clothes closet

And while she was away in the mornings, I knew where I could access all her stuff to study and stimulate my imagination. Thanks to her, I learned how to read and how to sound out words phonetically on my own. Before I turned five, I had already read *Curious George, See Spot Run,* and *Blueberries for Sal.* And when that wasn't enough, I would temporarily steal and read my mother's store catalogues and flyers, which thankfully she never seemed to miss. I was not the most beloved child in the family, and even at this formative age, I knew I caused my mother obvious annoyance with my "big mouth" at times. Janet was always ready to shush me when Mother was nearby. However, she personally found my responses both engaging and often weird for a four-year-old. She would remark that I could outsmart all her classmates if I wanted, and indeed, I wanted! I couldn't wait to turn five and start school.

Janet was the clear and obvious apple of my father's eye, and I was content to play second fiddle. When Dad was not on the road and was at home, he would take a break from my mother working in the kitchen, and he would spend his free time with Janet and myself in the front parlour. I was happy that my father adored Janet, as did I. She inherited my mother's good looks and fine features, along with my father's broad grin and his hazel brown eyes and brunette hair like myself. Janet was the only child that he liked to pick up and hold; she was referred to by everyone as "Daddy's girl." In those days, little boys like myself were not coddled by our fathers, at least in our neighbourhood. I suppose he was a little hung up on the gender conventions and stereotypes of the day. I would like to believe that it was not because he did not like me. It was just the way things were back then, when men were expected to be macho and not display any affection as the family disciplinarian. Clearly, this was a role that my mother annexed for herself, and she never relinquished it!

On the other hand, he loved to hold Janet on his lap in his dedicated chair at the front of the house, facing west to a large picture window that was covered in layers of drapes and curtains that obliterated the view out to a tavern on the other side of Sherbourne Street. Mother alleged that he

14

patronized the establishment after his work on the road and before he came home. Sometimes, the three of us would sneak a peek behind the heavily draped window coverings to look at the beautiful sunsets and the tavern when we were sure that Mother was not around. And it's no wonder why I continue to this day to feel happy when I watch a sunset or sunrise, and I thank my dad for this memory that repeats itself each day of my life. Although these small memories may sound mundane, the poetic nuance of those quiet moments was not lost on the three of us. We were at peace and thankful to have one another. Many times, we just sat in the room in silence, awaiting Mother to call us into the kitchen for dinner.

In August, which was the month before Janet started kindergarten, Dad took her on a special daddy/daughter celebration in anticipation of her first day of school. They'd gone for a full-day adventure to the Canadian National Exhibition (CNE), and when they'd returned home, they had found me eagerly waiting to greet them at the front door. Janet was waving this green bamboo cane with a beautiful miniature doll attached at the handle, and I was visibly apoplectic and speechless. I had never seen such a pretty souvenir as this in my life! But I knew that dolls were for girls, according to my parents and the social norm of the day, so I held in my gushing until later, when Janet and I were alone in our bedroom upstairs. I didn't want my father to think I was a "*sissy-boy*," but I suppose I was by his definition. "Michael the sissy-boy" would eventually become a familiar title, assigned to me by my mother in her passive-aggressive manner.

Meanwhile, I hustled the two of them into the front parlour so Father could sit in his favourite chair while Janet jumped onto his lap and waved her green bamboo cane like it was a hand-held flag. I ran and sat next to them on the floor so that I could share in their adventure through Janet's recitation of all the fresh details percolating in her head. The first thing I noticed was she used her souvenir like she was an orchestra conductor using her musical baton to punctuate the rhythm of her concert performance. She began reliving all the details of the marvellous food she'd eaten, starting with the sweet-smelling caramel popcorn. Then she moved onto her hot dog that was smothered in mustard and relish that dripped out of the bun and into a bunch of napkins that Dad had tucked into her dress collar. Then she remarked that she ate an order of French fries with ketchup for the first time and then chased them down with a Dairy Queen ice-cream covered in pretty sprinkles! As far as I was concerned, it was always a good idea to start talking about food. I was hooked after that, and I wanted to hear even more.

Her eyes danced as she then described the large wooden roller coaster called The Flyer for the big people, and then she described the much smaller Cup and Saucer ride that they had ridden together, which left her feeling a little dizzy afterward. And then there were the countless rows of arcade games, with so many different prizes to be won. "Father tried to win me a large white poodle, my favourite of all the colours," she commented. The game and stall where he'd spent the most money was the baseball toss. He'd tried so many times to toss baseballs into any of the milk cans, but they'd all bounced out.

This was the point that Father injected himself into Janet's story, adding, "All the games were rigged and designed to take your money. He said it was easier and cheaper to buy a prize to take home as a souvenir. And that is exactly what he did. Afterward, they walked toward the Princess Gates main entrance, where a bunch of hawkers without a stall stood by themselves, juggling a variety of souvenirs that included the green bamboo canes and miniature dolls. I made a mental note to go there the next summer with Janet and Father to celebrate my own start of kindergarten.

She continued with her story, and I learned that they walked past the Dufferin Gate's streetcar loop and then walked under an unusually simple concrete arch that led to the much grander *neo-classic Roman* Princess Gates, which was the main entrance to the Canadian National Exhibition (CNE) grounds. This is where they'd decided to sit and relax on an adjacent patch of grass, next to the automotive building. Janet loved the *Triumphal 1920s* arch with its statuary figures. "It all looked very grand and important," according to her. The most beautiful part she mentioned was a large-winged lady *on the Winged Victory* sculpture on top. Resting on the adjacent lawn, Father and Janet laughed about how the original modern-looking arch that they first passed under reminded them of a recent scene from the 1944 movie *Meet Me in St. Louis*. We were all big fans of Judy Garland's music and movies. Janet suggested that the Princess Gates arch was the grandest entrance and the most beautiful arch in the world, but years later, I begged to differ. Give me Toronto's non-geometric catenary arch, like the one in St. Louis, any day of the week.

Janet and Father continued to describe the CNE setting that was full of teenagers who were hanging out and having fun. Some were sitting on the lawns, but many others were up dancing to the music from a mobile CHUM Radio stage. They had loud music blasting out from large speakers while beautiful go-go girls danced on the stage in their hot-pink bikinis. Janet described a bikini contest with girls in high heels who pranced across the CHUM stage. At the end of her intoxicating story, I secretly wished that my father would have invited me to attend the CNE as well. After all, I thought we were the "three amigos" and did everything together. Perhaps next time, I thought. But unfortunately, I would later find out that next time would never happen for me and my dad.

Everyone seemed to gossip about Mother's *personal business,* according to Janet. While most of her schoolmates came from families of three or four kids, Janet would proudly volunteer that we were a family of ten kids at the time and then this would trickle down to our neighbourhood. Our neighbours started asking us, "How do you all fit into that tiny row house? "We barely have enough space in the same-size house!" And Janet would respond with, "No problem." She elaborated on the point by saying that nobody in our family had their own bedroom in our house. We all double- and tripled-up in the shared three bedrooms upstairs, and our formal dining room on the first floor had been turned into a fourth bedroom for our brothers Johnny and Kenny.

Whereas Janet could sometimes be a bit naive, I was always inclined to be suspicious of strangers and sometimes even of my own family members. Together, we had a healthy balance in our mutual thinking and exchange of ideas. Since I did not trust outsiders from my lack of exposure to the real world, I had little experience and reason to attract their attention. On the other hand, Janet was in school and meeting all kinds of new people that she implicitly trusted. I would often challenge everything she said with them. Like a teeter-totter, we would take turns going up and down with our assertions and opinions.

This is the foundation of how I learned to debate and argue, and I must credit my sister for this invaluable life skill that she gave me at such a young age. While Janet's head was sometimes in the clouds with her stalwart belief in fairy tales, mine wasn't so much. There were times when I had clear evidence to debunk her fantasies that I refrained from sharing. I have no idea how I could be so skeptical at age four. I was always a precocious and curious kid, with a rebellious streak from the get-go. On one occasion, I can recall catching Mother sneaking into our bedroom when she thought we were both asleep. She went over to Janet's bed and then removed my sister's lost tooth that had been placed under her pillow and she replaced it with money from the alleged "Tooth Fairy." The following morning, Janet was so joyful to find the Tooth Fairy had come and left her some money, and I didn't want to spoil her happiness with the truth, so I played along and learned a lesson about generosity of spirit. The same thing happened when it came to hunting for the magical Easter Egg Bunny, who had, in theory, hid his chocolate eggs and colourful jellybeans around the house for us to find.

It was almost like my mother did not realize I was around when she did these things before my very eyes. More likely, she assumed I was too stupid or naïve to put two and two together! It did not really matter. I knew from early experience that she did not have high expectations of me. And she told me so as I got a little older and started school. As a result, I would try to read anything and everything that I could put my hands on around the house: comic books, store catalogues, coupon flyers, almost anything except the romantic Harlequin romances that were hidden under my older sisters' pillows.

On one occasion, outside with my mother, I noticed a sign on one of the old wooden hydro poles on Sherbourne Street advertising a children's picnic on Centre Island, which I phonetically pronounced as "Is-land." My mother argued it was pronounced "I-land" and I recall telling her she didn't understand spelling as well as I did. I was so obnoxious for such a young person when I think back now!

Unfortunately, there were times at home when my mother investigated my whereabouts and then openly chastised me for being a nosey parker for going into other people's personal books and magazines. I was now branded by my mother as the busybody of our family! Further, she scolded me when I asked her to buy me my own books to read. She got so ticked off that she reiterated her busybody comment in the company of my siblings to shame me with the intention to break my spirit down. But I refused to be broken by her or anyone else, for that matter. She would say to the family, "Look at him! He thinks he's better than the rest of us!"

To which I would much later, as an adolescent, cheekily reply in jest, "But I am, Blanche, I am!" My sister Janet would just grin and roll her eyes back; she had my number!

Mother would emphasize that *normal kids* waited until they started school to learn to read and write, implying somehow that I was abnormal. I recall that she said, "How on earth did you get it in the back of your thick skull that it was my responsibility to buy you books? Shame on you." Apparently, for some reason she thought I should know that money does not grow on trees. I was not afraid when she threatened to tell my father about my audacious behaviour. She claimed that I would surely "get a licking" if he ever found out how I spoke to her. From my view, Father was never unkind or hard on me. I was one of his two biological sons, unlike my other half-brothers and sisters who he spent no time parenting. I knew my mother's con when she was bluffing, and I despised her for this game.

I never really understood what I had done to offend Mother at such a vulnerable young age. My intentions were always honourable, in my humble opinion. I knew I might have had a unique personality that she'd not been prepared for, but to suggest that I thought I was "better than the rest"? Well, her unfair statement just got stuck in my craw. Her negative opinion and cruel remarks pissed me off at times. She generally lacked any warmth and kindness toward me, which was not a joyful experience in my young heart. And out of frustration and hurt, I decided to take creative revenge on her with a box of crayons and put my feelings into words for the very first time. I picked up a bright red crayon and rewrote my own version of "The Old Woman Who Lived in A Shoe" on the back of a large brown paper bag from our local Dominion grocery store. I can't remember the exact phrasing, but it went something like this:

> *There was a young mother*
> *Who lived in a shoe,*
> *With so many husbands, we didn't know what to do.*
> *She filled us with fear and no love to spare.*
> *So, we hid in our rooms with great shame and no care.*

Later, when my sister returned from kindergarten, I told her what had happened, and I showed her my scrawled-out poem, which made her jaw drop to the floor! For a few seconds, she said nothing in disbelief. "You can't show this poem to anyone!" Then she reminded me how Mother always threatened me if I didn't watch my big mouth. Instead of being reprimanded by her one more time, I would be sent to my room to wait for my eldest brother to get home from work. Janet warned me that I would be strapped over the bed with one of his heavy belt buckles as our mother always threatened. "For your own good, I am going to tear this up," she said. Although I had no clue that my mother would ever follow through with her threats, I could tell by the anxious look on my sister's face that she was afraid for me. I knew she was trying to protect me, and I nodded my head in approval. But there was still a tiny part of me that wanted my mother to see my poem! I wanted it to be seen despite her hair-trigger temper. I struggled early on to articulate my feeling of inadequacy to my mother. Often, she would let me know that the doctors who delivered me had warned her about a possibility of a brain defect or delayed learning problems created by my premature birth. Consequently, she never had any high expectations of me and only showed pity toward me, with a not-so-subtle intolerance. Older siblings would likewise adopt her insidious assessment of me and leave me alone. Everyone, that is, except my sister Janet. We were extremely close to each other and looked so much alike that it was not uncommon for strangers to assume we were twins.

My early dysfunctional family life was no fairy tale, for sure, but neither were the lives of many of our neighbourhood peers and acquaintances who lived in the same vicinity of South Sherbourne Street and Queen Street. An unbridled sense of chaos and neglect was the operative status quo for many of the down-and-out families on *Toronto's skid row*. However, it was the only concept of what "normal" was to me, and I simply got on with it. I was taught that whatever happened behind our family's closed doors was private and nobody's business.

We were typical of your everyday white Anglo-Saxon Irish family. We shared a long history of bearing a stiff upper lip and keeping our emotions bottled up inside. And indeed, I modelled my behaviour on what I saw all around me at the time. I was grateful to have my sister, who was the only person that I felt comfortable sharing any sentiments with, and I didn't have to worry about controlling my emotions around her. I was curious why I couldn't be more like Janet. She seemed to never get into any kind of trouble, and my mother never yelled or threatened her until years later when she became a teenager. On the other hand, I was on the cusp of just starting school and I was already branded as a "little shit disturber."

Both my parents struggled to find work in areas suitable to their limited skills and education. From an early rocky beginning in my mother's adolescence, she'd managed to pull herself up by the bootstraps after getting pregnant as a young teenager. Despite not attending high school, she used her Irish grit and passion to flee to Toronto and escape from her stern, affectionless parents who had little patience for a female child who could not contribute to hard farm work in rural Listowel, Ontario. In fact, when Mother first hooked up with my biological dad, she had already birthed six half-brothers and sisters from various men following her early marriage to this mysterious husband in her life known as "John Taylor." She would then go on to add four more hazel-eyed kids with my biological father, and she did not stop there. She subsequently produced two additional blue-eyed half-brothers: Ricky and Greg. All my older sisters were convinced my mother had cheated on our father during their time together and leading up to the birth of Ricky. Ricky had blue eyes like my mother, while all of Father's other biological kids had hazel/brown eyes. My older sisters speculated that Mother had cheated with a neighbour who had similar colouring and facial features with comparable sparkling blue-eyes.

In our neighbourhood, we were just your typical large family who happened to be blessed with many half-truths, half-brothers, and half-sisters. Although I felt sometimes embarrassed and ashamed of my circumstances in life, I never wore a heavy mantle for the adult choices made outside of my control. And on the occasions when curious neighbours or other kids would ask about my family in a condescending tone, I would say, "It is what it is, and it is not what it is not." I am not so sure they got my four-and-a-half-year-old drift. And for that matter, I am not so sure that I understood where my words came from, either. Most of the time it was like verbal diarrhea falling out of my mouth as the family-branded little shit-disturber. And I was so relieved a few years later when people started referring to my spontaneity as "witty." It always sounded like a prettier way of saying "shitty."

There was always a sense of goings on and madness during this time, and emotions ran the full gamut from laughter to meltdowns. There was one particularly dramatic accident involving me playing with a ball near a refrigerator that someone had left out on the street. Somehow, it had tipped over and knocked me unconscious. I was apparently rushed by ambulance to the hospital with blood rushing nonstop from my nose and ears. I vaguely recall background screaming and seeing bright flashing lights, but nothing more. Evidently, I had almost died, and I can't remember anything about this accident.

Regrettably, my younger brother Jackie also had his brush with death, thanks to my ignorance and stupidity at the time. He stands out in my memory because I was the one who gave him Drano beads to taste and see if they were candy. Although they had a weird perfume, they looked like candy, and I thought that since Halloween had just passed, maybe someone was hiding their stash of trick-or-treat candies in the bathroom. This mysterious Drano looked like a rainbow kaleidoscope of tiny sugar-candy beads that looked like birthday-cake sprinkles. I thought I would get him to be the guinea pig and taste a few first. The next thing I recall was a hurricane of household chaos. Everyone was running around my mother, who was busy holding Jackie upside down while he foamed at the mouth and gasped for air. Someone was screaming for her to bring him to the front door and others were crying hysterically. Everyone seemed to look at me in disgust, and I felt such guilt and shame that I tried to hide behind the sofa. Everyone seemed to be spinning out of control and nervously pacing.

Meanwhile, I must have gone into shock myself, as I felt paralyzed with fear for my three-year-old brother's young life. It was unbearable and excruciating to hear that I had tried to poison my little brother. For God's sake, why could they not accept that it had been a horrible accident that haunted me for many years? I should have tasted them first, and I gladly would have if I could do it all over again. Both of us were feeling burned deep inside. In the background of all this chaos, I could hear the chipper voice of Judy Garland on the kitchen radio, and in that moment, I concentrated all my attention on her joy. She was merrily singing a new song from the movie *Meet Me in St. Louis*. It was the last voice I heard before the ambulance rushed my brother Jackie and my mother off to Sick Children's Hospital.

Clang, clang, clang went the trolly,
Ding, ding, ding went the bell,
Zing, zing, zing went my heartstrings...

Other than these near-fatal accidents, our family life on Sherbourne Street went off without a hitch. Moving forward, I felt a compelling need for a sense of security and comfort that came with knowing what to expect.

When the streetlights came on, I knew that it was time to come in from outside. I would then take a shared back-to-back bath with either my younger brother Jackie or my elder sister Janet. Afterward, we would change into our flannel pyjamas and end the day with a shout out of goodnights to all at 8:00 p.m. sharp. The next morning, we would get up early and start another adventurous day. My young life was no walk in the park. But who wants to walk when they are young? I mean, Moss Park was literally at the corner, and I wanted to be a part of the action and run around freely like an unbridled wild stallion. The park accommodated a small military hall for the army cadets to practice their drills, a seasonal ice rink, and a small family community centre with two large protective lions at the entrance. It was an exciting place to me. But Moss Park was not a place where my parents allowed their kids to loiter. Anyone could see it was a seedy place that was run amok with unruly teenagers, addicts, and predators who were looking for an opportunity to pounce on the young and defenceless. It was a definitive "no go" for my family. It was bad enough that we had to step over passed-out bodies on the street.

So, what to do? Our neighbourhood in 1958 was no verdant green Rosedale with wide, winding streets and homes with beautiful, manicured gardens and lawns. We lived in a proverbial shoebox of a home in what I believed was the most densely populated slum in Toronto. However, our community included Canada's largest housing project and national pride. In my neighbourhood one could find densely packed blocks of high-rise apartments integrated around the dilapidated and pre-gentrified Victorian-era row homes that were congested with family housing for underprivileged families.

The physical, spiritual, and nutritional needs of the massive amounts of homeless men were supported by local institutions and religious-based community centres. Basic human necessities that most people took for granted were not always readily available for the homeless. The only way to access such luxuries was to voluntarily enter the nearby Salvation Army shelter for men, or as an alternative, the Fred Victor Mission that was one block west at Queen and Jarvis Street. The two options were both faith-based organizations, primarily run by volunteers. We all knew that inside these Christian-based charities, the indigent were safe and their physical and spiritual needs were attended to, whereas on the streets they were ignored and shunned.

This was the only option from their frequently abandoned family, and they always appeared grateful when they peacefully lined up each day to enter.

Although my family would frequently remind me not to stare as we passed by, I couldn't help but notice that they reminded me of the older school kids lining up at school; they appeared calm and quiet and were simply a little down on their luck. I would agree there were a few who were more seriously impaired with mental-health issues and heavy alcoholic substance abuse, but most of these men looked burned out and grateful for the community's support. It was sad to see that they had been neglected and abandoned on the streets to die. As a sensitive preschooler at the time, the issue of homelessness shook me to my core. I would gratefully hold my mother's hand and look at the homeless with an irrational sense of guilt and shame that was imprinted on me at an early age. Poverty was everywhere, and my family implicitly knew that we were only one paycheque away from missing rent and being bounced out of our home.

My Sunday School at Fred Victor Mission was one of the local Christian charities that provided the destitute with hot meals, warm showers, and a cot. Sometimes when I was bored, I would slip out of the service and sneak around the men's shelter. I discovered the homeless men had access to basic toiletries, hygiene products, and there was even a locked room with a window, and I could see shelves of what appeared to be new clean or recycled clothes. Across from the main floor chapel, I could see into the homeless men's cafeteria, which I would occasionally enter out of curiosity. The gentle-looking men ate in a social environment that did not seem any different than a public restaurant or cafeteria, and they would often look up and say hello to me as if they knew me. And their smiles always made me feel good.

In comparison, I realized at a young age that my family struggles and hardship seemed trivial. Our humble beginnings on skid row and food vulnerability were no less of an issue for our family, but our family's problems were not ever discussed inside my home (or at least when I was within earshot). As far as I knew at my young age, this was the way everyone must live in the real world, which was a far cry from what I knew from storybooks and TV. It just seemed unfair. For the most part, I was secure with the knowledge that we had a roof over our heads, basic nutrition, recycled clothing, and hand-me-downs. Most importantly, I had a range of siblings that I could count on as surrogates for mothering and support. By all appearances, we did not necessarily look like we lived on Skid Row. We were always cleanly dressed and schooled with impeccable manners. I had always been instructed to put my best foot forward with a smile, which was not always easy. According to Mother, appearance mattered, and I would take this to heart. In retrospect, I think our family approach to distancing ourselves from our circumstance by putting on a good face was a lesson that served me well in life.

However, at the time, I could never fully escape from the reality of our poverty and the chaos in our neighbourhood. The close-by sirens from ambulances coming from St. Michael's Hospital never eased up from dusk to sunset; even from inside my house where it was comparatively quiet, I was constantly reminded of the outside noise of where I lived. Many of the unfortunate souls who lived on Skid Row were psychologically incapacitated with severe behavioural issues and were often dumped off by the police at St. Michael's active emergency room. Every day I saw them suffering, scream-ing, and talking to themselves. According to my mother, it was customary in the late 1950s and early 1960s for St. Michael's hospital to assess patients in the emergency room and then transfer many of them over to what was orig-inally known as the infamous and draconian *Asylum for the Insane* which was opened in 1871 and eventually revised to the *Ontario Hospital* in 1919, and more commonly referred to as "*999*" when I was a child. Mother may not have been formally educated, but occasionally she would know some amazing things about the history of our local hospitals and other fascinating random bits of knowledge as well. Anyhow, the name of the original asylum was eventually changed one last time to the *Centre for Addiction and Mental Health* (CAMH). No matter how many times the medical community tried to destigmatize the institution, the boomer generation will always recognize CAMH as the vernacular "999."

Later, as pre-adolescents, Janet and I would terrify our mother by telling her the address was inverted 999 to disguise the fact that the original address was reported to be 666, which was a symbolic sign of the devil, and the asylum of hell was where the patients had to endure for the remainder of their life.

Generally, the three of us would stay up late on Friday night while the younger children were upstairs sleeping. Mother would order a pizza while we watched old black-and-white movies, huddled together under a blanket on our old sage-green three-seater sofa. *The Snake Pit* starred the frail and traumatized Olivia de Havilland, and she reminded us of our mother. My sister and I sensed this movie resonated in a profound way for my mother, as she curled herself into a fetal position in the corner of the sofa. We thought we were joking when we innocently scared her with our stories about 999 and the similarity to *The Snake Pit*, but somehow, we recognized the movie truly terrified our mother.

In our overdramatic minds, the three of us saw how our local 999 Queen Street could have easily stood in as the movie set for *The Snake Pit*, complete with all the internal bells and whistles, including electroconvulsive therapy (ECT); frontal lobotomies; hydrotherapy; and shackled screaming patients left alone in their soiled and tattered clothes. We could see that mother saw herself in the helpless and vulnerable patients portrayed in the movie, and we knew she felt anxiety every time she went to see her doctor to get her prescriptions refilled. Her eyes sometimes looked so intense and glazed over that we believed if she sustained this appearance for any long period, her doctor would surely give her a one-way ticket to the funny farm. Janet and I made a pact to remain silent to everyone about Mother's mental illness. Meanwhile, Mother would take extra time to gussy herself up with make-up and styled hair to put her best confident foot forward whenever she went to see her doctor.

During the Christmas season, when we all needed a break from the drudgery of our everyday life, my mother always had one more trick up her sleeve to bring us a little seasonal joy. Her suggestion was we take a respite from the cruel, hard streets surrounding the economic circumstances of our reality. Her simple and cost-effective solution was located within walking distance and just two blocks east at the intersection of Queen and Yonge Street. This was the central location of Toronto's flagship department stores that were transformed into a fantasy wonderland at Christmas. Many families from our neighbourhood would anticipate going there for a little window shopping over the festive holiday season, and it gave everyone an opportunity to abandon skid row momentarily. The joyous sights were wonderfully special with the additional holiday elements of coloured lights, piped-in street music, and chestnuts roasted by street vendors on the packed streets. It was all very intoxicating for everyone to be in an exuberant and merry crowd.

I was always enthralled with how the department-store windows were bedecked in a variety of magical scenes and home vignettes inspired from Hans Christian Andersen's *Christmas Fables* and Christian biblical stories. In my young mind, I thought it would be a miracle if I could have an actual family Christmas that closely resembled the scene showing a crackling fireplace with ornate Christmas stockings on the mantle and a live spruce tree situated in the window, loaded with beautifully wrapped toys beneath! I could only imagine what it would feel like to gather round a candle-lit table with a roasted turkey with all the sides and trimmings, followed by yummy home-made mince-meat pies and other rich desserts displayed on a grand mahogany-wood table, festooned with decorative branches of spruce and holly. These holiday windows gave me the inspiration to dream about creating a new vision for my future. As Walt Disney would say every Sunday night on TV, "Dreams really do come true if you believe." And in my young, impressionable mind, I was fully invested in the power of imagination. I dreamed of a destiny that reflected more about what I saw on the other side of the Christmas windows.

On rare occasions, when it was very cold and we were a little weary from the crowds shuffling along to the piped-in street music and annoying handbells being rung by the stalwart Salvation Army soldiers, we would shuffle our cold butts into a warm banquette window table at the nearby *Dominion Grill*, just a block north of Yonge and Queen. Since Mother was working at Eaton's department store, a few of us would be chaperoned, either by older siblings or on occasion, by Granny Kirk. Although she did not live in the city, Granny always seemed to mysteriously pop in and out during times of family celebration or crisis. She reminded me of the Wicked Witch of the West with her haggard old face and intensely piercing eyes. I was on my guard with her. While my sisters got to wear white gloves, I was instructed to "Wear a smile on your sourpuss" which I *always* wore in fear of Granny Kirk.

My favourite memories of 1958 included my dad's rare demonstration of kindness and gentle physical affection toward me. I don't believe his lack of physical touch in front of others was any personal flaw in him; it was just the convention and practice of all heteronormative fathers, at least in my neighbourhood. Anyhow, in the evenings when the kids were in bed and my parents were relaxing in the first-floor parlour or kitchen, Mother would send Dad up to check on all of us, with special instructions to check in on my infant brother, Ricky, who was alone in their bedroom and sleeping in his cradle. There were a few occasions when he caught me outside of my bedroom and nestled inside Ricky's crib when I instinctively didn't want to see my infant brother wake up all alone in the dark. Any psychologist with half a brain could connect my need to provide him comfort resulted from my own traumatic start, isolated in an incubator that was devoid of parental touch. It was decades later when hospitals finally figured out it would be a good idea to have volunteers come in to provide body contact and warmth to the infants. But at the time of my birth, it was hands-off the babies for non-medical staff. There was no such thing as "baby rockers" in my day.

But even as a four-year-old child, I intuitively knew that human contact was vital to an infant. And I would stealthily climb over the rails to his crib and ever-so gently snuggle in close for a few blissful moments of mutual comfort. Periodically, I would fall asleep, and then it would be Dad who would discover what I had been up to. Instead of being annoyed and startling me, he would lovingly rub my arms or legs to wake me up without disturbing my swaddled brother laying soundly next to me. Without any words, he would smile and lovingly scoop me up, stand me on the floor and nudge me in the direction of my room, where I would peacefully fall back to sleep. There were no words and no reprimands. This was a revelation to me. He must have sensed that a loving approach to parenting was missing in my life, and he somehow understood that what I needed and craved most of all was protection.

I am confident that my father never shared his moments of tenderness toward me with my mother. We both knew from her emotionally reactive history and from the shared understanding from my other siblings there would be serious consequences for anyone who disobeyed her orders. Her go-to response would most assuredly be, "I will knock your lights out for not following my rules." Furthermore, she would have called me a sissy for not sleeping alone in my own bed throughout the night. Like a deadly sniper, she knew this would emotionally kill me and stop me in my tracks. Just the humiliation of her saying this in front of my father would be enough to destroy his support and affection toward me. Not to mention the pain and shame that I would feel as a result.

Unfortunately, our secret nighttime routine with brother Ricky in his crib would come to an abrupt and unwelcome end. Later one evening after a tender episode in the cradle, I awoke in my own bed to loud noises and chaos coming from my parents' bedroom. I could hear threats and physical fighting, swirling like a hurricane out of hell in everyone's direction. It was visceral and frightening. I remember fearing for everyone's safety. I knew there was nothing I could do to stop the path of destruction. I knew that there was nowhere for me to hide and take shelter in the dark of my room. For a brief second, I thought I could hide in the closet, but I was paralyzed with fear that they would hear me and open my door to the eye of their hurricane. The best I could do to protect myself was to stay quiet under a useless blanket, clutching it tightly at my chest, hoping it would soon end. When I woke up in a wet bed the following morning, I somehow assumed that I had been the origin of the storm. It was instantly clear that I had snuck into my infant brother's crib at night for the last time.

As I got a bit older, I finally started to realize that I'd had nothing to do with that hurricane of hell that rained down from my mother, and she put the recent devastation of Hurricane Hazel to shame. The genesis of my mother's wrath was revealed after my father recognized that Ricky's blond hair and blue eyes had no resemblance to himself, and he was understandably furious over my mother's infidelity and deceit. In retrospect, even at my young age, I felt that he should have known and expected this. According to my older sisters, they had both cheated in their marriages and neither one had a leg to stand on. I was curious to know if their infidelity and anger impacted my sisters and brothers in any way. I know that I cannot speak for Rosemary, Janet, nor my brother Jackie, who was the closest to me in age. What I *can* say for myself is that I became a habitual and closeted bedwetter, and this filled me with shame. I carried this unmanageable curse until the age of nine, even though my sister Rosemary never made an issue of it when she had to change the bedsheets.

My place for a little stress relief was a simple patch of concrete paving on Sherbourne Street, directly in front of our small rental home; it was thought of as the family yard and playground. As I recall, there was no back yard; it was rented out as tenant parking. I would open the front door and voilà, I was right in the thick of things, playing in pedestrian traffic and spying on transients, hanging outside an adjacent beer tavern from across the street. Sometimes we explored the alleys and laneways, and I recognized all the nearby banks and shops, which acted as my landmark boundaries. Various sisters and brothers were charged with monitoring this crazy carnival of pedestrian characters and vehicular traffic while supervising my sister Janet, who was five, myself who was four, and my younger brother Jackie who was three. For additional security, Mom and Granny Kirk were content to yell at me from inside the parlour window or threaten me from the front door with a licking if I disobeyed or accidentally ventured beyond their sightline. Granny Kirk was good at striking the fear of God in me when I did not meet with her approval. For dramatic effect, she would snap her false teeth, or "choppers," which would then rattle loose and scare me. Any one of her unique quirks and expressions was enough to scare me into minding my manners or *P's and Q's.*

Heaven forbids I would grow up to be a "Nancy-boy" as they would be inclined to say within earshot. I may have had no clue what I wanted to be when I grew up, but I knew that it was my decision to make on my own terms—if I was to be a Nancy-boy, well, so be it. I had no clue at the time what this expression meant. What others may have thought to be a negative start to my humble and precarious life on skid row didn't matter to me; I regarded coming from the school of hard knocks as a badge of honour. Everything I endured as a child strengthened my resolve to get the hell out of Dodge as fast as I could. I rarely suffered from any serious depression, and the difficulties I faced served to motivate me more. Most of my short flirts with depression have essentially been attributed to situationally based anxiety and a fear of failure. As with my mother before me, I would change my environment or flee from a threat, and I pretty much have stubbornly remained that way to this day. It's how I operate best.

I have always relied on my intuition first, and only then will I commit to doing my fact-finding to either support or debunk my decisions in life. Intuition has saved a lot of unnecessary time being wasted falling down rabbit holes that could have easily led me astray from my goals and design intentions in life. My personal philosophy was simple: If I felt good, then I had no need to change, and if I felt bad then I would remove myself from the equation. It was a rather simple but effective decision-making strategy that served me well.

3
FALL FROM GRACE!
137 FIRST AVENUE, 1959-1962

As the time drew near for us to move, Mother took Janet and I on our very first ride on the streetcar and subway, starting from our current home in downtown Toronto, then over to our new home that awaited us on the other side of the *Don Valley Parkway*. The easiest and least expensive way to get there was by the Toronto Transit Commission (TTC), and it cost ten cents for school-age kids to ride, back in the day. En route to the corner of Queen and Yonge Street, Mother would check our shoelaces and make sure that they were secured with a double-bow knot (which I had just learned to do on my own), and then we were good to go upon her orders. I was instructed to always walk on the outside, Mother walked in the centre, and my sister walked on the inside, close to all the shop windows and buildings. Janet and I had only ever seen electric streetcars on Queen Street, but we had never ridden on them! Of course, we had watched them many times, especially when there was a problem! It was fascinating to see how the whole thing was so beautifully engineered, yet still required manual assistance when things broke down. The metal wheels would frequently grind in the tracks, and it would get our attention every day when the overhead connection to the power line above would become disconnected.

When this happened, the streetcar conductor would have to come outside of the streetcar and manually jimmy the connection back onto the electric wire. Meanwhile, the passengers would look quite bored with the whole stop-and-go situation. Janet and I found the streetcar operations fascinating and amusing.

Once we reached the southwest corner of Queen and Yonge Street, we entered through the revolving glass doors of Eaton's flagship store. Mother continued to tightly squeeze our hands as insurance when we proceeded toward the escalator and then down to the lower level. I felt excited and jubilant and just a pinch nervous, while Janet seemed quietly withdrawn and unsure of what to expect. Following Mother's countdown from three, Janet and I were prepared to jump onto the moving steps of the original-wood escalator exactly like the one I would discover decades later when I lived in NYC when I would shop on the seventh-floor men's department at the back of Macy's.

My first impression as a young child was the old wooden escalators looked and sounded positively medieval and threatening, but exciting, nonetheless. Taking a quick moment to double check our shoelaces, Mother alerted us that she would bark out when it was time for us to jump in unison. When she did this, we would all land as rehearsed on the first moving step together. I would then awkwardly clamp my left hand onto a flat, black-rubber handrail, which seemed to suction the nervous sweat from the palm of my small hand. My other hand remained tethered to my mother's firm grip, and I could feel both her and the escalator chugging like the old steam locomotives I had seen in my Saturday-morning television cartoons.

I was so entranced by the escalator mechanics and design that I momentarily forgot my mother and sister were with me. I tried to take everything in with all my heightened senses and awareness. I could physically feel the clunky vibrations behind the escalator side panels, and I could make out the faint scent of the oil that lubricated the mechanical and operational parts. We lived near a gas station and an auto-mechanic shop, located maybe half a block south of our Sherbourne Street home, so I was familiar with the smell of oil. As I looked down, I could see the stairs disappearing under the floor. It was like magic how the large, ominous-looking metal claws on the steps that reminded me of a bulldozer, and mechanically disappeared at the bottom. As we approached the end, Mother counted down from three as the steps were swallowed up like quicksand. The only scary part of the ride down was the thought of getting my shoelaces caught and pulled under the floor.

My introductory escalator ride in Toronto was indelibly imprinted on my consciousness as we quickly repeated the same routine on another escalator, moments later. Following the first ride down, Mother ushered and navigated our way through the crowds of people. She stopped, briefly, to look at the route to the next escalator on a framed poster attached to one of the large rectangular structural columns clad in grey tiles with candy-apple red lettering. I could read at this point, and I noticed the sign indicated the subway stop as "Queen Street" and included directions to the next escalator. Upon getting our bearings, we took the second escalator further down one level to our subway destination onto the northbound-train platform. I can recall feeling I had ants in my pants as I was consumed with the biggest adventure in my life. However, when I looked over at my sister's cautious expression, I could see she wasn't feeling the same; she appeared apprehensive and nervous about the crowds of people.

As we waited close to the inside wall on the platform for the train to arrive, Mother mentioned that we were riding on Toronto's first subway that opened four years earlier, just a few short months before I was born in 1954. And like my sister, Mother admitted that she felt a bit stressed even though she had ridden the subway a few times before. This news about the inaugural TTC opening in the year I was born would always be memorable in my mind, and I joked with Janet that it was created in honour of my birthday! Without any words, she simply rolled her eyes back in her head and plugged her nose; she was not amused and gave me the evil eye to cut it out!

Apparently, she had learned some effective non-verbal communication strategies from her kindergarten classmates on the school playground, and I was impressed. Indeed, this was just one more valuable skill that I noted as we awaited the arrival of the train. Well, that is up until I heard the blast of the train's horn, and the braking of the screeching train wheels. I felt a powerful gust of cold air that blew my hair back, and I told Mother that I loved the subway blow job, and that I couldn't wait to feel it again. I thought it felt like a tornado from the Wizard of Oz. For some unknown reason, my comments netted me a stinging smack in the back of the head. When the screeching train finally stopped, my mother snorted something to the effect, "Good grief—shut your mouth, Michael!" The doors opened, and she commanded us to "Get-on." The doors quickly shut behind us and we rode silently on our way.

Our new Toronto subway line had twelve stops and we had to travel two stops to reach our first transfer stop at College/Carlton Street. From there, we escalated our anxious butts up to a nearby exit from an Art Deco-inspired building to a smaller Eaton's store location, which catered to the more expensive taste of the well-to-do from nearby Rosedale. Today, the secondary Eaton's location is now occupied by a *Winners* store, regrettably. Thankfully, the historical architectural bones and the interior gestural nods to Art Deco remain. Once outside, the three of us transferred onto an east-bound streetcar, and we rode into our aspirational dream of an exciting new future within a larger home and a more kid-friendly neighbourhood. Perched on the inside window seat, I saw a whole new world opening before my eyes, and it was breathtakingly beautiful and exciting. First, we rode by Allan Gardens and through Cabbagetown. Turning southbound, the street-car turned onto Parliament Street and continued eastbound onto Gerrard Street. Eventually, we crossed over the Don Valley ravine and stopped at the main intersection of Broadview and Gerrard Street. While we were stopped at the red light, Mother alerted us of membership cards that she had in her purse so we could visit the Riverdale Public Library for the children's reading hour every Saturday morning. And I remember thinking to myself how thoughtful and kind she could be when I least expected it.

Our new home was on a beautiful tree-lined street, located at 137 First Avenue, next to St. Matthew's Church, which immediately became my new Sunday School. The first difference I noticed was how quiet the neighbour-hood was! The homes were all free-standing, with short front lawns and long, narrow backyards. It was a sanctuary compared to where we had lived on Sherbourne Street!

After a few short weeks in our new home, I was pre-registered and ready to start my first day of kindergarten. I was beyond happy, and I felt all grown up. I was pretty much speed walking toward my first day of kindergarten with Janet, who was entering grade one, along with my sister Rosemary, who was entering grade five at Withrow Junior Public School.

It seemed like an endless walk; first we started walking east from our home on First Avenue toward Logan Avenue, and then we proceeded north for ten long blocks to school. On the way, we joined a cavalcade of other first-day students in the procession to our school. While most students entered from either ends of the building, my sister Rosemary escorted me around to the back of the school yard and led me to a central dedicated entrance for kindergarten. She introduced me to my teacher, who was outside and ringing a handbell while waving us inside. My teacher's name was Miss Snow, and Walt Disney couldn't have picked a more fitting person to match her name; she looked just like a fairy-tale princess.

Once, all the kids were safely inside, she told our class that it was her first year and she was fresh out of teacher's college; we were her very first kindergarten class. After the first few weeks, we slowly got to know each other and learned the class routine, and the remainder of the year seemed to go by in a flash! Initially, I thought we would be doing a lot more independent reading, but instead Miss Snow would have a daily story hour like the Riverdale library that we attended on weekends. We would all sit on the floor in front of her chair, and she would read to us. Since I had already learned to read some of the exact same stories from Janet, I frequently found myself nodding off to Miss Snow's soft, evenly modulated voice after an exhausting walk to the school, frequently on an empty stomach.

There were two other things that stood out in my impressionable young mind during the first few weeks. The first outside-class guests were two police officers: one male and one female. They introduced us to their mascot *named* Aylmer the Safety Elephant. The police spent the better part of the morning explaining how to be safe on the street and how to get help if we needed it. We were then invited to participate in a bunch of "what-if" situations. If *this* happened, then *what* would we do? Afterward, we had time to go and beep the horn in Aylmer's toy patrol car and ask questions directly to him. I was too shy to go up with the other kids, who were acting a little crazy. I thought they were in playschool with all their laughing, joking, and basically acting like fools in front of our guests.

The second highlight that sticks out in my memory was this girl in my class named Anne, who spelled her name just like *Anne of Green Gables*. She had straight, jet-black hair, chalk-white skin, and a resting smirk-like smile. I can't recall ever seeing Anne's teeth, and I became obsessed with waiting for the moment when she might let her guard down. I noticed that Miss Snow would always come to stand next to Anne and softly whisper whatever question or feedback she had for her ears only, while the rest of us kids would respond to her inquiries from the front of the room, and we would shout back our response to what we had heard. We looked like heathens compared to Anne. She looked refined and elegant for a young person. Anne's eyes weren't like mine, yet they were not like a typical Asian person, nor how I perceived them to be at the age of five. I would have guessed her eye shape was somewhere in between. Without question, she was unique, not resembling anyone else from class. I liked her because she stood out to me. She was an introvert with a little bit of a dark edge, and I was happy that she felt comfortable sitting next to me.

Anne always wore a distinctive type of dress, unlike what all the other girls wore. Her dresses were plain and simple, without pattern, prints, or bright colours like the other girls in class. I believe this was the first time I'd heard Miss Snow refer to her dresses as either a jumper or a tunic. Oddly enough, two years later, Janet had her own park-bench-green-coloured tunic when we attended Winchester Public School. And this confirmed my belief that Anne was cool and ahead of her time. She was a kindergarten trendsetter, just like my teacher.

Anyhow, I remembered Anne's unique personality and quiet perspective on things was not conventional and did not comport with the rest of the kids in our class. So, being a little different meant she was already in my good books! And I knew she liked me, as I was one of the very few classmates that she would have any direct eye contact with. Although I was only five, I kind of felt like her protector and made sure I was always nearby. If I wasn't so madly in love with my teacher, I knew Anne would have been my first school crush.

Following one of our routine naps on the floor mats that we would find in a stack at the back of the room, Miss Snow asked everyone to collect their paints from a display of individual tiny glass jars that she had collected from recycled baby-food jars over the previous summer. It was a smart move and provided us manageable-size jars with lids that we could carry without spilling. She seemed so organized and prepared; I figured she must have worked all summer in anticipation of her first year of teaching, and in my opinion, she did not disappoint. Our assignment was to paint a picture of our home and family.

Everyone, including myself, was using lots of colours: red for the house, green for the trees, and so on. But my friend Anne painted in lots of grey and black, with dark blue tones as an accent colour. Her house was painted in black, with no embellishment other than a front door and one window. She did not show a white picket fence around the garden like everyone else copied, nor did she have any stick figures to represent family members. I had no idea if she lived alone or if she had parents, and I was taken by her unique approach that did not imitate anyone else, whose work all looked very similar and plagiarized.

Her work made me stop and think about what she was trying to communicate. Were all the family members inside because it was a nighttime scene? Most of us painted a bright-yellow sun but she'd omitted it. Some of my classmates snickered and talked about her alleged "weirdness," while I just assumed she had painted a cloudy dark day or night. And instead of joining in with the other kids who began to tease her behind her back, I thought holy moly! I really liked her more than anyone except for my teacher. I had a silly crush on her the entire year without saying a word to her.

As my first year was coming to an end in early June, Miss Snow announced that she had been promoted and would be a teacher in grade one for one half of our kindergarten class, while the remaining half would have someone new. Nobody knew who would be in what class section, and this gave me something to think about over the summer. Maybe there were some who looked forward to another teacher, but I did not. Following my birthday, our family spent our summer vacation residing on First Avenue, and I dreamed about returning. When the school year ended, I was curious to see what room I would be in the following year for grade one and who my teacher would be. The only thing my family did all summer was hang out, go to Sunday school, and make Saturday morning pilgrimages to the Broadview Street Library. That was pretty much our routine.

However, one highlight that comes to mind is when my eldest sisters, Lois, and Edna, got confirmed next door at St. Matthews. I thought it looked like a mass wedding with all the girls dressed in pure white. Toward the end of the summer, Edna got all gussied up one night in this beautiful royal-blue satin, form-fitting dress that was sleeveless. The big surprise was there was an over-skirt attachment that wrapped around the dress, and it was secured with a big fabric rosette clip, allowing the skirt to cover the sides to the back, revealing an open front to showcase the figure-hugging dress inside. Everyone in the family gushed but none more than me. I sat on the flat top of the backside of the living-room sofa as all the girls made a big fuss over her new "cocktail dress."

Around the same time, my favourite sister Janet had won some sort of contest, and the prize was innumerable stacked wood crates loaded with green glass bottles of Coca Cola stored in our basement for special occasions. Somehow, her prize was connected to a radio-station-sponsored street party where everyone attending was looking at my sisters and neighbours who were holding vibrantly coloured new transistor radios up to their ears. I can recall desperately wanting to have one for myself. According to my sisters, the radios were given out only to teenagers.

Meanwhile, I found my own joy in preparing for my first day of grade one and drilling Janet about what I could expect and the new clothes that I would wear in anticipation. The two of us played a lot in the back yard and we passed the time by putting on make-believe plays and talent shows, per the programming and direction of Janet. Our plays were for our own amusement, essentially. Although, on hot days I can recall my mother bringing us sandwiches and lemonade outside while inspecting the mischief we were up or seeing why we were stealing chairs and blankets from the house. Janet and I were making stage curtains.

Janet would always tell Mother it was my idea, and she was probably right. But it was her suggestion, and I was her apprentice doing all the grunt work. Mother would let it slide, as she wanted us to spend the entire day outside. She would tell us that she didn't want us "nipping at her heels, and under her feet all day long." Whenever I was accused by Janet of stealing the blankets or any other household infraction, I would secretly look in the backyard lawn for a worm or spider, and when Janet's back was turned, I would slip the harmless creepy-crawly down her back collar. Then I would run and take cover as she screamed and shimmied the earth dwellers out from her clothes, shrieking like a banshee. I figured we were now even-steven. And neither of us turned our back on one another in front of our mother. We pinky-crossed our fingers that we would act like twins who instinctively understood one another.

Finally, the day arrived when I could return to school for my first day of grade one. Down the school hall in front of me, I could see Miss Snow, and my heart raced with excitement. She was holding a class list and waving her students into the classroom. As I approached the class door, I got her friendly hand invite to come in. My dreams and prayers were answered! There she was dressed like a movie star. Her clothes reminded me of those worn by Lucille Ball from *I Love Lucy*. There was no way she was just a teacher, being dressed so fancy. I imagined she must have been a model or a movie star before she started teaching. She was even more breathtakingly beautiful, graceful, and kind than the year before. And I loved the way she stood out from all the other teachers.

Later in the day after I returned home, I shared my excitement and observations of my first day at our overcrowded kitchen table for supper. I was all about

Miss Snow this and Miss Snow that, blah, blah, blah. And my sisters then made comparisons to the beauty and style of our sister Edna. They compared her stunning beauty to that of an actress named Sophia Loren. I recall not understanding who she was, but I nodded my head in agreement. As a six-year-old kid, I had first-hand knowledge of Edna's high fashion potential when she got all dolled up in her blue satin dress, but she wasn't my teacher, after all. Miss Snow was flawlessly dressed every day. And my big sister Edna was, as far as I was concerned, was just my plain old everyday sister. I saw how she dressed like everyone else on the block. No question she had occasional style when she went out, but not the everyday kind of flair of my teacher.

I noticed that throughout the course of our informal family meal, my brothers had not spoken a word. Some of us were still eating supper when Kenny and Johnny abruptly got up from the table. As Kenny pushed in his chair under our late 1950s chrome-and-grey Formica kitchen set, he said "time for the men to leave the "girly-girls." For a brief second, I wondered if he was talking about me, when he gave me a parting side glance that looked like I had done something wrong. I didn't dwell on it, and I eagerly jumped back into our table conversation.

Meanwhile, the next day in the school lunchroom, I recall none of the other boys in my class were talking about anything, really. And I was bored sitting with them. On the other hand, I could overhear the girls gossiping about how beautiful our teacher was. And that's when I planned to start sitting with the girls the following day, and every day thereafter. I preferred to be with "the girly-girls," as Kenny had described. The girls were simply more observant of things that mattered to me: style, art, beauty, fashion, and design. They were clearly smarter than the boys, in my young mind. And that's when I began hearing whispers from kids in my class who thought I was "odd."

When I asked Janet if she thought I was odd, she responded by telling me that she loved the way I saw things. But she was surprised that I liked to sit with the girls in my class for lunch. She told me we should take advantage of our time at school to make new friends and that I should try to hang out more with some of the boys. We agreed that we had lots of time to hang out together at home. Besides, we shared a bedroom where we could freely gab about our different experiences at school.

I bet if my previous kindergarten friend Anne, who had been placed in the other section of grade one with a different teacher, was in my class, we would have happily curated a strong friendship that we would cobble together, leaving everyone else behind. I missed being inspired by her nuanced and solitary approach to learning and her artistic creativity. In my view, the two of us were clearly the most creative and forward thinkers in our class, and I was sad not to have her alongside me in grade one. As I reflected on her for a moment in the lunchroom, I imagined Anne must have been an only child with parents who treated her more like a young adult, as I wished my family would have done with me. At least, that's what I conjured up in my mind.

Playground recess activities were a complete waste of my time. I would have preferred to stay indoors and do more independent reading and experimenting with the art supplies. I knew I did not want to kick a ball, and I certainly did not want to always sit and gossip with the girls. I noticed that kids in my class were already starting to separate from me because I was spending too much time with the girls, and it took personal courage to sit in my own feelings and not run from my own desires and personal interests—despite what was expected from others.

Meanwhile, back in class I continued noticing every visual detail of Miss Snow with a critical eye, and it was clear that she was flawless. She was wearing a black shirt-waist dress covered in large pink flowers, and it was breathtaking! I recall all the details: the top part of the dress had short-capped sleeves; the front was very form-fitting with pointed boobies and buttoned up to the top with a tiny Peter Pan collar. She wore a wide cloth belt and buckle in the same matching printed fabric that cinched the dress in at the waist while the bottom of her dress flared down and out to about her mid shins. As she walked into the classroom wearing her black pumps, her dress appeared to swirl. I had only seen people dress like her on TV, and Miss Snow was *my* star. She became my first role model on how to dress differently than other people. I recall thinking that when I grew up, I wanted, in my own way, to be as fabulously beautiful as Miss Snow.

I thought to myself, why dress in boring daily clothes when you could dress to the nines any day of the week? I returned home that day and informed my mother that I would only wear clothes that I bought, and I refused to wear any more hand-me-downs from the local thrift store. I even went as far as to steal money one time from my mother's pocketbook and headed over to a little nearby bargain shop at Gerrard Street and Logan to purchase a pair of black polished shoes for myself. When I returned home, Mother saw what I had done and, surprisingly, she did not scold me. In fact, she did just the opposite, and once again this took me by surprise. She quietly told me that if I promised *not* to go into her purse, she would secretly take me shopping to pick out my own clothes. The only mandatory requirement was that I had to promise not to tell anyone, and if any of my siblings asked why I was getting brand-new clothes and not them, I was to tell them that Mother had found these almost-new clothes at the local thrift store, and they just happened to be in my size.

To make it look even more credible, she would immediately wash my new clothes and let them air-dry with wrinkles and remove any labels or tags. It was our secret, and the very first time she made me feel noticed and loved. However, she took the wind out of my sail when she expressed her take on the situation. She claims she did this out of frustration and didn't know what else to do with me. She warned me that she couldn't afford to do this with the other kids and if they found out, she would never allow me to have my way again. So, even my conventional "Hurricane Mom" had calm, gentle moments between her normal storm of chaotic behaviour. I quickly learned how to watch out for her emotional swings, and strategically I knew everything was about monitoring her unpredictable timing of her moods. I learned at an early age to adapt my behaviour accordingly.

Back at Withrow Public School, everything was sailing smoothly along, and I was quickly becoming my teacher's pet. I sat in the centre row right in front of her desk and I could see everything she did. Every day, she would put a delicious-looking red apple just a kiss away from my grasp. Whenever she asked for a volunteer to read aloud, I always raised my hand first, and invariably she would pick me to respond. Even in my first report card, she mentioned that my reading comprehension was well above average. And she also mentioned that I was a sensitive child with an active imagination. I could not tell if this was a compliment or not; I overheard other adults and my mother refer to me this way.

Anyhow, I was soon dethroned of my status on one fateful day. Since I was a little late for school that day and had missed my breakfast at home, I was hungry and became laser-focussed with the apple on my teacher's desk in front of me. It was a miserable, snowy, wet day and I had refused to go to school unless I could take the streetcar. After the other kids went, Mother had acquiesced and gave me ten cents to ride the streetcar along Broadview, insisting once again that this was just between the two of us. I was a little out of sorts, and I wondered if Miss Snow would notice if I helped myself to her apple. As recess approached, I put my desperate plan into motion. I waited until the last student was ready to leave while Miss Snow stood at the door ushering everyone out for recess. I thought she was distracted just enough not to notice me as I snatched the apple into my fist and then hid my hands inside my coat pocket. As I met Miss Snow at the door she asked me, "Michael, do you have something in your pocket that doesn't belong to you?" In a flash I believed if I did not speak, then technically I could not be accused of fibbing, so I just shook my head side to side. I instantly felt the heat of blood rushing into my cheeks and was embarrassed for not telling her the truth about the reason why I helped myself to her apple.

I knew it was wrong and, in a heartbeat, Miss Snow picked up the wall-mounted phone located next to the door and called for the vice-principal's assistance. When he arrived, they both escorted me back to his office without saying a word. My stomach was in a knot, and I felt like a hive of buzzing bees were eating me inside out. I couldn't find an exit to escape to, and I felt like a shackled convict walking toward his execution. I didn't know what was going to happen, but I knew it wasn't good. When we arrived at his office, I was surprised to see my sister Janet there.

That is when I was informed that I was going to be strapped for my lying and theft, and my sister was there to act as a witness. When the principal grabbed my hand and held it out straight in front of me, I understood what was about to unfold. I stoically bit my lip and closed my eyes, and that's when I heard and felt the leather strap brand the palm of my hand with unimaginable burn. I was humiliated and felt like a failure. Regardless of the stinging pain that felt like a thousand bees burrowing into the palm of my hand, I resolutely stared forward without shedding a tear. I could sense everyone present expected me to cry as I started to feel my eyes on the brink of welling up. A few years later I would feel the strap on another two occasions before I finished grade eight: once for walking on the wrong side of the steps and once for using my loud outside voice while wearing an untucked shirt inside the school while I was acting out with a few classmates in the hall.

However, the very first time I was strapped in grade one, my post-traumatic shock didn't kick in until afterward when Janet and I stepped outside the school. I remember breaking down and crying like a snotty-nosed baby as I tried to gain my composure and suck back the shame of my self-disappointment. I had embarrassed my sister and humiliated myself. I had severed my reputation as the teacher's pet. Clearly, I felt deserving of everyone's hate. I earned my punishment for lying, and from Sunday School, I knew it was a cardinal sin. I tried to explain to my sister how I was hungry, and this was the reason why I took the apple. Janet came to my rescue as usual and mentioned that we should not share this bad incident with Mother, as "she would never understand." To appease my hunger and pass a little time, we stopped at the corner store at her suggestion, so that she could buy us some penny candies to make me feel better while I composed myself. According to Janet, everything had to be synchronized with the normal end of our school day, and it was important that our timing was not off to indicate we had been let out an hour earlier than normal. By the time we got home, everything on the outside appeared normal as ever, but on the inside, I couldn't wait to go to my room and collapse on my bed.

The remainder of my year in Miss Snow's class was a pitiful blur. I was too ashamed to even look her in the face after that fateful day. I don't recall volunteering to do anything in class. The summer could not come fast enough for me! As good fortune would have it, the City of Toronto did a rezoning over the summer, and instead of returning to Withrow, I would be transferred south to *Dundas Public School* for grade two. Clearly, my new school was not as memorable as my first two years at Withrow, but two things did stick out in my memory.

My new teacher had a name that most of the other kids pronounced incorrectly. Mrs. Tomasina was a lyrical and pretty-sounding name and that is the only thing I can recall from grade two, other than learning how to sprint and run class races on the track outside. I was there for just the one year, and the most significant thing to happen was not about me; it happened to Janet. Although she was a year ahead when we'd started out at our new school, she'd unfortunately had a terrible year with chronic ear infections. Eventually she was referred for a surgical skin graft over her eardrum at the Doctor's Hospital, out west on Brunswick Avenue. Because of so much school time missed, she'd been held back a year, which crushed her spirit and made her feel stupid, although it was no fault of her own. Anyhow, our family would be moving over to *Cabbagetown* on the west side of the Don Valley and back to our original stomping grounds. Janet and I knew we would both be in the same grade at the new school, and it was my idea that we could let people assume we were fraternal twins. It was nobody's business, and if it would make her feel less self-conscious that would be a good thing (for both of us). She did not say yes or no to my idea and just gave me one of her sheepish grins that she'd inherited from our father. Her quirky smile let me know that my hare-brained idea made her feel a little better. I could always pull her out of a mood.

The other major takeaway from that year is I had this selfish little secret that I had uncovered about myself at the mom-and-pop shop across from the school. I must fess up and alert you to the fact that I became an addict at age seven. Well, that was how I saw my situation, anyhow. I knew my mother had her "nervous pills," and my preferred drug that hooked me was the moment that I first tasted a five-cent bag of bacon-and-hickory flavoured *Humpy Dumpty* (Old Dutch) potato chips. There must have been several other available varieties, but I never deviated from the chosen brand over the entire year at *Dundas Public School*. Each day I anticipated a nickel-bag fix on the way to school and another nickel bag on the way home; that was how I spent my daily allowance of ten cents. And like a true addict, I waited until I was walking alone on the street to scarf down my fix of salty chips. There was no way I was going to risk having to share my coveted stash on the school playground! There would be nothing left for me, and this was reason enough to make me withdraw and force me to get my fix in the shadow of public view.

Later that school year in early May, I was admitted into *Sick Children's Hospital* for an entire week as I recovered from an unnecessary appendicitis removal, predicated on a tiny white lie I told over a melodrama that I had created in my mind at Sunday School. This lie triggered my mother into rushing me to the hospital like she had done when my sister Rosemary's appendix burst a year earlier at Withrow Public School. The genesis of this unfortunate and unnecessary surgery was manufactured in my mind. It was a legitimate-sounding reason to escape from my *St. Matthew's Sunday School* class on a specific day when my teacher was absent and out sick for the day. I was randomly selected as the only boy to sit in an all-girl group, and I knew I was going to be relentlessly teased. And true enough, the moment I sat in the assigned circle of girls, the snickering from the other kids began, my new teacher for the day did nothing to stop it, and I felt pissed-off!

Instantly, I knew that I had to take control of the situation and use the power of my creative imagination to end this disastrous predicament. And presto, my sister Rosemary's episodic experience with a burst appendix came to my mind. So, I dramatically pointed out to the replacement teacher that I was not well, and my stomach was hurting. She recommended that I go home to rest, and I thought to myself Halleluiah! But this fooling everyone did not last long. After I returned home, my mother recognized the alleged sharp pains I was having in the very same area that she recalled from when my sister Rosemary suffered from a burst appendicitis. And boom, before I even had a chance to explain my lying little ass, my mother went into full commando mode, and she called my bluff.

Immediately she rushed us off in a cab with great panic to the emergency room at Toronto's *Sick Children's Hospital.* I was quickly assessed by a young-looking doctor who kept pressing his fingers into my lower abdomen, which hurt, and I genuinely winced from his examination. From the tiny examination room, I was wheeled out on a gurney down a dark corridor and parked outside an operating room for a moment to say goodbye to my mother. I did not know what the hell was happening, but I knew it was too late for me to admit that I was faking almost everything except the excruciating pain from the doctor's examination. I simply could not admit my guilt and shame for lying. I figured it was better to face my chances with the operation rather than face the consequences of my mother at home. The last thing I recall hearing as I was wheeled into the room and transferred onto a table was a nearby voice of someone from behind who held a mask over my nose and mouth; I was instructed to "Breathe in and count back from ten."

Later I woke up in a four-bed ward in a bed next to the window, and I noticed my mother and older sisters standing around. I had no clue whether they had learned the truth about this unnecessary surgery from my doctor. In my groggy state, I assumed they did not, as everyone seemed genuinely concerned and happy with the result of the procedure. Shortly after my family left, I reflected on the serious consequence of even a little white lie. From everything I'd learned at Sunday School, I knew I was a sinner, and I kept my fingers crossed that God would forgive me yet one more time!

For the remainder of the week in the hospital, I followed my day nurse around like a lost puppy dog, even going as far as to track her down in her small office where she filled out her reports. She lifted me up onto her knees and proceeded to update her written notes in the patient files. But she told me she had to get on with her work and that I could go hang out in the playroom down the hall, or I could go back to my ward. She reminded me that dinner was in an hour, and then later, at seven p.m., I would get a lemonade just before I had to settle down for the night. I thanked her for her kindness and patience and then sauntered off back to my room.

At the end of the week, I returned home, and I faithfully cited the Lord's Prayer every night, asking the Lord for forgiveness. Why could I not act normal like my siblings who knew better? Many times, I concluded my bedtime prayers by asking God to bless various people while sensing my soul's real purpose was to be noticed and simply be loved and to share my love. Although I did not specifically ask God's help for myself, I hoped he would still accept my apologies for my sins. There were prayers that I conjured up when I needed an escape hatch from my alleged childhood sins. On those occasions, I would simply end the Lord's Prayer with a request for more tea parties and an opportunity to play with Janet's beloved first-edition Barbie doll, who was sporting a black-and-white swimsuit and large sun hat to hide her face from the sun. That hat was everything a girl could want to protect herself from the sun, and I wanted one. However, later, at Christmas, I had to settle for a Mexican sombrero, which didn't quite measure up to Barbie's elegant sun hat.

Not too long after the apple incident, our playtime tea party was used as a ruse to discuss how our mother and father's demonstration of any affection toward anyone ended abruptly. On a random Sunday summer afternoon, my dad whisked my sister Janet and I out for a rare drive without any other family members in his 1950s Ford two-toned blue car, during an imminent thunder and lightning rainstorm over Lake Ontario! We thought he must be crazy, but we jumped at the opportunity to share some special time with him outside the home. We drove past a large neon Tip Top Tailor billboard near the baseball stadium, then he parked at nearby Sunnyside Beach, close to the lake. There were no other parked cars or people around; it was as if he planned this to be our very own private bonding time with a spectacular and panoramic view of the lake.

As soon as he turned the engine off, he positioned us on either side of his crumpled white shirt and rolled up his sleeves. He then wrapped his arms around us and pulled us in close to his side while we all stared out in silence, watching the rain pour down as sporadic lightning cracks danced upon the water's rippled surface. It was scary and beautiful all at the same time. At one point, my sister and I simultaneously looked up at our dad's face and could see a few tears slowly running down his cheeks. We had never seen him cry and silently we both knew that something was terribly wrong. We bit our lips and remained silent as he stared out at the lake. It was all too confusing, but I was so happy to finally have his hugging arms around me.

Shortly thereafter, we returned home and discovered the truth of his melancholy over our family supper. Ironically, and for the first time that I can recall, he picked me up and placed me on his lap at the head of the table after finishing another one of our typical 5:00 p.m. sharp meals. He affectionately secured me on his lap, his crumpled white shirt, and warm, hairy arms on full display to all my brothers and sisters. Normally, it would be my sister Janet on his lap, and I felt it was clearly a special occasion that he finally included me in this ritual going forward. Or so I thought. The kitchen seemed busy that night. Not only were my brothers and sisters sitting around the table, but my granny also stood near my mother with maybe one or two other adults lurking in the background, and I didn't really pay much attention.

For that one brief, indelible moment, I was in so much bliss and happiness that I failed to notice anyone else! I was basking in the warmth of my dad's lap with his protective arms wrapped around me. I will never forget how secure and invincible I felt for the first time in my life. I felt loved by him. While the adults engaged in "grown-up talk," I was keenly zoned in on the gleam of my dad's articulated metallic watchband, which he wore on his left wrist. At first, I would carefully expand it in and out like a Slinky toy. Then I pulled on his watch band extra-firm for one final time and released it. As it snapped back, it caught a few hairs from his wrist, which made him swear and jump up with dramatic force. I fell off the chair in a fit of pure laughter and happiness as he stood by, pretending to be hurt in front of his neatly pressed shirt and uniform, which hung on the back of the kitchen door leading down to our cold cellar.

The evening ended for me with pure happiness and my prayers for the promise of a closer relationship with my dad. To my misfortune, he was gone the following morning, clothes, and all. No discussion and no explanation for his disappearance from our lives. And sadly, no more visits from my dad. The only conclusion that Janet and I could conjure up was the only thing that mother wanted from my dad was his financial support. Based on the gossip from our older siblings, our father had no legal dog in the fight for a parental role, as they assumed that he had another family to return home to, and this left Janet and I feeling abandoned. I was profoundly devastated when he disappeared from my life, and I knew Janet was as well, but we never talked about the hurt.

Grade One (age six), *Withrow Public School*
Sketch of 137 First Avenue-Toronto.

137 First Avenue—Toronto
Childhood Home. Grade 1
Next to St. Matthews Church

4
SISSY-BOY
7 LANCASTER AVENUE 1963-1964

The New York Times once described Cabbagetown as containing the largest collection of Victorian homes in North America. Most of the homes were originally constructed between 1860 and 1895, and in 1963, a house could be purchased for as low as $15,000 if you were not too picky. A laneway row house would have been even lower in value at the time. After three short years of living on the east side of the Don Valley, my mother found herself single and free from her common-law relationship with my biological father and his financial support.

As a struggling single mother with so many kids and mouths to feed, Mother could no longer independently afford the rent on our spacious free-standing house on First Avenue in south Riverdale. I suspect she felt it was important to move the kids back to the west side of the Don Valley, where she was much more familiar with the proximity to downtown and she knew there would be cheaper rents in the pre-gentrified working-class ghetto of Cabbagetown. As her anxiety and stress increased, so did the frequency of her mood swings. On any given day she could be sweet as pie, and then, out of nowhere, the tiniest thing I did could set her off. I would tell her, "I can't understand why you chose to have so many kids that you can't afford to keep." And when I was really pissed, I would tell her I thought she was selfish and her "craziness" hurt me and the other kids. Invariably, that would make her snap and grab whatever was nearby to beat me: a wooden spoon; a spatula; a shoe, and even a wet dishrag (her favourite weapon). However, the physical abuse that hurt the most was when she smacked me with her hands, or pulled my hair, and by far the worst assault was when she plunged her jagged fingernails into my flesh. At the age of eight, the imprint of her fingernails was embedded into my left arm and hand, and although the marks may have faded over the years, the scars remain forever etched in my memory. And when I reflect now, I know her corporal punishment and physical abuse was not applied to the younger family members. Clearly, it wasn't something I believed happened to other kids in the neighbourhood.

To be brutally candid, Cabbagetown was once considered Toronto's largest urban slum, and naturally there were many over-stressed parents and large families who lived in the once-stately homes. Heaven only knows what went on inside their households. Many of the neighbourhood homes had been converted into tenement rooming houses after the Depression era in the 1930s. When we moved into the neighbourhood, entrepreneurial real-estate agents and landlords like ours were chomping at the bit to take advantage of an untapped hotbed of historical Victorian homes, while most of the inhabitants, like our family, simply saw it as a ghetto for people on welfare and the struggling blue-collar working class. As kids, we just thought of our socio-economic circumstance as normal; so long as we had a roof over our head, food on the table, and a warm bed, then all was good in our world. We had many neighbours and peers who had much less than our family, and we felt grateful that we were not in their shoes.

However, things were about to change and blur our distinction from other poorer families. Mother was forced to go onto *family welfare* as a last financial resort, and she gratefully accepted the taxpayer's dime. She stretched out every penny the best she knew how. She said it was nothing to be ashamed of since a significant amount of our neighbours were in more dire situations and found themselves only able to afford rented rooms and illegal basement apartments that were not up to required building codes and safety regulations. They were what Mother referred to as fire traps. She remarked that it wouldn't be this way forever and took on extra part-time jobs, cleaning the local billiard hall on Parliament Street and cleaning a nearby bank in the middle of the night. She claimed she never slept and that we could use a little extra unreported income for incidental and emergency expenses.

It was a mixed blessing when my mother finally rented us our own home, even though it was a tiny hovel of a place that was tucked away in an obscure back laneway called *Lancaster Avenue,* which no one ever noticed. My sister Janet knew immediately that things looked grim for us and much less inspiring than she had anticipated. "We are living in a lane. Can you believe it?" she asked. But for some inexplicable reason, I told her that I found our new home and neighbourhood very exciting and different. In my mind, this could be a whole new adventure and beginning for us. There was so much more for us here to explore and take advantage of in our new downtown location. I saw the possibilities, while my dear sister sank into the poverty of our circumstance. But things would eventually look up for her.

Our new address at 7 Lancaster Avenue was situated in a short lane just north of Winchester and west off Parliament Street. It was anchored by the very popular Brewers Retail Store to the east and by Winchester Public School on Rose Avenue to the west. Or as we preferred to say in terms that made sense to us, "the adult side and the kid's side." Random strangers would ask, "Where's Lancaster?" And according to my sister, my smart-ass response was always, "Just look behind the beer store!"

Our little pied-à-terre consisted of four very narrow row houses adjacent to a loud, smelly auto-mechanic shop that would later be converted into a boxing club and community drop-in. The entire walk would take a senior citizen two minutes on a slow, arthritic day! At the age of seven, I could literally hold my breath and make it to my front door from Parliament Street.

We didn't know anyone or have any neighbourhood friends at the time. The only thing that was familiar and brought us a measure of reassuring comfort was the nearby *Parliament Street Library,* which we were well indoctrinated with from our recent and joyful membership at the Riverdale branch. One of the first things we did was to visit our new library and immediately take out a membership. At least we were assured of something familiar, and it provided a continuity in our previously established Saturday morning routines, while Mother and the older siblings did their big weekly cleaning of the house from top to bottom. Meanwhile, Janet and I continued to spend our glorious Saturday mornings in the sanctuary of the children's wing of the library, as we sat by a fireplace while the librarian read us stories. Afterward, we had a dedicated opportunity to explore the children's picture-book section, but most times I wandered off, exploring the books for the older kids and adults. Those peaceful childhood memories at the library were our best recollections about the transition to our new neighbourhood. More importantly, it was the first time a librarian tutored us on how to use the large wooden card-catalogue console with the *Dewey Decimal system* of numbering and shelving of books; this gave us an advantage when we later were introduced to this with our classmates at the library inside *Winchester Public School.* We looked knowledgeable to our peers and were happy to show our new classmates who were struggling at first with the alpha-numeric coding. Learning the Dewey Decimal system made me feel grown up and no longer tethered to children's books. It meant freedom to expand my growing interests and curiosity.

I believe that I was eight and Janet would have been nine when we both saw a notice that the library was casting for a children's production of *Cinderella,* and we decided we just had to give it a go. "No more playacting in the backyard for us," we said. This was professional theatre as far as we were concerned. Performance was in our DNA, and I knew it was in my destiny to be in the theatre someday. I was one of the two children who were cast as Prince Charming, and Janet was one of the two girls who were cast in the coveted role of Cinderella. We knew this would give us something to talk about with our new classmates at Winchester Public School, and we believed it would help gain us new friends quickly. However, shortly after we started school, I found out that my fondness for theatre and plays were for "sissies and gearboxes" and "for guys who preferred playing with sticks." While my male peers at school threw terms at me like "sissy-boy" and "fairy," the older adolescents preferred calling me a gearbox, queer, and of course faggot, the most egregious, pejorative term that continues to this very day.

I learned a fast lesson that it was not safe to share anything that I was interested in with the other boys. Particularly since I had nothing mean to say about girls, nor anything good to say about sports. I knew many guys were limited in their capacity to think beyond the confines of their limited view of the world beyond the dominant standard role they assumed as toxic young men. Much of their ethos was predicated on what had been passed down to them of socially accepted norms for masculinity. And because of this, there were many times when I felt marginalized, and I wished someone would have taught me how to physically fight back. Of course, when Janet was nearby, she would intervene and stop the bullying on my behalf—which earned me the name of sissy-boy. "What's wrong? Got to have your sister protect you, little sissy-boy?" was all I seemed to hear in the school playground.

Regrettably, my family had drilled into me that "sticks and stones may break your bones, but names will never hurt you," which was a big fat lie, and I knew it! Even my own mother was suspicious of me not doing what were considered normal boy things, and despite her claims to the contrary, I believe she found a secret pleasure in hearing outsiders curse and make crude sexual comments about girls! But that would never happen, as I had four sisters whom I adored, respected, and valued as equals in my family. Their inner strength, courage and power of conviction outshone any of my older brothers and the other guys at school—and those were the qualities I pursued.

Without a shred of doubt, Mother knew that I was perceived as a Mama's church-boy as well. She had raised me that way, but she was not prepared to help with the consequences that I suffered outside. However, she damn well knew this because I could see it in her side glances and disapproving look at me when were out together; just like my eldest brother, Kenny, had done the previous year.

Everyone in the community seemed to foist the loaded terms of "church boy" and "sissy-boy" on me throughout my journey from childhood to young adulthood. By the age of nine, I realized that their taunts were certainly not terms of endearment but rather intentional slurs to show their disapproval of me acting as a non-conventional boy. I was simply not like other boys. I was no different than any other marginalized minority, and it became my personal mission to find a way to be accepted. I had no choice if I didn't want to bullied and terrorized, no matter what price was exacted on my individual soul and spirit.

In almost every report card from grades three to seven, my teachers would reference my sensitive and artistic nature as if it were a gift and not a curse. Although I liked who I was and had no intention of totally blending in, the only friends I made who could appreciate my unique character and personality invariably happened to be girls. And I could not help but feel that my teachers' character assessment of me played a role in my growing anxiety and self-consciousness as I was struggling with my identity as a young child.

I was originally branded a "gearbox" by the garage guys who worked in front of our house. Most of the men, I was told by my mother, were paroled prisoners who had been locked up at the Toronto Don Jail and were on a work program that trained parolees for occupational trades upon release. And as bad fortune would have it, I would have to endure their name-calling, daily. I pretty much got the gist of the term, and it wasn't friendly. They were an unsavoury lot of pit-boys servicing motorcycles and cars for the likes of *Hell's Angels* and other societal outcasts. There was not one worker who wasn't covered in crude homemade tattoos, and they all had what we euphemistically referred to as Pepsi smiles (stained, decayed, and missing teeth). These guys were my nemeses as a helpless and innocent young boy in grade three, and I couldn't understand why they didn't know better.

They were among the first adults who bullied and terrorized me. And when my sisters or mother happened to be with me, the guys would switch out their monikers of gearbox and sissy-boy in favour of church boy, which my mother took as a compliment, but I surely did not! It seemed like every day when I quietly snuck out my front door for school, the toxic, foul-mouthed garage guys would be out there like clockwork, with the garage's overhead door open, rain or shine. Frequently, there was at least one of them out front, smoking and taking a long break followed by another. All three mechanics continuously rotated their breaks throughout the day. And God forbid I should come home at lunch when all three would break together and open their metal lunchboxes for a good hour. From what I could see, they never harassed my younger brothers. My sisters, on the other hand, were the recipients of occasional cat calls and whistles, until my mother would eventually stick her head out the front door and give them the hairy eye, shutting them down.

I was their favourite diversion and target for harassment. I would pretend not to notice them and distract myself as I opened the front door, fussing with my clothing or shuffling my books. Clearly, I was capitalizing on my recent community theatre experience at the nearby Parliament Street Library to help me! Unfortunately, my feeble charade at pretending to be immune to their insidious taunting and bullying fooled only myself. My miserable acting garnered no applause and clearly made no difference to the continuous snickering and taunts that made my everyday life a living hell. By this point, my only refuge was to make a quick dash over to Winchester Public School as fast as I could walk! My home was situated maybe five hundred feet from the school's front door, but it felt like miles.

Unlike many of our classmates who openly accepted that they were poor, our family did not; we always thought it was a temporary situation. We were indeed poor, and just like many of our neighbours, we wore hand-me-downs and would switch out typical Irish dinners of meat, potatoes, and vegetable for economical pancakes or eggs at least once a week. My mother and I also collected occasional groceries from the church food bank at the *Fred Victor Mission*. For a couple of years, we received charity *Christmas Star boxes* and presents that were delivered in person at *Fred Victor mission* and this would make Christmas something to look forward when money was short. Personally, it gave me a reason to attend church during the holiday season. We never went hungry that I can recall, thanks to the church food bank. We always attended the Sunday services, and it was sometime around the age of nine when our entire family was baptised at the Fred Victor mission. All our names were recorded into a large, white Bible that I believe one of my siblings eventually inherited.

From my early design perspective, our rented, postage-size home on Lancaster Avenue was one of the four row homes that gave a minimal nod to Victorian design. Unlike most of the larger surrounding houses with tall, sloping, peaked rooftops, ours was one of the few that had a flat asphalt roof that was trimmed with a heavy parapet cornice. There were no fancy bay windows or stained-glass. Maybe they were designed as servant quarters or cottages way back in the day. Who knows? Anyhow, all four of the homes on this ridiculously small avenue were occupied by families of different minorities and ethnicities that included: an Aboriginal family; an Italian Canadian couple; our large Irish family; and an Eastern-European-sounding childless couple whom we rarely saw.

Even as a young child, I was interested in how things were functionally designed in our house and how our interior household features compared to other homes. As I recall, all four of the row homes had dirt cellars with modest-sized windows at the front and back. My family was lucky, as we had additional side windows in our end-house. The largest side window was in the main-floor living room, and a second window facing west was situated in my second-floor bedroom. There was also a very tiny third window in the unfinished basement facing out to the lane running north/south, while another service window, like in all the other three houses, faced out onto Lancaster Avenue.

My earliest recollection of design discourse was with our furnace repair man, and he discussed how the small basement windows were originally designed for delivery trucks to unload coal down a chute as heating fuel for the houses. However, over time, the old coal furnace had been converted into oil and the updated replacement came with a small metal container attached to the side of the new furnace, about the size of a narrow letterbox. It was my job in the winter to fill it with water, as it was engineered to provide a little humidity and offset the dry winter heat. I filled this every weekend when I joined the family's Saturday morning chore day.

Out back, each of the four homes had a small, 200-square-foot yard that was securely contained behind high fences and a brick wall. Except for our end house. We had a small backyard that had an ungated narrow opening to the north/south lane, which I would use as a safer alternative to the front of the house, especially in the warmer weather. The interior of three of the four row homes that I had been inside had a very familiar footprint; we all had the same rubber-stamped room sizes and functional locations on two levels with floors that were covered in decades of old linoleum. There were no beautiful hardwood floors like the nearby larger Victorian homes. Fortunately, our end house had those additional windows to allow additional natural light. The first floor's typical configuration was a small sitting room at the front, a tiny dining room in the centre and a small kitchen with just enough room for a table to comfortably sit four to six people at any time.

However, when it came to how families used the available space, there were at least two families that I knew of that annexed the sitting room in favour of an additional first-floor bedroom at the front. In my home, my elder brothers Kenny and John would sleep in the converted bedroom on the first floor. Our middle dining room became the new family sitting room and the kitchen remained at the south end of the house. The second floor consisted of one small bedroom at the back facing south, and next to it was an adjacent small narrow bathroom, then another small bedroom in the middle, and finally my mother's room-facing north. I shared the middle bedroom with my sister

Rosemary, who was five years my senior. Our bedroom had a window facing out toward Winchester Public School and a small, doorless closet with a drawstring curtain that housed my sister's clothes. Meanwhile, all my clothes were stuffed into two of the four available shared small dresser drawers. Seasonal/additional clothing storage was available in a large cardboard cylindrical drum located in the basement. And I got plenty of exercise running up and down those well-worn linoleum- treaded stairs!

Our bedroom provided a measure of quiet comfort most of the time. Rosemary inspired me as a great role model; she was extremely immersed in her faith of God and was well-disciplined with her evening routines. From under the bedcovers, I would watch every night as she laid out her clothes for school the next day and did a few stretching exercises. Afterward, she said her prayers and then she would come to bed and request me to recite the Lord's Prayer as she pulled up the covers and turned toward the inside wall. I felt comfort with her rituals every night. Many times, we both overheard our mother and her latest paramour shouting and fighting next door. Rosemary would cry into her pillow, and I would curl up into a fetal position. Although it had a profound impact on Rosemary, I was a little too young to fully understand what was going on, and I never asked. I think I didn't want to know, as I sensed it all looked terribly bad and I didn't want to cry from finding out the truth. I was taught early in life that "boys don't cry."

There were many nights when I would go to bed with my brain rattling around with not understanding what was happening in my mother's bedroom that she now shared with her latest and unfriendly paramour Norman, who I assumed was the biological father of our youngest brother. I worried about my brother Gregg, who cried alone in his crib, which was situated by the door to my mother's room. Ironically, their bedroom overlooked the noisy mechanic's garage across the lane where vehicles were brought in to be repaired. And I secretly wished that my mother and her partner would take their troubles to the mechanics so they could fix their problems. I was confident those unruly pit-shop guys would loosen their rusted-out nuts and bolts and tell them it was time for a new replacement.

Sometime in the fall of grade four there was a mini renovation in our home. As conveyed by my mother, this was the result of a tiny building health-code infraction that was cited in a report from the Toronto public housing inspections. The team of two inspectors had come to visit our home while all the kids were at school or work. Mom had not been amused whatsoever by our rental slumlord, and she called Toronto city hall to complain. Our end-house was painfully lacking in sanitary health and safety conditions, but most egregious was the fact that we had only a tub and a toilet in the upstairs bathroom and no sink. The City of Toronto issued a report to our landlord's attention, and he was finally forced to install the smallest sink he could possibly find after much complaining from my mother and her assigned family services caseworker. The new and absurdly small stainless-steel, airplane-sized bathroom sink was installed in the only available corner across from the toilet. It was a perfect size if you were a small child but impossible for any adult to wash without splashing water everywhere. It was, for all intents and purposes, useful for one thing: brushing your teeth!

We continued to empty the contents from the dirty cotton diapers into the toilet and rinse them out in the tub, before bringing the soiled diapers down to our dirt-floor basement where we had an old-fashioned wringer-washer. It was so dysfunctional that I often would accompany my mother for a walk down Parliament and Carlton Street to the nearest laundromat, and I can remember her saying that she would be a terrific owner of a laundromat one day. That was about the extent of her personal dreams and ambitions. Well, that and winning big at the Woodbine horse track in the east end of Toronto.

Grade four was the year that I decided to wear my Sunday-best clothes to Winchester school for our class photo day. This turned out to be a huge mistake! The neighbourhood's roving band of young teenage thugs managed to corral me just outside the fence of the schoolyard property before I had a chance to enter through the gate, which was just three feet away. And just like the garage mechanics, they started taunting me with shouts of "church-boy, gearbox, and sissy-boy!" There was no escape route for me to be found. The inevitable confrontation escalated into them physically volleying me back and forth between the guys standing in a circle surrounding me. I started to feel dizzy and light-headed, and their faces started to blur from one to the other.

Before I knew it, and for the very first time in my life, I felt the onslaught of vicious punches and painful kicks to my nuts, which knocked the wind out of me and sent me into a downward spiral, hitting the ground with my face planted on the cold cement. Part of me was grateful to be knocked down, and I hoped they would soon stop kicking and laughing at me. What hurt the most was the realization that the older guys thought less of me than they would a dog. I really wanted my sisters and brothers to show up and rescue me from this nightmare, but they were nowhere to be found!

What the hell, I thought. I was an innocent victim, and this was my first battery assault that would impact my future ability to go to school without the impending threat of violence. I was now a target, and it just made no sense to me! As the school bell rang and the playground supervisors made their way toward the outside fence to see what was going on, the thugs took off, and I stood up to the stabbing snickers and laughter from my nearby classmates in the schoolyard. I'd thought they were my friends but apparently not. They wanted a scapegoat, and I was it. I made things even worse by losing a bit of my composure when I started to cry. I quickly self-corrected my emotions, telling myself that I was acting like the sissy they'd accused me of being. I stopped crying and became angry with myself. Somehow, I managed to stand up. I mechanically brushed off the embedded leaves and dirt from my special Sunday-best fashion … not knowing what else to do at that moment. No one came to my rescue. I was numb and really can't recall how I mustered the courage to walk into the school and attend class for the day. I did my best to fulfill my desire to smile and look the very best for my class photo.

When class was over at 3:10 p.m., I scanned the playground and quickly proceeded to speed-walk the two-minute walk of shame. It was only then that I finally sensed a crusty wetness on the backside of my upper right thigh with a sharp pain from where my pants were sticking. When I reached behind and touched my backside, I felt a very sharp pain and I knew something was wrong with my ass. I must have been in shock all day and hadn't realized what was going on back there. I knew that I would be in big trouble with my mother. I could feel a tear in the back of my nicely pressed grey-flannel pants. As I further examined myself with my hands, I felt a lot of blood and became nauseous. All I could think about was the impending response from my mother. I knew for sure that she would slap me for sneaking out in my Sunday clothes. Then she'd accuse me of purposefully ruining my best pair of grey flannel pants. And finally, she'd forcefully remind me that money did not grow on any of the non-existent trees on our property.

And of course, I was right. My mother was so angry when I arrived home that she refused to take me to the local *Raxlen Clinic for medical treatment*, just steps away and one block south on Parliament Street. She insisted that my tomboy sister Janet escort me as the loving responsible adult.

I may have thought of us as twins, but Janet would most assuredly let it be known that she was my big sister. Although we were unescorted children, we walked bravely over to the Raxlen Clinic reception counter, stood up on our toes and checked in with a whispered "emergency situation" in the back of my pants. After going into an examination/procedure room, I dropped my pants for the doctor and nurse to have a look. There was a quiet consultation between them and then I was dutifully informed that I would require a little cleaning, probing, and removal of glass from the area. In addition, the doctor mentioned I required a few stitches to close the wound.

In my vivid imagination, I fancied this would be my biggest surgery next to my previous appendectomy. I thought perhaps I might have to be transferred by a blaring ambulance to the hospital emergency at Toronto's *Sick Children's Hospital*. My mother would surely feel bad about ignoring me. Meanwhile, the next thing I saw in the tilted-ceiling mirror above me was a big silver needle of Novocain, which the doctor painfully injected into my tiny ass. This was followed by subsequent heavy-duty threading going in and out of my flesh to make four or five gross stitches under my right cheek. Hours after returning home and the effect of Novocain had worn off, I could touch the lumpiness of what would become a grisly scar. I knew this doctor was not skilled in the art of stitching, and I wondered how he'd got through medical school; it was a mystery to me! He would not have passed a basic home-economics class at *Winchester Public School,* where twelve-year-old girls learned to sew by hand. Meanwhile, I had the souvenir of an inept and ill-trained Dr. Frankenstein, who'd created a roll of scar tissue that would forever remind me of this tragic day.

Life went on, and my incident was never mentioned again. As a welcome distraction, suppertime was generally the best time to be at home; Mother seemed to be happiest when she worked in the kitchen. We always giggled at one thing or another when we ate, and it was the only time when our family was together. Everyone sat together except for my mother, who never really seemed to eat. Afterward, Janet and I would wash and dry the dishes and then be dispatched upstairs for our evening bath before changing into our pyjamas for the night. Weekends were a little different and special. Our regular nighttime schedule got postponed for an additional hour of TV-watching or playing games like *Yahtzee* around the kitchen table; those would be the happiest moments in our home. Mother would normally budget her money to make a glorious Sunday pot roast dinner or a roasted chicken, served with potatoes and vegetables. We always ended our meals with home-baked pies and cakes. The Sunday dinners were usually a time when my married eldest sister, Edna, would drop by with her husband, Herbie, and my niece Sandy, who was five years my junior. I loved brushing Sandy's long red hair as I regaled her with my stories out front of the house.

I pretended that no one in my family knew I had been branded a gearbox by the garage guys, and I knew damn straight they didn't know my eldest brother, Kenny, called me a big fairy behind my family's back. He would mention this under his breath when no one else but myself could hear. He thought he was tough like the local street thugs. He was such a deceitful ass, or at least he was until he met his wonderful fiancé, Darlene. Thank God! She changed him for the better, for sure! And they endured a long and happy marriage together.

I was also grateful and much relieved when summer would arrive, and I would be dispatched to exciting summer camps for underprivileged kids for several weeks. Over the period of five years, I was very fortunate to have attended many charity-sponsored sleep-away camps for the *underprivileged,* and I loved them all. Unlike my younger brothers, I was resilient and determined to pivot as necessary to succeed. I excelled in swimming, archery, canoeing, hiking, and building campfires. Most of all, I fit in with all the other campers and was admired for my skills. I felt great sadness when camping would end. On the other hand, my younger brothers Jackie and Ricky despised summer sleep-away camp and they would do everything in their power to be sent home within the first forty-eight hours.

Spending time in the Huntsville and Algonquin Park areas was simply breathtaking. The natural beauty of the pristine lakes, forests, and wildlife were all a magical escape for me! I was accepted by my camp peers as no different than any other guy, and I always felt such a brotherhood and a sense of belonging, which I'd never felt in the urban schoolyard hell that was my childhood. Feeling unheard and unnoticed at home, I welcomed all the favourable attention I received at camp, as it gave me a respite from not feeling like I belonged. I figured out then and there that I should get it where I can…and I did! I was free to stand in the sun with my head held high alongside my fellow cabin mates; we were a great team of underprivileged kids who intuitively felt privileged to be in a porridge of racial and socio-economic diversity. Our spirits were rich, and we were all equals. That was all that mattered.

5
GRANNY'S CLUTCH
NEW LISKEARD, ONTARIO,
SUMMER 1964

Although summers at sleep-away camp were joyous and fun, there was one horrific summer I spent at my grandparents' farm, and life was far from great. When my mother was a young girl growing up on her family's farm outside New Liskeard in rural Ontario, she learned from her mother that girls were not deemed as desirable as boys, as they were somewhat more problematic to raise. As a result, Granny Kirk and my mother explained how girls were more expensive to clothe and educate and they both considered girls to be moody chatterboxes, demanding of unrelenting attention. And even more offensive, they admitted that they believed girls were dirty. According to the family matriarchs, girls were good for only two things: making babies and homemaking. And money spent for higher education was a waste of time.

It was clear that Granny Kirk and Mother preferred boys, who could work on their large family farm and assist Grandpa Huey with a plethora of daily farm chores: various crop seeding; seasonal fertilizing, watering, and harvesting of the crops; daily milk collection, and the subsequent transport of large, heavy galvanized steel milk cans to the end of the long driveway; swine and dairy feeding, followed by mucking out the livestock stalls on the main barn level; and stocking and the storing of baled hay on the upper level. These were just some of the daily chores for the men, and their work was frequently exacerbated by continuous maintenance and repairs of the facilities and equipment. Getting dirty and exhausted was integral to a farmhand's honest good day of work, and girls weren't cut out for it. I thought to myself that if I had the choice I would gladly work outside as far away from my grandmother as possible.

My grandmother had her own outside responsibilities and chores as well. Granny took care of the daily feeding and cleaning the large chicken coop, along with the early morning collection and sorting of farm eggs by size and colour, which was now handed over to my caretaking. In addition, she managed a significant household garden that was filled with many rows of assorted berries, vegetables, and produce that required daily weeding and watering. And that is where I was duped into summer service on the farm; my grandmother and mother had secretly arranged and appointed me as Granny's dedicated farmhand for an unspecified amount of time, as I would soon discover. I was a scrawny, fifty-pound, nine-year-old-kid and had no clue as to what was ahead of me.

I was in grade four when my mother first invited me to chaperone her and my uncle Kenny, along with my two younger cousins Debbie and Diane, for a 500-kilometre drive and overnight visit to my grandparents' farm. Although Granny Kirk could strike the fear of God in me, I felt protected by my mother and therefore accepted her invitation. Upon arrival I was told that I would be sleeping in the lower bunk in my brother Dale's bedroom; he was a brother I knew nothing about, nor did I ever learn exactly how he'd come to be raised by my grandparents. Although I am not clear on the nuances, I understood from my older siblings that Mother had given up Dale as an infant to be raised by my grandparents as their own son. My grandparents needed farm help, and they were not going to hire and pay a farmhand when there were grandchildren to exploit. It was perplexing to me as to what sort of secret trade agreement had been made between my mother and Granny Kirk.

Was money exchanged? Or was it simply a quid pro quo and penance for my mother being underage and pregnant as a young girl? Of course, I was happy to be introduced to my adult brother Dale. He came across as a very decent guy, and I noticed that he didn't resemble anyone else in my family. When I went to sleep in his lower bunk, he remained downstairs with the other adults. I assumed my cousins were put to bed in another room somewhere on the same floor and that the other adults would be up later. But apparently, at some time during my overnight sleep, everyone I'd come with secretly disappeared in the dark of night.

The next morning when I realized the truth of what was going on, I felt personally devastated, abandoned, and hurt by my own mother's lie! She had kissed me goodnight the previous night and said that she would see me in the morning! My trust in her would be forever shattered because of her deceit and abandonment of me. How could she lie to me, and I asked myself what I had done to deserve this? All I could think of was that I was the worst child in the family and that my mother had finally had enough of me. And like my father, I was dismissed without word from the family. My head was reeling.

Early the next morning, I went quietly downstairs and walked hesitantly toward a large, round, oak kitchen table with unknown relatives sitting around and eating breakfast. At first, I didn't focus too much on who exactly was there because I was transfixed by a singular strip of severely encrusted fly tape hanging down from the ceiling in the centre of the table. I had never seen anything like this before and I was instantly mortified! I knew something was ominous when I couldn't see my mother and uncle anywhere, and so I kept my focus on the fly tape, knowing it was now my turn to be stuck like the suffering flies.

As I nervously walked toward one of the empty, mismatched wooden farm chairs, my mind began to race. I felt both nauseous and sad that all those flies were at very different points of being slowly tortured to death, and it pained me to know that I had to sit and pretend that I was not witnessing this tragedy. Deep inside, I could relate to their struggle to escape a slow, torturous death!

Fortunately, I was momentarily distracted by the whistle of a large aluminum kettle boiling water for the brewing of tea on a massive cast-iron, wood-burning stove. As I soon found out, Granny used the wood-burning stove for everyday baking and the slow-cooking of stews and various meats. During the summer, she cooked in the early morning hours before the day reached unbearably hot temperatures. All the screened-in windows, which ran the full length of the far north and west walls, were open and you could feel a modest breeze from the cross-ventilation. The south wall, which anchored the wood-burning stove at one end, also had a pass-through window at the other end that opened into a smaller modern kitchen with white appliances and a double stainless sink where Granny did all her washing and the preserving of vegetables and fruits. She rarely used the modern stove, and the cast-iron, wood-burning stove seemed to run every day, fuelled by cords of wood that were piled from the floor to the ceiling on the inside wall of the garage.

As I sat at the table without any recognition or acknowledgement from anyone, Granny appeared silently from behind and dropped a bowl of steaming hot oatmeal in front of me, and then she returned to make tea for the thermoses that the men would take out to the field. From the table conversation, I gleaned that all the livestock had apparently been fed and milked earlier and the cows were momentarily ready to be released to various designated pastures. Everyone at the table excluding myself was on their first workday break and enjoying a hearty morning breakfast.

Meanwhile, I was trying my best to focus on what was now happening, after the cruel and cowardly departure of my mother while I was asleep. I did my best to follow the table conversation with the men's barely audible, grunted-out accomplishments and summary of the upcoming chores for the remainder of the day. I followed their lead by sweetening my own bowl of hot oatmeal with several heaping teaspoons of Red Path brown sugar as they sipped on cups of hot brewed tea from a huge brown betty teapot that sat in the centre of the table, under a tattered old tea cozy. Grandpa Huey and Uncle Norman deeply inhaled their hand-rolled EXPORT 'A' cigarettes, exposing their gnarly, chipped, and nicotine-stained teeth.

Thankfully, my brother Dale did not smoke, and he was careful not to load up on all the brown sugar, which I realized was why he probably still had his beautiful white teeth and rosy-cheeked complexion. Maybe I would follow his lead on the brown sugar and cut back! Later that day, Dale demonstrated how I could drink water directly from the hose that was located by the water trough for the cows; he claimed it was more refreshing and beneficial than pop and juice, and I was grateful for the advice. He must have done something right because he claimed that he had never been to a dentist, yet his teeth looked perfectly straight and white.

Meanwhile, as the three adult men finished their meals and headed out to the fields, Granny Kirk came and sat so close in the chair next to me that I could smell what I assumed was her caffeinated breath, which caused me to involuntarily retract my head. Her first words were to inform me that I would be spending the entire summer under her watchful supervision, and that if I maintained my Sunday-best behaviour and followed her rules while I did all my chores to her complete satisfaction, then she might consider allowing me to return home in the fall for school. If I did not do what she demanded, then I was assured that I would never return home to Toronto to see my family again and I would live with them until I was old enough to go out on my own. On the outside, I remained cool as a cucumber but inside I was a mass of jelly without a structural bowl to contain my worst fears. My mind was swirling with disbelief and absolute horror at the prospect of never going home. More importantly, I had no understanding what I had done to be so brutally discarded by my mother. I instantly knew that there was no one there to help me, outside of myself, and I was prepared to silently figure this all out and plan my escape, one way or another.

Granny's first cardinal rule for me was that children should be seen and not heard. I was only to talk when asked a question by her. I was to assist under her strict supervision when we worked side by side; fertilizing, weeding, watering, and harvesting the garden's bounty. I would also be responsible to get up at the crack of dawn to go to the henhouse and collect the eggs every day. The one chore that I was not required to help her with was making the winter preserves, and the sterilization of countless mason jars. However, I was required to always stay within her sightline.

I was instructed that when I was compliant to her satisfaction, I would be granted permission to sketch and draw on a tiny, wall-mounted chalkboard located on the east wall, adjacent to the back door. The back door was used as the main farmhouse entry and led out to a sidewalk path that was lined with a singular row of her prized dark-green hostas, (plantain lilies) nestled against the outside wall of the garage.

Unless invited indoors, I was ordered to stay outside all day, unless it was raining. On sunny days, I was to eat my lunch, which she would place on top of the concrete well-pad. I was fortunate to have the companionship of their German Shepard, *Buster*. If I had to use the toilet, I would have to ask permission to come inside, and she would monitor me while I went up the stairs to make sure that I didn't put my dirty hands on the protective plastic-covered, wall-papered walls. I was to touch nothing in the washroom but the toilet and the sink, and I was never to lock the bathroom door. If I took too long, she would shout for me to return, which always made me anxious and pee shy.

Eventually, I learned to covet the simple reward of the chalkboard and was grateful for the opportunity to escape in my mind. Furthermore, when I was deemed good, I was allowed to share some of the results of our hard work from the household garden. I was rewarded with samples of some of the yummy preserves that she had made and served as a dessert following our evening meals together. Raspberry, strawberry, and rhubarb compote remain my favourite to this day. If I was not good enough, according to her, well, then it was no dessert for me, and I had to sit and watch everyone else eagerly indulge. Granny Kirk oversaw me, and none of the men at the farm ever got involved or participated in her decision-making and farmhouse rules. To the men of the household, I was a persona non grata.

Eating would be the only sweet part of my farming experience. When I was denied sweet treats, I would use strategic deception to get back at her. I would sneak a few sips from the fresh lemonade and use my pocketknife to slice undetectable ends from the lunch treats that I would have to walk out to the fields for "the men." She had her rules, but I always found a way to outfox her! They didn't refer to me as a juvenile city-slicker for nothing.

Walking out to the fields every day, I would think about the family mystery of my estranged brother Dale. It was a secret that was just too much for my young childhood brain to wrap around. Moreover, his features led me to believe he could possibly have been fathered by someone unknown to me. All I knew was if Mom and Granny could do this to my brother Dale, then what might be in store for me? Maybe there were just too many children who lived in my mother's shoe and due to overcrowding, perhaps I would be the next to be literally farmed out to granny's permanent custody. Clearly, I did not want to risk this, and I remained vigilant about pleasing my granny, the Wicked Witch of the West! During my summer residency on the farm, I had lots of time to think about my siblings back home and wondered if they missed or even thought about me. My anxiety grew about Granny's rules, especially the one where I had to stay outside all day and had to knock on the back door to ask permission to use the washroom.

The washroom problem quickly became unbearable; I was not used to being monitored and supervised for my bathroom functions. I figured I could avoid this and outfox her by crapping outside and pissing (unobtrusively) under the leaves of her prized hostas. I also found the leaves a purposeful alternative to toilet paper. I thought I was clever and had her fooled until the day when she demanded to know why I no longer asked to come in for the toilet.

Granny demanded to know why she smelled poop whenever she came outside. And like a dog with a bone, she wouldn't let go of it! She frantically searched everywhere for the source of the smell around and inside the garage. I finally redirected her to her prized garden plants, and I took great pleasure when she gagged in horror at what she found amongst the leaves. Before I knew it, she grabbed the scruff of my neck and flew me up to the second-floor bathroom and threw me into a cold shower, wearing all my clothes. When she turned the shower off, I opened the curtain and stepped out onto the mat, completely drenched and shivering. Without a moment to catch my breath, she then grabbed me by the ear and pulled me over to the sink where she immediately washed my mouth out with a bar of ivory soap. I now fully understood that she meant business, as I frantically *tried* to cry but couldn't from the bubbles that burned inside my mouth and throat. After I caught my breath, I sputtered out an apology and promised never to do it again. With that said, she sent me to my room to change out of my wet clothes and instructed me to remain there for the remainder of the afternoon and evening without any dinner. I went to bed on an empty stomach burning from the soap I had ingested, earlier. I learned my lesson that Granny was not to be messed with. She felt no remorse for what she had done to me, and as she later said to me, "I was simply doing God's work by not sparing the rod and spoiling the child." And in penance, she demanded that I read passages from the Old Testament at her bedside every night before I was allowed permission to go to my own bedroom.

Eventually, the summer was coming to an end, and I desperately wanted to go home. All I could think about was how I did not measure up as a normal boy to either my mother or my grandmother; I had no idea if I would ever see my family in Toronto again. It was clear that they both had it in for me, and I really did not know how much more I could take. I was so young but felt so old and helpless. Later that evening, as everyone went upstairs to prepare for bed, Granny Kirk called me into her bedroom to talk about the day and to pray for my soul. She confessed that she did not think I could ever change my God-given character and stubbornness to adapt. She said that she'd had enough of me and that she and Grandpa Huey would be taking me back to Toronto and returning me to the custody of my mother the following Sunday. She had one last request before I left her bedroom: She asked me to sing a verse or two from the hymn "Jesus Loves Me."

It may not have been a Judy Garland showtune, but I knew this Christian song by heart from earlier lessons at St. Matthew's Sunday School when we'd lived on First Avenue. Without any hesitation, I let it rip as though I were performing on stage in front of a large audience. When I finished the song she said, "Enough of you!" and directed me out of her room. In an instant, I knew that I had served my time at the farm, and I was finally going home; just as if it was like I was returning home from prison! Tonight, was going to be my best night of sleep, and I wasn't even concerned about wetting my bed. In fact, I welcomed leaving her a reminder so she would never entertain the idea of her tricking me back for a visit ever again. But I knew it was better to remain calm, as I did not want to risk losing my well-earned opportunity to return home to Toronto. In fact, I made a point of saying my prayers and apologizing to God for refuting him over the summer.

The final week on the farm flew by as if I were on a cloud. I could feel a smile start to return to my face as I did my daily chores with a newfound sense of joy. By this point, I had grown quite fond of their dog, Buster. He shadowed my every move and would not leave my side. I knew he was the best thing about my summer on the farm, and I felt a little pain knowing I would be leaving him behind. He had taught me a valuable lesson about a dog's loyalty and massive affection; he was a constant and a trustworthy source of comfort when I couldn't depend on the emotional kindness and affection from nearby family members. Following dinner, Granny announced that I would have the privilege of unfettered access to the chalkboard for my remaining time on the farm and I thought to myself, *maybe* she's finally realizing that I'm a good kid, although I knew she would never admit to it. Everyone seemed to be in a better mood during my last week, and I would occasionally get a smile or the odd smirk. Maybe it was just my imagination! Even better, maybe Granny and my mother would no longer tag me as the "black-sheep" of the family because I was considered a little different!

The following Sunday morning we headed back to Toronto. The smoke-filled car and drive home seemed to take forever. Grandpa Huey calmly inhaled his hand-rolled cigarettes one right after the other, and the sound of his huffing and puffing were the only sounds in the car. I noticed how Grandpa seemed to avoid the main roads and took all the back dirt roads instead, which of course only added to my misery. I wanted to tell him to get the hell on the highway and drive as fast as the car could go! But I feared Granny would pull out another soap bar of Ivory Snow from her pocket-book. It was agonizing to see only farm after farm after farm. Neither of my grandparents spoke a word the entire trip, and the car radio was never turned on; the silence was excruciating! I had such ants in my pants that I could have hopped out the back door and run on my adrenaline faster than driving on the backroads.

Eventually, we made it back to Toronto, and just in time for lunch. There was no fanfare or family recognition of my return other than I was instructed to go wash my hands as my mother quickly ran my suitcase down to the laundry space in the basement. It was all I could do to sit silently throughout the predictable summer lunch of bologna and cheese sandwiches, pickles, and Kool-Aid. Table conversation was reserved for the adults. The only solace I could find after lunch was hanging out with my sister Janet, who agreed that Granny really was a *wicked witch* after she heard what I had endured. We promised each other that we would never allow either of us to be trapped into going out for a visit again. It was clear to us that family adults could not be trusted and that we only felt safe when we were together.

6
FIRST LOVE
7 LANCASTER AVENUE 1965-1967

After my summer farm experience, I was grateful to be back in Toronto and return to Winchester Public School in time to start grade five. As the school year progressed, my academic and social life seemed relatively easy and enjoyable compared to my miserable time in the summer. Not since kindergarten had I become a teacher's pet, yet, for some inexplicable reason my teacher, Miss Sharp, who was a battle-axe to most students and did not hesitate to crack you on the skull with her large black Alaska-diamond ring, took a shine to me. I became the official student hall monitor for grades one to five in the old Winchester School building. I got to leave class early and ring the old-fashioned pull-bell for recess and lunch. In addition, I was relieved from class to deliver the mini milk cartons stored in metal crates that were assigned to the various classrooms. My class also had some pet hamsters, and I was responsible to find volunteers to take them home over the weekends. I loved all my new responsibilities at age ten and felt confident I wouldn't let my teacher down. After the summer from hell, this work was a cakewalk in comparison.

Toward the end of grade five, I remembered my classmate Nora Cotter announcing to me and her close girlfriends that I was her boyfriend, much

73

to my surprise. She made this official one day after she had pulled me behind a big old oak tree and kissed me unexpectedly while I was walking her home to Hillcrest Avenue. I kind of just followed her home like a lost puppy dog, not understanding what was expected of me. Her family lived at an end house that faced the Hillcrest Park ravine, and their yard backed onto the St. James Necropolis. Her calm and quiet family was headed by a storybook-type father, who was an Anglican minister at St. Simon's Church, which separated the haves to the north of Bloor Street in Rosedale from the have-nots in Cabbagetown and *Regent Park* to the south.

The Cotter family seemed rich in comparison to my family. Mr. Cotter and his wife had two children, Nora, and her brother, Christopher, who was always in his room studying and reading. I was impressed they could afford a full-time live-in nanny who was a lot less exciting and certainly more grounded than Mary Poppins. At dinnertime, they always ate white rice instead of potatoes as was the custom in our Irish Canadian family. In my mind, I thought it was so exotic, as they were not Chinese. Sitting at their table for family dinners elevated me and made me feel singularly important and worthy to be a part of their upper-middle-class family. So, I learned to like rice as a starch alternative with the main course, even though my mother thought it was odd. At home, the only rice we ate was in the form of creamy rice pudding with raisins as a dessert. And I sure as heck loved a good rice pudding.

Over a few months it was clear that Nora and I were more like brother and sister, and I became a fixture at their dinner table a couple nights of the week. Eventually, Mr. Cotter moved his family to a new parish in Parkdale but not before ensnaring me to join St. Simon's all-male choir, composed of privileged, Ivy-league schoolboys from Rosedale. Back in 1966, I was the first boy south of Bloor Street to join the ranks of the ultra-WASP and prestigious Rosedale South Church's all-male choir.

The best thing to come out of my introductory girlfriend experience with Nora was that I now had an intellectual inkling of what having a girlfriend did not entail. However, I was emotionally primed and open to pursuing an authentic girlfriend in my life and that's when I first saw my future girlfriend Lynne in grade seven. In 1967, I felt an instant emotional and physical spark for the first time in my life when I saw her sitting next to Cathy Lepper in Mrs. Crysdale's music class. I felt compelled to win her attention.

I discovered we all lived a few short blocks from each other, and we began to hang out a bit at Cathy's house after school, listening to various musical soundtracks like the Sound of Music and West Side Story. Compared to them, I felt like the village idiot. Lynne was effortlessly intelligent, and Cathy was highly competitive and studied hard. Other than school, the only thing I had in common with them was that Cathy and her two younger sisters were Brownies, and their mother may have been a Brownie leader, if I am not mistaken. Anyhow, I was a Boy Scout at St. Enoch's, and I think this gave her parents a modicum of assurance that I was a responsible young man. Their father, Mr. Lepper, was a teacher out in the west end who I would see on occasion when he got home from work, or at choir rehearsals at St. Simon's.

In my young mind, the more I got to know Lynne the more I adored her, and I started spending more and more time alone at her house on Metcalf Street, and less time at the Lepper residence. I would do anything to protect Lynne from her feelings of loneliness or sadness. She was an only child, though I soon learned that she had been born with a twin who had not survived. We both found a strong chemistry and attraction to each other. She brought me a sense of calm and peace, and in return, I seemed to bring her laughter and happiness. In many ways we were opposite, yet we seemed to fill in the voids of what each of us was longing for: to be loved and celebrated. We seemed to be the perfect fit, and this relationship grew over time. Eventually my friendship with Lynne led us to take confirmation classes at St. Simon's Church. Thereafter, we would try to spend all our free moments together. We were a legitimate and sexually curious boyfriend and girlfriend. Whenever we could find a private moment, we messed around. Moreover, Lynne's doctor put her on birth-control pills to attenuate her severe monthly cramps and pains. And this provided us some assurance that she would not accidentally get pregnant.

The truth of the matter is that we were more afraid of being discovered by her mother, Peggy, who considered our friendship a passing phase in her daughter's life. She was clearly immutable in her belief that we were simply class friends and nothing more. However, Lynne and I were in our own safe bubble and busy imagining our long-term future together, along with the children we might parent one day. I recall Lynne even went so far as to pick out the name Timothy as a great girl's name. She said the name sounded so pretty, and I thought she made a good argument. I was always impressed with Lynne's unpretentious intelligence, her beauty, and her creative imagination. She was the real deal, and I was blessed to have her in my heart and potential long-term future. She was the quintessential first love of my life.

The other great thing that came out of grade seven at Winchester Public School was a once-in-a-lifetime class field trip to *Montreal's Expo 67*, the International and Universal Exposition and World's Fair. People from all over the world went to see ephemeral design concepts and architectural buildings imagined for the future. Of all the installations, my favourite was a monorail that took us through Buckminster Fuller's Geodesic Dome; it felt like we were living in the age of *The Jetsons*. It was nothing like I had ever seen or could have imagined before, and I tucked that experience in the back of my curious mind, considering future design possibilities for myself.

Unfortunately, the year of 1967 also brought some devasting news to our family. I learned from my sister Janet that our older sister Rosemary would not be making the upcoming family move over the summer from our current Lancaster Avenue location down to Carlton Street and just a few blocks south. She had taken an intentional overdose of my mother's pills. As a result, she spent many months at the Wellesley Hospital recuperating and continuing with her high school classes at Jarvis Collegiate, directly across from the hospital. After several months of hospitalization, the rest of our family was asked to join Rosemary at what was known then as the *Clarke Institute of Psychiatry* (prior to the current renaming to the *Centre for Addiction and Mental Health* or CAMH). The purpose was to discuss our dysfunctional family situation and the impact on the attending family members. The result of this was that she was legally emancipated and allowed to go live with a Christian couple, located up in northwest Toronto on Schell Avenue. The impact on me was profound and her disappearance was never discussed with anyone in our family and her name was rarely mentioned. Only in subsequent times of anger, my mother would refer to Rosemary and me as the black sheep in the family. She would assert that we both had big mouths and maintained that we both thought that we were better than the rest of the family.

"Me in a gold blazer & choir crest"

Class photo *with Choirboy Michael (back row, far right)*

7

SURVIVING CABBAGETOWN

393 CARLTON STREET,
TORONTO, 1968-1969

During the summer of 1967, we picked up and moved without Rosemary
to south Cabbagetown, located at the end of a red cobblestone road that
transitioned at the end of Carlton Street and the west side of Riverdale
Park. Once again, due to school neighbourhood zoning, I had to switch
from Winchester Public School and transfer to Lord Dufferin, which was
located on Parliament and Gerrard Streets, directly across from Regent
Park. Our new house was one of four nearly identical grand Victorian row
houses flanked on either end by two larger houses that shared a firewall
between the interior row houses sandwiched in between.

Our new home was located at 393 Carlton Street and was situated near
the corner of Sumach and Carlton Street. It was shockingly grand and spacious, compared to our former shoebox on Lancaster Avenue. We had a
white-painted historical wood porch, which framed a large front-parlour
window and a beautiful Romanesque, arch-shaped stained-glass window
at the top. Details of the stained glass featured hand-painted swallows,
raised geometric glass buttons, and various rectangular and square lead-
glass inserts. Our Victorian house had all the original hardwood floors and

a beautiful staircase with a heavy, dark-stained wood handrail, anchored by an ornate newel post and beautiful crown mouldings above that set off the original hand-plastered ceiling. Our house faced Riverdale Park and onto what was then an established old zoo, occupying 3 hectares (7.5 acres) in downtown Cabbagetown. It was a terrific place for a young teen like myself to live, and I frequented the zoo as often as I could. At the end of my street, it opened to a large hill that went down to two large baseball diamonds and a path to a large bridge that crossed the Don River over to the east side of Riverdale. Currently, the old zoo has been transformed into a working farm and Toronto's new replacement zoo is now located in Scarborough, Ontario, and occupies over 280 hectares (700 acres) as Canada's largest zoo. From my viewpoint, it was a win/win for everyone, but especially for the poor zoo animals I witnessed suffering and isolated in cramped quarters across from my home. Even back then, I felt tremendous empathy for the caged animals living in what was virtually a concrete prison.

Meanwhile, not long after moving into our new home, there was one specific summer morning when I sent my younger full-brother Jackie out to play with our younger half-brothers Ricky and Gregg in our backyard while I was busy doing my household chores. Mother, as I recall, had gone off to the Woodbine racetrack for the day. I could easily monitor my younger brothers from either the first floor back kitchen or the second floor back bedroom. The windows were open, so I could hear them mucking about and having fun with our adopted black-and-white border collie *Beauty*. Much to the consternation of my mother, we'd only had our dog for a few months when Beauty had gotten out of the yard when she was in heat, and consequently she was now pregnant.

During the summer she was relegated to staying outside in her own secured pen in the house niche that jogged back next to the kitchen, which was designed to let natural light into the middle dining room on the first floor. This narrow cut-out at the back of house is where Beauty slept and was fed. We heard that she was pregnant, and *Beauty* mysteriously disappeared the following weekend. My mother claims she was adopted by an anonymous farmer who wanted our pregnant dog sight unseen, but in my gut, I was highly skeptical and suspicious that she had been taken by someone on the behest of my mother and dumped off to fend for herself. I was devastated; Beauty was the first and only dog our family ever had. And now she and her unborn puppies were gone. Poof! I just couldn't believe she could do something like this to a poor helpless animal. But I wasn't shocked by it, either. And here's why.

When my sister Janet turned sweet sixteen, we had a small birthday party with a homemade cake and a family-sized bucket of KFC. Afterward, Janet asked if I could keep a secret, and she confided that some of her girlfriends and the local boys who hung out in Lord Dufferin's schoolyard were throwing her a surprise party at her classmate Karen McGuire's house, just south of our home on Sumach Street and situated across from the Kiwanis club where I used to hang out. She looked very pretty and radiant that day.

After the birthday lunch, she explained to Mother that she was heading out for an hour or two to go for a short visit to her classmate's home. She promised she would be home in time for dinner and that she had completed all her daily chores. What none of us were anticipating is that Janet had other secret plans, and she hooked up for the first time to lose her virginity to Danny Rose, who lived nearby with his family in Regent Park.

A month later, Janet confessed to me that she was pregnant and didn't know what she was going to do. She looked terrified and fearful about telling Mother. I recommended we should wait until none of the other kids were around and I would be there by her side when she told her. Later that day, when Mother was alone in the kitchen having her cup of coffee and a cigarette at the table, we decided this would be the best time to speak with her. And it did not go well. The first words out of our mother's mouth were, "I knew you have been up to no good and I should have known better than to trust you!" In my very presence, Mother then told my sister that she could not afford to take care of her and her unborn child and that she had to leave before the birth of her child. Mother then stood up and picked up the load of freshly washed laundry and headed out to the backyard to hang the clothes out on the line and never spoke another word about the matter.

Here we go, I thought; from one generation to the next, history was repeating itself. My beloved sister was terrified but had no choice but to move out and temporarily live with the family of her boyfriend, Danny Rose. Midway through her pregnancy, Janet went on welfare and was able to secure a tiny one-bedroom above a shopfront on the south side of Queen Street, just two or three stores east of Parliament Street. I wasn't sure how I felt about her living in one of the worst parts of town, but it was all she could afford, and it would be a place to set up home before the arrival of her baby girl. Part of me was happy that both Danny and she appeared to be so in love and ecstatic about living as a new family unit. My sister and I both realized that our everyday close relationship would end but we pretended it wouldn't. I realized our time as a co-dependant brother and sister was over. I didn't fully understand the implication, but I knew it was going to be tough on both of us. We were both facing adult responsibilities without parental supervision and guidance.

Even though I was barely fifteen, I was the next in line to share the adult responsibilities of running the household and taking care of my younger siblings. I felt totally inept. And my mother wasted no time adding Janet's previous responsibilities and household chores onto my ever-growing list. Meanwhile, Mother was pulling herself away from her current boyfriend, Bob Jack, who made a respectable living as a truck driver for Canada Post. He resided at the nearby Winchester Hotel. Outside my own dad, he was the only boyfriend/companion of my mothers who I ever truly liked and who treated me well.

I can recall coming home from the woodshop class when I was in grade seven at Winchester School with a wood lamp base that I had turned on the lathe. Mother didn't say much about it. But Bob, who was generally a shy and soft-spoken guy, suddenly got animated and told me that we were going to turn my "handsome new wood lamp base," into a real functioning lamp. The next thing I knew, he took me down into the basement, found an old, discarded lamp, took it apart and took the internal electrical threaded metal tube and brass light socket and harp, and repurposed them for my hand-turned wooden base. And when he asked me for the honour of switching it on for the first time, it was like magic. I was so overcome that he did this for me that I remember throwing my arms around his neck and crying (just a bit). He thought it was in appreciation for the lamp, and it was. But I was so touched to feel like his son for a moment; I wished this would have been the right man for my mother to marry.

But, a year later after we moved to Carlton Street, postal worker--Bob Jack would be cast aside in favour of an alleged rich guy called Harry Fissenden, who my mother had apparently met at the Woodbine racetrack. By this point, she was secretly spending more time outside the home and more time in his company each week.

Meanwhile, I was very much lost in my own pain and trying to figure out my own escape plan from our home; I had little inclination to care much about anyone else, which saddened me as I mechanically continued with my household chores and babysitting responsibilities. I was now a young teenager and the eldest child currently living at home. I had a plateful of adult responsibilities: school obligations; the choir; Boy Scouts; a changing adolescent body; a girl-friend; and a mother who was increasingly not on the horizon and left me as head of the household in her absence. And I was so angry and disgusted that she so easily broke off her relationship with my dearest sister, Janet, and now with Bob Jack, who I had come to love and respect. At the time, my younger siblings were simply clued out and would soon begin to see "Harry" as their new dad. I would certainly not. Just as I would never consider my mother as my "mom" ever again. And no matter how hard I tried; I could never do enough to please her.

In any case, on a random Saturday morning when my mother was out, and just before our pregnant border collie had been allegedly "rehomed," I had sent my younger brothers outside in the yard to play with Beauty. Meanwhile, I kept busy cleaning and organizing the household to my mother's standards and requirements. I wanted to please my mother and meet her demands, with everything in perfect order upon her return. I certainly did not want to give her any reason to get angry or upset with my younger brothers, who appeared to be blissfully unaware of all the adult drama going on behind the scenes.

If my younger siblings and charges suspected any problems, they did not show it. Nor did we talk about the ever-changing family politics and dynam-ics. I realized that once my beloved family members like Rosemary and Janet left the house, their names were never mentioned by my mother, and it terrified me to know that sisters could be erased from our family in a heart-beat. I was determined not to fail my mother, and I knew that succeeding in my chores provided a measure of calm and security for her. So, I buried my emotions in my chores while trying to prove my worthiness, all the while becoming increasingly aware of my enveloping sadness and loneliness.

Quite by happenstance, something quite random lifted my spirit. While I was cleaning, I made an unusual discovery of a secret hiding place. There was a built-in wooden linen closet at the north end of the stairs on the second floor, with ¾ inch cedar shelves for the bed linens and towels. I would use the shelves as steps to reach the freshly laundered towels on the upper shelves. I decided to climb up to the very top shelf and take a good look up inside the dark space hidden behind a wood valance. There was a good foot of additional space that extended up into the darkness above, and I could detect a small door-pull that was affixed to a discreet ceiling panel that gave me access to the hidden attic above. I was confident no one had ever noticed this when we originally moved in, and my mother, who generally organized the linen closet, had never mentioned seeing it. Normally, she put the linens away, but I assumed her responsibility when she was not around.

After I unsecured the pull and pushed into the space above, I could see all the way up to the interior side of our pointed roofline rafters and wood cladding. There were a few tiny holes and cracks that let a little natural light pierce through and reminded me of the laser lights at the McLaughlin Planetarium next to the ROM (Royal Ontario Museum). My curiosity was piqued, and I continued my way up, carefully stepping onto the wood floor joists and avoiding the old fibre insulation sandwiched between. Balancing my left foot on one joist and my right foot on another, I carefully emerged and surveyed my surroundings.

Once my eyes started adjusting to the cavernous dark space, I looked carefully and slowly turned around. Immediately, I discovered that there was one continuous long attic connecting all four row-houses; including the house that my neighbour Paul lived in. I could see the tops of four red-brick fireplaces and the firewalls that separated and delineated each home. Upon closer inspection, I could see there were open service portals through each of the load-bearing firewalls, allowing a draft of air (and potential fire) to move quickly through. I had learned about fires and backdrafts from seeing old episodes of the 1958 syndicated American action drama called Rescue 8, and from safety tips acquired at school over the years: "Never open a door or window when there is a fire; put wet towels at the foot of the door to avoid smoke from entering and wait for the firemen to come to your rescue." All that came flooding back to my memory as I looked at the unblocked service openings in the attic.

At one point as I was walking carefully above my next-door neighbour's house, I accidentally slipped and stepped down into the cavity between the two joists. As I did so, I sensed the crunching of plaster from the underside of the ceiling below. Immediately I envisioned breaking a hole through the ceiling and falling into the old, retired lady's home below, where she lived all alone. I jumped back onto the raised floor joists with my heart pounding out of my small chest! I shuddered to think of all the trouble I would once again find myself in. I needed to get back to the access panel above my linen closet and get back down before anyone returned home.

At that point I was spending a lot of my free time at Paul and Sue's house, conveniently located two doors west of my home on Carlton Street. They were becoming alarmingly suspicious of my mother's neglect and corporal punishment, so they started inviting me for regular dinners during the week, on the pretext that I was babysitting. Mother barely noticed that I was not showing up at home to eat and she frequently left the dirty dishes in the sink for me to clean afterward. She cooked and I did the dishes, and those were the rules. Paul's response to my secret request was neither a yes nor no. What he did say as the mature head of his household was that it would not be wise for me to go up to the attic anymore: "You could accidentally get hurt and no one would know where to find you." He made a good argument, but I still took an occasional peek up there to hide my coffee can with savings from my neighbourhood odd jobs. My savings were earmarked for birthday and holiday gifts for my girlfriend, Lynne. Having outside friends to hang my heart onto was my salvation, and it was important that they believed in me.

I even offered to sneak Paul into my house when I was sure no one was home, but he declined the invitation and said it was fine; he believed me about the secret access to the attic above. Neither his house nor the other two row houses had any built-in linen closets like mine. I was happy with the revelation and the possibility that he might notice my natural curiosity about architecture and encourage me to follow in a design path of my own one day. (A few years later, he would indeed send a reference letter off to Joan Harland, the department chair of interior design at the University of Manitoba, recommending me to the program).

To earn a little cash and leverage my cleaning and household skills, I plastered a few posters on some of the old-wood hydro poles at the end of Carlton Street. My advertisement said, "Odd Kid Will Do Odd-Jobs for $1.50 an hour/cash," and Paul and Sue gave me permission to use their phone number to avoid potential drama with my mother. My first client lived two houses east of my house. I was contacted by resident *Alan King*, a venerable movie producer who owned a unique Victorian-style farmhouse with a carriage house at the back. He said he would hire me to clean up some outdoor debris that went down his driveway and back to the carriage house. Afterward, he was so happy with my work that he asked me to go with him to his Yorkville studio to help with some organizing and cleaning in the basement.

So, I was off to a fortuitous start and made another connection through him that led me to a summer job the following year working backstage at the Avon Theatre as a dresser. Mr. Alan King was a friend of *John Hayes*, who was the director of The Stratford Repertory Theatre, and the two of them thought I could work alongside John's son, Elliot, who was about my age and just as crazy about the theatre. It was the best summer of my adolescence. Even my girlfriend, Lynne, came out for a visit.

Another client of mine was architect Noel Hancock, who worked on the architectural design of Ontario Place and lived maybe six houses farther east. He hired me to babysit his infant based on the recommendation from our mutual friends Paul and Sue. Noel's wife, *Yvonne,* was an architect as well and had designed a discreet women's halfway house and shelter with an interior courtyard on Wellesley Street and Ontario Street next to Mac's Milk. We were neighbourhood friends, and I would occasionally be invited to join them as a young adult for dinner when I wasn't babysitting. They took turns hosting a variety of their friends/colleagues, and invariably the conversations always turned to their latest projects and buildings.

In mid-March in 1971, we were invited by Noel to go on a pre-opening visit to Ontario Place as his guests. Paul took his wife, Sue, his daughter Josie, and me; the ever-appreciative and curious fifteen-year-old babysitter. After stopping at a security check for verification, we parked the car as close as we could to the futuristic-looking complex of angular pods linked together by external ramps.

The first thing that stood out to me was the geodesic dome, similar but smaller than the one I had previously seen at Expo 67. And based upon my experience in Montreal, I was happy to see Toronto celebrate the province with this new public venue and lakeside park called *Ontario Place.* My role for the day was to push Josie in her baby carriage and follow behind while Paul and Sue walked eagerly in front discussing the architectural merits of the design and the contextual data of the beautiful lakeside setting. I tried my best to stay up close so I could hear, but I had to be mindful not to accidentally ram them as I tried to navigate around the burping muddy grounds off the narrow, plank-wood boards leading up to the angular floating pods that ascended from the murky waters. It was an exciting outing, and I was mesmerized by our Sunday tour of Ontario Place.

My new life at *Lord Dufferin Public School* was fine for one year but the neighbourhood was unpredictable and risky; there was always trouble lurking like a homing device waiting to find me. However, the school environment made up for the daily journey. I had some wonderfully talented teachers, especially *Dr. Holland*, who taught grade-eight art. Still to this day, I have my grade-eight class workbook, which captured her theoretical design teachings and artistic underpinnings as topics for class assignments. Years later, her lectures and class assignments gave me an early context of what to expect in my first year studying interior design at the University of Manitoba (U of M), particularly as it came to our weekly "pinky-plates" on the elements and principles of design. All the theory I learned in grade eight was directly related to my foundational first year.

In grade eight I also had the fabulously inspirational Miss Anne Crysdale for music class. Her mother was an excellent music teacher and had previously taught me music at Winchester Public School. I knew Miss Crysdale would be the same as her mother. She decided to put on a musical following our senior grade-eight convocation ceremony. Having a reputation as a choir boy at St. Simon's Anglican Church, my teacher knew I had more training, history, and skill than anyone else in the class, and she basically assigned me the title role of Charlie Brown in *You're a Good Man, Charlie Brown* without bothering with an open-school audition. I recall that when I first saw the lyrics and I started learning the melody for "The Doctor Is In," I knew instantly that I was destined to be Charlie Brown—not just once, but for a second time a few years later in grade eleven at Central Commerce. It's a tune that has always stayed with me and has been my signature tune for most of my life: "I'm not very handsome or clever or lucid; I've always been stupid at spelling and numbers..."

Shockingly, my mother decided to show up unannounced to attend the convocation of Janet and myself. I'd had no clue that she was planning to come. Janet and I suspected that Miss Crysdale must have called all the cast parents to personally invite them, which was the only logical conclusion as far as we could tell. I know that I consciously did not invite her based on her track record of rarely showing up to parents' nights or any other school functions; I did not want to feel disappointed by her hollow promises. Incidentally, I never attended any of my own subsequent graduations after high school.

Anyhow, I think the reason our grade-eight convocation ceremony at Lord Dufferin's was over so fast is that everyone was excited for our school's production of *You're a Good Man, Charlie Brown*. Children had short attention spans, and the idea of putting on a show was much more appealing than sitting thorough a drawn-out convocation ceremony. In fact, we didn't even have to cross the stage for the brief ceremony, which was now set up for our musical. Our names were simply read out by the school's vice-principal.

Afterward, our school musical started. When I made my entrance from stage left and walked toward the front of the stage, I momentarily froze and almost crapped my pants. There was my mother sitting in the front row, directly in front of me! I recall feeling so flustered and self-conscious by seeing my mother that my heart raced uncontrollably. It was the first time I ever experienced a mini panic attack. Fortunately, everyone in attendance thought my agitation was a part of my role's character. Once the old piano sounded, my performance muscle kicked in and I began my first (depressing) solo: "*The Doctor is In.*" Immediately, I refocussed on my acting job and before I knew it the show had gone off without a hitch. It was over in a laser-like flash.

As the crowd applauded, I looked down at my mother, who was wearing a very short peacock-blue and white-paisley empire-waist dress that matched her customary blue eyeshadow. Her thick, auburn-coloured hair was in the usual Mary Tyler Moore Show-inspired hair flip, secured with extra-hold Aqua Net hairspray. Her hair colour contrasted with an accent pair of white-coloured clip-on hoops that coordinated with her bright-white sling-backs, freshly retouched with a coat of Kwik shoe polish. It was one of those rare times that I did not mind her dressing like someone half of her age; she kind of pulled the whole look off and certainly stood out from all the other moms!

If anyone recalls the 1968 music video of Jeannie Riley singing "Harper Valley PTA," well, that is exactly the image and lyrics that captured my mother perfectly when others described her as someone who was wearing her dresses way too high and reported that she was running round with men and going wild! This was essentially my mother, who was sitting in the auditorium's front row. For a moment, I got a peek inside her private emotional side when I saw a tear running down her cheek, nervously smiling in a self-conscious way. It was the first and only time I saw Mother publicly or privately proud of me. And for a fleeting moment, I also felt very proud of her unique personality and fashion sensibility. It was the only time she ever approved of the spotlight on me. I will always treasure that one very fond memory of my mother. I realized that outside the home, it was the first time that I could candidly admit I saw her as an attractive woman, which was a little hard for me to fully appreciate as her son.

After I wiped off the stage make-up and changed out of my Charlie Brown zig zag shirt, I returned to the auditorium, which had now been rearranged and set up with tables for food and refreshments. It was not hard to pick her and my sister (wearing a homemade pink empire-waist dress that she'd made in home economics class) out of the crowd. I was too self-conscious and a little embarrassed by all the attention that they were garnering, and so I held back so they would not see me for a few moments. I will never forget the last thing I heard her say to the group of strangers before we headed out to walk back home. Smiling more confidently now, with the most beautiful set of fake white choppers I had ever seen, she proudly proclaimed, "I am the proud mother of Charlie Brown!"

Other than my mother's unanticipated attendance, the person I loved best and wanted to invite as my guest was my girlfriend, Lynne. But we were attending different schools and she had her own obligations back at Winchester Public School. We spent most afterschool time at her aunt's house on Metcalfe Street in Cabbagetown. Although her mother, Peggy, and her future stepfather, John, temporarily lived there as well, it was clear to me that good old aunty was more of a mother figure to both Lynne and me. She was a rock to both of us in our early adolescence.

You never met a woman who was more nurturing or kinder than Aunty, and I loved her like we were kinfolk. She taught me through her British traditions and how to properly welcome family and visitors into your home. There was always a cup of hot tea ready from a large, cozy-covered brown betty teapot that was constantly refilled throughout the day. And on one very rare occasion when Lynne and I sat with Aunty for a spot of tea in the dining room, she read the loose tea leaves from the bottom of my cup. As she focussed on the pattern of leaves, she indicated that I would experience a fork in the road and get lost on some mysterious journey. But then she added I would find myself eventually going down the right path in life. It really didn't make much sense to me at the time, and all I could think about were the aromatic smells wafting in from the kitchen. Aunty made the best open-faced, grilled-cheese sandwiches and thick-cut homemade French fries in the world. And to this day, this is still the best comfort food from my childhood memories.

Whenever I see someone eating grilled cheese and French fries, which are becoming more and more rare on restaurant menus, it makes me happy to have a flirt down memory lane and to a more innocent time. I miss you, Aunty! And I know deep in my heart that Lynne deeply misses her as well.

Incidentally, speaking of Lord Dufferin, I must mention I still have the original copy of my very first attempt at an essay from my grade-eight class. The topic was to identify what I wanted to be when I grew up, and the purpose was to help the counsellors stream me into the appropriate high school based on my potential. The topic was something I had been pondering the entire year, and I had narrowed my focus down to becoming a future architect or a medical-arts illustrator. I'd always known that I loved design from the early age of four when I read how *Curious George* had creatively imagined and transformed his living room with objects and animal-inspired furniture that made him feel like he lived at the circus. It was a revelation and a bolt of lightning to my creative imagination.

I knew it was exactly the kind of imagination I would need in my professional career as an architect or creative medical artist for veterinarians. At least, that's how my little brain worked back then when I was heading into puberty. When I shared my career dreams with my sister Janet, she told me that storybooks had great whimsical ideas, but nobody lived in a home like Curious George, and I said, "Well, why not?" And I realized at that point that growing up meant I would have to start hiding my fanciful imagination and agree with her to make her happy. And so, I learned to hate the increasing responses from family members saying that I had to be realistic. Honestly, for a kid with an active imagination, what did I know about being unrealistic? As my earlier teachers used to say, "If you can dream it, you can build it!" And I coveted my curiosity and imagination!

By the time I reached grade eight, I was fully immersed in my school art class and my early homework assignment for an interior design concept made my sister Janet smile and feel giddy with delight. In my mind, I knew she would probably be my first client. I recall how I had sketched a conceptual glass-block bathroom that was designed as a feature focal point in the centre of my proposed future living room. When I had to show my work to the class, I understood from Dr. Holland's remark that my concept was clearly not "everyone's cup of tea." But I thought, God bless Janet and Lynne for their support, even when others thought my designs were considered too far outside the bounds of normal conventions. This was my very first attempt at an interior design plan and perspective sketch. And I could visualize it as if it was already built, but my drawings were frankly just a little too "sketchy." My imagination far exceeded my visual communication skills. Give me an opportunity to walk someone through my thinking and I am sure I could sell my ideas to just about anyone. The sad reality is that no one seemed to have much time to listen to a twelve-year-old kid from the wrong side of the tracks. In my young mind, I saw a creative and innovative interior designer-just like Curious George.

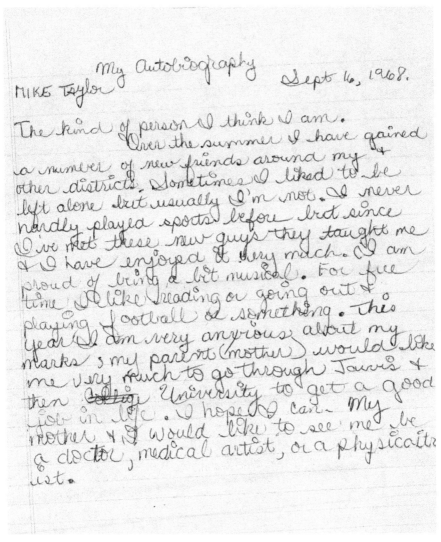

Grade 8. Lord Dufferin Public School

8
JARVIS COLLEGIATE
393 CARLTON STREET, TORONTO, 1969–1971

Because of my dream to be the first in my family to attend university, I had to do everything in my power to make sure I was one of the handful of students selected from Lord Dufferin Public School to attend the highly reputable and elite Jarvis Collegiate. *At the time,* many of the enrolled first-year students at Jarvis Collegiate lived north of Bloor Street in the established tony enclave of Rosedale. Their educational underpinnings were from private boarding schools and private schools, such as Upper Canada College and St. Michael's College for the boys; and Havergal College and the Bishop Strachan School for the girls. In contrast, I was from an inner-city public school.

As a Cabbagetown choirboy, I sang with privileged boys at St. Simon's Anglican Church on Bloor Street. I had first-hand experience interacting in extra-curricular activities with the upper middle class. Moreover, outside of the choir, some of my rich friends would on occasion take me to their nearby homes for lunch breaks when we had a full day that entailed morning rehearsals followed by afternoon/evening performances. We would often go next door and walk to the end of a very short dead-end street to enter a discreet entrance for the Glen Road pedestrian bridge connecting north St. Jamestown working class across to upper class Rosedale. The only people from Cabbagetown and north St. Jamestown who knew where to access this tunnel and foot bridge were the cleaning ladies and domestic help who would cross over to work as maids, nannies, and housekeepers. And although I was dressed in a blazer with the choir crest and could pass as one of the elites, I knew in my soul that I didn't belong and I wasn't any better than the hired help, no question about it. I thought passing as something you weren't like hiding behind a big mask.

Only two students from my grade-eight class were streamed into Jarvis Collegiate in the fall of 1969: Karen Lazotte and myself. That's how insanely impossible it was to get into the school for marginalized kids like myself. Most of my other male classmates were dispatched to vocational trade schools such as Central Tech and Castle Frank. Girls were sent off to secretarial business schools, such as Eastdale Vocational and Central High School of Commerce, where my sister Janet and brother Jackie attended and to where I would later transfer for grades eleven through thirteen.

However, my initial long-term goal was to go onto university, and it was mandatory for me to matriculate from nearby Jarvis Collegiate with its stellar reputation. Although students like my brother and sister were permitted to attend schools outside their neighbourhood, I preferred not to spend daily time commuting on the subways and buses.

I recognized the next five years of high school would be challenging due to my unstable family circumstances. The very concept and risk of failure kept me motivated. I would do anything to break free from my mother's perception that university was a waste of time and money, or that it was not necessary for securing a respectable long-term job. Blue was the colour of my mother's eyes, her dress, and her lower-middle-class DNA. And for someone like myself who aspired to wear a white collar one day, I knew that I would have to find support elsewhere. In my adolescent discourse with my mother, she continued to let me know in no uncertain terms that I thought I was better than the rest of the family. And I knew there was no point in arguing my position any further. Like a mastiff with a bone in her mouth, Mother wouldn't give up her beef; none of the other kids went to university, and according to her, "they all turned out just fine!"

Unfortunately, Mother was not alone in her misguided accusation and predictions for other kids from working-class neighbourhoods. By the early 1970s, plenty of high-school students from struggling working-class neighbourhoods went out to work directly after high school. We had no concept of a gap year for travel and exploration. Teenagers immediately started paying for room and board at home or simply moved out by age eighteen. Those were your two options. Rarely would I hear about poorer kids who were academically gifted students on scholarships to attend university. It was something I had to research and seek out on my own. Even back in grade eight, I can remember going to the library and talking to a counsellor about what kind of courses and grades I would need to attend university, and the bar seemed extraordinarily high for acceptance into the University of Toronto, but a lot less for community college. My guidance counsellor tried to convince me to consider a three-year diploma program at college as he did with all the other underprivileged kids in my school, and I ditched that counsellor's piss faster than a flush in the urinal. I may not have had any family or financial resources to support me, but there was no way in hell that I was going to be robbed of my dreams.

By the time I entered high school in 1969, Jarvis Collegiate was considered a very preppy, buttoned-down school, populated mostly by "WASPs" (White Anglo-Saxon Protestants) who abided with the strict rules and protocols. Because Jarvis was a publicly funded high school, they charitably accepted a few token kids like me from Cabbagetown and Regent Park, particularly those students who had the most potential of academically competing with the privately educated kids from Rosedale. Even the manner of how they formally dressed in their jackets, grey flannel pants, and penny-loafers at a public high school created financial and sartorial anxiety for me.

In my first year, the boys at school had to wear their shirts tucked in with the long sleeves unrolled, and the shirt had to be buttoned up to the neck with just a hint of a crisp white T-shirt showing at the top. Polo shirts were also acceptable, but T-shirts were frowned upon. There were a lot of grey flannels, khakis, and corduroy pants in those days, and rarely would you see denim jeans. Hair was neatly trimmed or buzzed, especially if you were a jock. However, everything dramatically changed by 1971 due to the impact of hippie culture on the high school landscape of new liberal norms. We had two distinct lunchrooms back then—one was for the boys and the other for the girls—as leftover British traditions.

Phys-ed was not co-ed at the time. In fact, strange as it may sound, boys were not allowed to wear bathing suits. Unless of course you joined the extra-curricular swim team where you got to wear one of those quintessential and recently invented Speedos, which was the standard competitive swimwear of the day. Jarvis Collegiate had their own varsity-branded red, white, and blue Speedos for competitions.

I can't think back to a single guy who was not self-conscious about his body in the locker room; everyone was at different ends of the spectrum in physical development and shy about puberty and penis size. The maturely developed guys were sometimes more painfully shy and embarrassed than guys who were a little slow in development. In the showers they were the first to feel self-conscious and often turned into the wall, whereas I would twirl around like a figurine on top of a jewellery box, slowly and methodically, allowing the shower to hit all parts of my body. However, I paid a price for my natural freedom of expression, and this did not go unnoticed by my teacher, who as far as I was concerned, lingered around the shower room far too long!

Our phys-ed teacher had sadistic tendencies with people who had a smaller frame and were perceived as weak. Although I loved swimming, I dreaded water wrestling in the deep end of the pool. And why would that be, you might ask? Although I was not uncomfortable being naked and wrestling in cold water, I was concerned about being matched with someone who could not swim and had a fear of deep water; particularly someone who was way outside my division weight.

At the start of class, we would all have to sit around the pool with our legs dangling in the water, ready to jump in at a moment's notice. I always tried to hide behind one of the large square columns flanking the pool so my twisted teacher couldn't see me. After the first experience in our swim class, I knew his sick agenda of pairing opposite weight classifications, like David and Goliath. His strategy was to pair someone small like me with the most obese guys in the class, like Luke or Peter, who were both around 250-300 pounds at the time. I was a puny runt of maybe 120-135 pounds soaking wet.

He would gesture at either one of the two of the larger guys to get into the water and then take a moment of silence and dramatic suspense. Then he would walk around the pool until he found me with his piercing evil eyes.

He would lock onto me like a laser and emphatically gesture for me to jump into the deep end while blowing his pacifier/whistle like it was some sort of police raid that he was conducting. I knew exactly what he expected of me and my much-larger wrestling opponent.

I remember Luke being the kinder of the two; he was very shy, and I could tell he hated this just as much as I did. When Luke would grab me from behind, he would pretend to hold me tight as he pushed us both below the surface. Once under the surface, he would relax his hold just enough for me to squirm out of his sweaty embrace, allowing me enough time to swim to the shallow end. We worked well with our pre-planned choreographed routine out of mutual concern for each other.

Unfortunately, my other opponent, Peter, *was* different; he was a non-swimmer and easily panicked in the deep end. His powerful and non-relenting hold on me always led me to quickly tap out, but he ignored me and frantically tried to climb on top of me so he would not go under without a fight for his life. Thankfully, we had a class volunteer/look-out who acted as a safety spotter and carried a long aluminum safety pole. He would extend the pole down into the water so anyone who was panicking could grab onto it and be pulled to the side of the pool. I never needed the safety pole to grab, but Peter always depended on it with every inch of his life. The moment he saw the pole, he would flail himself toward it, giving me an opportunity to swim safely to the shallow end of the pool, feeling exhausted and drained.

My saving grace was that I was an excellent swimmer and very nimble. And as a lifeguard in training at the time, I knew how dangerous it was for one-on-one contact with someone panicking in the water. It never ended well for either person. Because of this, Peter was my biggest fear in water wrestling, even though part of me felt a little sympathetic for him. I always ended my round in the pool with an equally serious laser-like stare right back into my teacher's eyes. I thought he was a despicable person and I wanted him to know, by mirroring his behaviour, that I thought of him as one sick, sadistic puppy!

Later in the change room, I confided in Luke that I would gladly take our teacher on as my opponent in the pool any time of his choosing. We both laughed and agreed that "Mr. Butch Teacher" was a pathetic coward, and he would never get into the pool with me even though he was a fully grown man and outweighed my weight division. He was a loser! Thank God we had more than one teacher in gym class!

In the shower room, *Mr. Butch Teacher* would stand outside our communal shower and whip these tiny hotel-sized bars of soap and intentionally hit select students in the legs and buttocks. There was lots of frenetic hopping around while the charade went on, and whenever I got hit my classmates would laugh unmercifully at his tactics. The truth of the matter is they did not want to be identified as weak and become the object of his weird little shower games. Invariably, I shared the brunt of his stinging bruises each week, but my friends Michael Nespiak and Calvin Mercer got their fair share as well. Back in the day, his behaviour was accepted as "having a little fun" and not considered abuse, unless you were the unfortunate recipient. This would go on twice a week when phys-ed class was scheduled to use the pool. In retrospect. I did love phys-ed, and I excelled in gymnastics, wrestling, and track and field. Ironically, my very favourite activity was swimming. I believe it was one of my top marks in grade nine, which was a revelation to both my mother and me! However, I detested my teacher.

I'd thought I was destined to be a lonely, fearful sissy-boy when I started out at Jarvis Collegiate with no competitive spirit and with a fear of bullies. But as my body developed and I grew stronger, so did my confidence and success. Looking back to this time, I would argue that this was the greatest gift I received in my first two years there; I discovered a newfound confidence in myself while knowing that I was equally good as the jocks. Despite the authoritarian approach and strict rules, my take-away was that I had moments of great acceptance and admiration from the other boys, and this was a huge awakening to my self-confidence. I said to myself, "Bring on the school cheerleaders and the marching band!" More specifically, I said, "Bring on our school's star cheerleader!" Miss Sally Sevetachnos was the winner of Miss Congeniality for Jarvis's intramural cheerleading competition. If I could have been a male cheerleader, I most certainly would have applied! But Canada was not quite as progressive as the United States back in 1969-1970. Looking back, I can see just how much I stood out from the other guys, and I would not understand why until my final year of high school.

The one last thing that stands out from my first year phys-ed class is that we were all placed on teams with a peer-team captain who had a rather particular duty. Before each class began, the team captain was required to inspect each team member in his line to ascertain that we were all wearing the issued class uniforms: white T-shirt with Jarvis logo, very tiny blue shorts, a mandatory jockstrap, and white socks and runners. Most of the boys who came from private school were acclimated to this type of control and regimented uniformity. I was not accustomed to this at first. Individual freedom and choice were unheard of at Jarvis Collegiate and not tolerated, especially in the lower school. Therefore, I abided by all the rules. If not, the consequence would be a class detention, or I would be sent home where there would be hell to pay from my mother.

Unlike public school, Jarvis encouraged all students to join extracurricular sports. I stuck to sports like swimming, track, and wrestling. Team sports such as football were a definite "no." The one thing that I liked about the uniform was that I could blend in with the team and avoid the stares of looking sartorially different, outside of class. It was bad enough that I came from a "welfare home" and that I was perceived by some as "a loser," by their definition. *À chacun son goût!* What did they know of me? They were more interested in interrogating me as to who my father was and what he did for a living. If I really wanted to cause them some discomfort, I would mention that my father had abandoned me for another family and mistress and that my mother made babies for a living. I would let them know she was a manic-depressive who popped a lot of pills! My canned response shut them up!

What did they know? In fact, the few disadvantaged students from marginalized households were sneered at in the late 1960s by peers who genuflected at the temple of British traditions and elitism. It was just a little too much at times and more than enough reason to ignore many of my peers at school. It was as though they were film extras from the British 1954 movie *Lord of The Flies*. They functioned like a wandering group of elitist misfits, stranded in the school corridors without supervision by adults. For the most part, this mindless mob was a small minority of anemic-looking, pasty-white dickheads from Toronto's private boarding schools. And somehow, they felt entitled to dispense slurs and vulgarities as their rite of passage. It wouldn't have hurt for them to get outside in the sun. Clearly, a little vitamin D would have helped their mood and added a little colour to their faces.

I would have given anything to see them pass through the actual back lanes and school yards of Cabbagetown and Regent Park where the bullies were *actual* thugs looking for an opportunity to strike and physically assault the weak. On the other hand, this group was merely obnoxious and rude. I never perceived them as a physical threat. They were simply intrusive and annoying with their determination to conquer and destroy anyone they deemed inferior to their pedigree and societal standing. Unfortunately, they presented themselves as content to ride on their parents' coattails and felt no remorse for hurling insidious slurs and negative comments about "the commoners and peasants" from South Cabbagetown and Regent Park.

Personally, I took great exception to their remarks. I could not fathom how so much affluence and privileged education could turn a small minority into a miserable lot of bullies. They were clowns, all right, but nothing was remotely funny about their suspended sense of reality. And if truth be told, they were utterly despicable and ungrateful pricks who pretty much went unchecked. As my choirmates at St. Simons liked to say, they were a bunch of "royal turds." I loved this expression for its British bite. No one does lethal sarcasm quite as well as the British, particularly from the best of the best, my much-beloved Dame Maggie Smith. So, royal turds became my temporary sword to slay with; it was a witty comeback and provided leverage. I had learned a good lesson that not all boys from Rosedale were cut from the same cloth. In fact, many of the upper-crust students I considered as friends and allies. We shared the gift of kindness and manners.

From the onset of grade nine, I was determined not to be assimilated into a destructive type of mentality and self-criticism, not then and not ever! Maybe my mother was right all along. Maybe I did think at some unconscious level that I was better than the rest of them. The hard truth is I never understood when my mother would say "sticks and stones can break your bones, but names will never hurt you." She was a hypocrite and knew very well that she often referred to me as a sissy herself. Her unkind words not only hurt my feelings, but they also consumed my childhood spirit and innocence. And by the time I went to high school, I'd developed a coping strategy and learned how to appreciate my quick wit and sarcasm to combat bullying and taunting. Kids were drawn to me and laughed. There were bullies who found me amusing and eventually stopped. I was beginning to appreciate the power of humour against complacency and the internalization of painful shame.

Make no mistake, the high school instructors and administrators passively contributed to the insidious ethos of acceptable behaviour from bullies and turn a blind eye to what they were witnessing in the school halls and cafeteria. They never intervened when they were requested by student class monitors. Invariably they responded with some pat response like, "Well, I am sure they were just joking and ribbing you. Boys will be boys!" In my view, this crazy-ass bullshit was ubiquitous and insufferable for vulnerable kids at Jarvis Collegiate, and I had a fundamental lack of trust in the adult's ability to protect me when I was periodically bullied. By all appearances, they were more interested in preserving the status quo and not rocking the boat. Personally, I felt it was despicable to leave me to fend for myself. They clearly did not understand the difference between a joke and ridicule, or maybe they did! Either way, I felt betrayed.

By the middle of grade ten, my family circumstances had reached an existential crisis, and I pretty much couldn't see any way out of the incredibly stressful circumstances caused by the ongoing threats of maternal abuse. I was physically and emotionally depleted and saw no way to pick myself up. There wasn't anyone I could trust or turn to for help. All my older siblings were gone from the house and had their own family obligations and financial responsibilities to deal with. More important, I couldn't bear the thought of any more family members rejecting me. Mother increased her frequency in calling me a sissy in front of my siblings, and she told everyone that my lack of interest in team sports like baseball and football were not normal.

After many early childhood years of neglect and anxiety, I came to the belief that my life was untenable and worthless. There was no hope in the world for someone to extricate me from my profound despair. My spirit and my will to live quickly deteriorated after my uneventful fifteenth birthday. This was a turning point for me, and I no longer valued my purpose in the world. My mind was focussed on how I could kill myself. I knew my sister Rosemary had previously overdosed on my mother's medications and ended up with a new home and a new lease on life. Maybe the same could happen for me, but I did not really care. I cried alone and wanted relief from my existence as I knew it. My solution was to likewise use my mother's medications, and I attempted suicide and was rushed off to the Wellesley Hospital across from Jarvis Collegiate.

9
ACCEPTANCE
CENTRAL COMMERCE
HIGH SCHOOL, 1971–1973

The Wellesley Hospital and Toronto Family Social Services had determined that my home was categorically unsafe for me to return to, and they threatened to take my mother to court if she did not voluntarily give up her legal parental guardianship. In the interim, I was assigned a social worker who provided a temporary place for me to stay in a regimented halfway house for ex-prisoners! I couldn't believe municipal officials thought it would be a good idea to have me socializing and living with men on probation, but they did, nonetheless. And because the hospital's psychiatric services were desperate to get me away from the constant threat of my mother's abuse and melancholia, I had no choice but to temporarily relocate to Ossington Street, just north of Queen Street. The only good thing I would have to say is my new temporary residence was inside a converted old firehouse that I found fascinating, and it was within walking distance to my new high school at Central Commerce. That meant it would help cut down on my travel time and expenses. The place was a little intimidating with all these older men, and it very much felt less like a prison and more like a military bunker. There were so many house rules that I barely had time for any interaction with the men, other than at supervised meals.

Most of the residents shared a room with bunkbeds; however, I was secured in a room without a roommate. We were allowed in our rooms only at night and we were never permitted to be in anyone else's room. Ignoring this rule was grounds for removal from the house and a loss of probation for the ex-cons. There was a security guard positioned at the end of the second-floor corridor off the bedrooms throughout the night. And whenever I got up to use the washrooms, all the bedroom doors were closed, and the guard was always there. He spoke to no one and kept a clipboard with a record of his nightly watch.

After the first two weeks, I finally managed to get permission to call my former neighbours, Paul, and Sue. Inside the main office and under the watchful eye of the daytime supervisor, I nervously explained to Paul how I had attempted suicide, and I could hear him gasp on the other end. I continued to explain that I was removed from my home and provided temporary accommodation in this halfway house until something more permanent could be found. At that point, I heard Sue jump in to see if I was okay.

They were genuinely shocked to find out about my suicide attempt and without missing a beat, they demanded to know the name and phone number of my social worker and the doctor from the Wellesley Hospital. At that point, I handed the phone over to the female supervisor who attentively monitored my conversation. Within forty-eight hours, they'd managed to arrange for me to move in with them, and I was so overcome with relief that I could not hold back my tears in gratitude. I remember how the stern supervisor stood for a moment in front of me and gave me a gentle smile. She remarked how happy she was that I was leaving, and that I would soon have an appropriate home to go to. She said she didn't want to see me there one day more than was necessary.

Before I knew it, I was living back in my old neighbourhood, and although it was just two doors west of my family home, it felt a world away. I immediately felt rescued and safe within a familiar environment, and I could now envision a future for myself as a valued and cherished member of the Barnard family. I could refocus my energy on completing high school and eventually fulfil my childhood dream to go on to university with their encouragement and support. For Sue and Paul, this was a normal aspiration for any kid, and they insisted I didn't need to feel ashamed for dreaming and expecting more from myself.

In fact, they made it a point to transform the back bedroom into my very first private sanctuary and study. Paul designed a work area for me to do my homework, with custom millwork, and he provided me his old clamp-on drafting lamp from when he was studying architecture at the University of Toronto. Sue was equally talented and transformed my room with a woody textured burlap wall covering. She painted my bedroom ceiling an emerald green that looked like a canopy of a tree, and it looked very trendy and youthful. In addition, she designed a custom bedspread for me, made from various geometric-cut pieces of Finnish-designed Marimekko fabric.

Sue had me pick the patterns and colours for myself and she insisted I go with her to a fabric shop located next to Honest Ed's Bargain Warehouse. She stitched together a beautiful graphic new design, and her kindness resonated with me. It was the first time any adult included me in the decision-making process about things that affected me. I was not accustomed to having adults consult me for my opinion. I felt like I was living in a sitcom, and everything seemed just so perfect and exactly what I had prayed for.

Their inclusion of me in the design process meant the world to me, and I have never forgotten this courtesy when I much later had an opportunity to extend the same respect to my clients, colleagues, and students. Truly, they made me feel loved and supported as a member of their family. It was almost too much for me to take in so soon. At one moment, I was identified as the neighbourhood babysitter and now I was welcomed into their home as an adopted new family member. My only responsibility was to finish high school and pursue my goal to go to university.

Meanwhile, my sister Janet was also out of our family home and trying her best to complete high school after dropping out to have her baby at age sixteen. When I would run into her in the school halls, she intimated that she felt she was being judged by the other girls, and I could sense the erosion of her inner spirit. Externally, she focussed on what she looked like, but all I could see was the collapse of her self-value, and this scared me. Most of her classmates had supported her while she was pregnant, but now that she was a young mother, they felt she no longer belonged at school. She went from being one of the most popular, well-liked girls to a bit of an outcast. And there was nothing I could do to remedy the situation and make it safe for Janet to continue with her studies without making her feel awkward and self-conscious. She was now expected to be a mature adult, but she was more of a little girl and still afraid of the boogie man. She tried to put on a good face and even went so far as to mention how happy she was to hear that I didn't die from my failed suicide attempt. As we said, "catch you later," she mentioned that she hoped my new home with the Barnard family worked out well for me. And that was pretty much was our last conversation. Shortly thereafter, she quit school and we lost track of each other for a year or so.

On a more positive note, my arrival at Central Commerce was welcoming and warm. I no longer felt under siege from peer bullying. The heavy mantle I previously wore simply vanished through a transference of high schools. The tables had turned, and the atmosphere at my new high school was remarkably lighter and infinitely more cordial and pleasant. I went from being an outsider to an appreciated insider. The school's demographics were mostly of Canadian-Italian heritage, along with a good smattering of Portuguese and Polish. Perhaps I was a welcomed new minority to them. Most students were from similar blue-collar working-class families and had little to be pretentious or snobby about. They had not been exposed to peers from upper-middle-class and white Anglo Saxon Protestant backgrounds, and I was certainly considered a person from humble beginnings who seemed to fit right in.

Although the school had varsity sports, they were not popular as there weren't too many boys enrolled in business school, and those who were enrolled at Central Commerce generally spent their free time assisting in their family-run businesses that were related to construction or the food industry. Unlike my experience at Jarvis Collegiate, many of my Italian classmates who turned sixteen took on part-time work to pay for their first car, which seemed to be a big priority amongst my new comrades. Their dream was financial independence from their family and to entice a girlfriend into becoming a fiancée, with marriage as their end-goal after completing high school. University was not even on the horizon for most guys back then.

This was so unlike anything I had ever seen or experienced in the white, WASP culture of my previous high school, where the student focus and emphasis was placed on higher learning and competitiveness and a goal to match or surpass the professional success of their parents. Jarvis grads came from professional households comprised of doctors, lawyers, politicians, corporate business executives, investors, and property owners. Instead of part-time jobs, Jarvis students had enriching holidays in Europe. Many of them had private tutors in anticipation and preparation for a full day of university entrance exams, which everyone took in the last year of high school. They were groomed for success, and I was a quick study.

Post-secondary education for most guys at Central Commerce was not a priority, and this made me stand out as a minority in the school. More importantly, my new school had a very strong theatre arts program as an alternative to varsity sports or high-school bands! The school had a definite creative energy and a sense of nurturing versus competition. It seemed like a natural fit for someone like me who was not into team sports. Most importantly, I wasn't bullied or looked down upon when I decided to go with the theatre electives. I was very grateful for the relief from my intense unwillingness to participate in extracurricular sports. The new theatre option was lifesaving, and I was willing and able to contribute whatever extracurricular time that it took to act and co-produce plays. If I had known better and hadn't had my own nose stuck up in the air, I would have transferred to Central Commerce earlier.

I was also developing a friendship with a close clique of new buddies who, unbeknownst to them, contributed directly to my well-being and my daily struggle for companionship. They never had a clue how profound the simple gesture of inviting me to lunch in their homes restored my faith in male friendships. I always counted my blessings with my new friends, particularly Joe Catalfamo and Rose Cuda. They made my days in high school memorable and fun, and I was so glad I had made the decision to transfer.

Although I was treated as an honorary Italian, there were plenty of customs that were foreign to my way of thinking. The men were traditionally waited on hand and foot when it came to meals. Clearly, this concept was not a part of my experience, nor did I subscribe to the practice. So, it did feel strange to sit at their dining room tables with just the men while the women hung out in the kitchen. Their unique customs never interfered with me accepting ongoing invitations for lunch. I found their delicious Italian family meals and lively conversations so refreshing. Moreover, my new comrades maintained that the cafeteria food that the school prepared at the school was absolute garbage! And after tasting their homemade meals, I would have to agree. Unlike my old peers from Jarvis Collegiate, the students at Central Commerce did not eat rabbit food from family prepared brown-bag lunches. They ate with gusto and pride with their robust portions of hearty, carbo-rich foods. I noticed I was starting to put on a few extra pounds; just enough to go up to another size in my clothes. And it was worth every bite!

When we weren't eating lunch at their homes, my friends would take me to the local hangouts for the best pizza from local corner mom-and-pop shops, or for a dessert from a selection of nearby bakeries. I really don't remember eating much in the cafeteria for the following three years. As a teenager with no disposal income, I was sure appreciative of their hospitality and kindness. For them, it was just normal, everyday hospitality to welcome school friends into their homes. My new friends were eager for me to share in their Italian culture and home life. They exposed me to their heritage of flavourful and hearty meals, and the conversations always centred around their secret family recipes for homemade sausages, gravy (sauces) and homemade wine made in the basement of so many of their homes.

In terms of school curriculum at Central Commerce, we had the same standard classes as Jarvis Collegiate: math, sciences, history, and languages. But my new school had a much broader variety of options and electives to select from, including keyboarding, computer science, and accounting integral to the business school curriculum. Theatre classes were also an alternative to music and art. There just seemed to be a much richer and fuller approach to a well-rounded education. Surprisingly, I took all three options: music, theatre, and art over my three years.

From my art class, I was selected to represent our high school in a fabulous painting and sketch class at the Ontario College of Art and Design (OCAD) every Saturday morning for one term. In theory, this opportunity was for gifted students throughout the city of Toronto, and who the hell would ever think that I would be selected to be the one student dispatched to represent my high school? Not me! I had not studied art since grade eight at Lord Dufferin, when my class was comprised of theoretical lectures for the most part. I knew nothing about hands-on studio art, thanks to the eccentric Dr. Holland. Regardless, I had a good eye for the elements and principles of design, and I was a quick study. I loved to be in this new milieu, and happily dabbled, sketched, and painted away on life drawing and artistic compositions involving nude models. The lesson I learned early on in life was to take risks and be fearless, especially when there was nothing to lose and everything to be gained by keeping an open mind. I was happier than a pig in shit with all these new educational opportunities.

The friendly and collaborative culture at Central Commerce was unique to me. All the students worked together in problem-solving, whether they were asked to or not. We all helped each other along the way in my grade-eleven class, and it was the first time I'd felt like I belonged as an equal and valued member of a group. It did not take long to become popular with some of the brightest students in the class, and this became very important in helping me keep up my grades with a competitive interest in school. The students couldn't care less about where I came from or what my parents did for a living. They knew nothing of my personal family or back story, nor did they stick their nose into it.

My first impression of my theatre class brought back familiar memories of Lord Dufferin Public School and the Parliament Street Library where I had gotten my earlier exposure to acting and singing. This class magically ignited my artistic leanings, and I began to percolate with enthusiasm that was palpable and infectious to my fellow classmates. I stood out because I appeared to others like I was openly comfortable with my natural flair and body mannerisms, which were not so butch! I may have been perceived as a little different as an outsider, but I was never referred to as a sissy-boy at my new high school. Being in the theatre, people assumed you were gay, anyway. Even though this wasn't true, I tucked this observation away in the back of my mind for later consideration about possible future careers in the theatre.

Meanwhile, I had found my new family tribe at school. I said to myself, "What a difference a change in high school can make!" My classmates, for the most part, admitted to taking the theatre class as an easy "bird course." But not me; I was steely focussed on our theatre-class exercises and work-shops, and I became a serious budding actor in the making. I had found a new passion.

By the end of my first term at Central Commerce, my theatre teacher, Miss Collett, had asked me to consider auditioning for the school play that she was going to put on. So, I showed up at 3:30 p.m. for my first audition in the school auditorium. It was only then that I asked what the title of the play was. And then she said those words I'd thought I would never hear again:

You're a Good Man, Charlie Brown! I was momentarily apoplectic, and I am sure my face turned a crimson red. Of course, I was a slam dunk, as I had just done the title role three years earlier at Lord Dufferin Public School! After one of the first read-throughs, she mentioned that her best friend disclosed that she had also previously found the perfect Charlie Brown. It turns out her best friend was Anne Crysdale from Lord Dufferin, and when my name was revealed, they both could not believe that it was me. After all, Miss Crysdale had assumed that I was a student at Jarvis Collegiate and had not realized that I had transferred out of the high school to where her friend Carol taught. Coincidence? I think not! It was divine fate and another example of my guardian angel watching out for me.

Miss Carol Collett took me under her wing for some reason that was not obvious to me initially. She would invite me to her apartment north of Broadview and Danforth, overlooking the Don Valley Ravine, on the pretext of giving me more one-on-one coaching outside of regular school hours. I saw for the first time that she considered me special and unique; I knew it was unusual to visit a teacher's home, but she convinced me that the extra coaching of my songs and acting would improve so much from when I had originally played the role a few years earlier. And because I was the lead, she wanted me to give the best performance of my life for the benefit of the school.

I knew sitting in Miss Collett's apartment that I wanted to pursue an acting degree upon graduation. She showed me a light toward new aspirations for myself. I believe she may have served me a light lunch as a reward for travelling across the Bloor Street viaduct to her apartment. This made the not-so-long subway ride from Castle Frank to Broadview worth my time and effort. Most of all, she gave us an opportunity to get to know one another in a relaxed atmosphere away from the school and the nosey eyes of her colleagues and my classmates. I felt singularly special and coveted the gift of her friendship. I came to suspect that her friendship with Anne Crysdale from Lord Dufferin might have been the source of some of her background information about my family's hardships. By this point, after developing a mentor-type relationship with her, I became comfortable volunteering a little of my ongoing struggles and challenges.

I discovered that both Carol Collett and my high-school guidance counsellor, Mr. Evans, had some sort of a conspiratorial agenda and joint mission to do whatever it took to not let me fall through the cracks again. Prior to this realization, I believed Miss Collett simply admired my creative talent and natural flair for both theatre performance and production design. However, Mr. Evans disclosed to me that Carol Collett had stomped into his office one day and demanded he do everything in his power to watch over me and keep me in school! He confided in me that it was a direct order and not a request, and so he'd agreed to comply with her demand. I was thrilled to discover that Miss Collett thought I was a "very special soul." Their combined attention inspired my accomplishments; the more accolades and attention I received, the harder I worked. And my love of Central Commerce as a creative haven was so much more than I could have ever dreamed or hoped for in a business school.

Shortly before the *Charlie Brown musical* went on, Mr. Evans called me down to his office for a check-in about my stressful living accommodations that evolved from the emerging marriage problems between Sue and Paul and to confirm my university aspirations. After a few sessions, he suggested that since I lived in his Cabbagetown neighbourhood, I could come and spend a quiet weekend at his nearby two-bedroom apartment in City Park. With a little bit of hesitation about his intentions, and the encouragement and blessing of Carol Collett, I did just that. Since I was familiar and had grown up in the neighbourhood, I thought why not? He knew Miss Collett, and I loved and trusted her, so maybe they were friends outside of school.

Anyhow, I was in my last year of grade thirteen, so I accepted the invitation and it turned out to be a lovely weekend. I had my own room, and he took care of all the meals. Our conversations never dealt with the immediate present but rather future opportunities and other culturally rich areas of interest to stir the imagination. He started with live theatre (which he knew I was interested in), but we also discussed architecture, and art and design from around the world. He emphasized the promise of an exciting future ahead for me. He wanted me to know that no matter what was happening in my personal life, he would always be available as more than just a guidance counsellor at school; he would also be an adult male friend and mentor. I realize in retrospect that both he and Carol Collett were acting in concert behind my back to keep my life from going off the rails. They were both angels on earth and manifested when I needed them most.

Anyhow, whether it was talent or just the watchful and loving eye of Miss Collett, I ended up being in every single play and musical thereafter. I starred as Charlie *Brown* and then as Captain Keller in the *Miracle Worker,* and by grade thirteen I co-produced The *Wizard of Oz* and took on the re-imagined role of the Wicked Witch of the West and designed the costumes. I wish I had hung onto my old photographs from The *Wizard of Oz* to illustrate the creativity and design imagination that emerged at the time, but I will use my words as best I can to paint a picture. For my make-up as the Wicked Witch, I had designed a bald skull cap with veins and arteries popping out of the head (like varicose veins), and at the back of the bald head a fiery red high ponytail stuck out; it was so effective that Miss Collett commented that little kids had left the show crying in fear when they saw me on stage. Instead of a witch's black dress, I custom-designed burlap pants and a top that were sprayed with glow-in-the-dark paint splatters that would show up under the black lights. My top was inspired by memories of my little baby brother Rick's shirt that he had worn in his crib when we lived on Sherbourne Street. It was a wrap-around with two little ties at the side. I had turned a pair of long women's gloves into veiny skin texture like my head, accented with long, gnarly fake talons.

By the time I had put the entire creation and ensemble together it was quite a vision to behold! Our play successfully performed over three evenings. However, opening night no doubt scared the audience and me the most. You see, what I had not planned for is an unanticipated accident when Glinda the Good Witch shows up with a lit fire sparkler, per my lighting and production special effects. She was supposed to simply let the magic wand sparkle in front of me as she chanted the classic line: "Be gone or I will drop a house on you too!" At that point, the tornado's path of destruction and the stage was strategically illuminated from hidden black lights that revealed random psychedelic colours and chaotic abstract splattering on my burlap costume and the set design. Unexpectedly, a spark from her sparkler ignited my costume into flames, and as I dropped and rolled on the ground to extinguish the flames, I knew no matter what, the show must go on! I delivered my final line: "I'm melting! I'm melting!"

My nearby brother Jackie, who played *Toto* the dog, knelt beside me and said, "Burn, baby! Burn, already!" Then the curtain dropped, thankfully! And I was relieved! Good old Jackie was so on point with his humour and quick wit. It was a personality characteristic we both shared, and because we had so little personal contact, I had never noticed this trait in him before. It was illuminating to see that no matter our differences, we had something in common. I knew he would be fine with or without me in his life.

But back to The *Wizard of Oz* for a moment. It was no wonder the kids went out screaming at intermission. I thought at first it was my unconventional approach and costume as a male witch, but then when you factor in the accidental torching of my costume, I realize it was the entire performance that had scared them. Their parents thought the flames were just a part of the special effects in the production! They were very lucky to see the first show, because on the following night, "Glinda" stayed well back and twinkled her magic wand sparkler toward the audience ... and not directly at me. There were some wonderful times back then, and best of all, I would see brother Jackie auditioning and loving the theatre as much as I did. He was still living at home but having a personal experience that appeared infinitely more positive than mine. We had an unspoken boundary between us to not talk about what was going on at home. And we never did. We were one grade apart and had our separate friends and identity.

When I turned sixteen, I became certified as a lifeguard by the City of Toronto and was hired part-time by my high school to assist our phys-ed teacher as a lifeguard during my swimming classes. He was not a swimmer, and he unofficially allowed me to teach swimming techniques to the boys in my class. I was perceived as an expert in the eyes of my classmates. All the big, hairy, macho dudes were like putty in my hands; they depended on me to teach them how to swim, and I could see so many of them just struggling to stay afloat. I never anticipated this type of adulation from my peers. By the end of the term, all the guys in my class could swim with a measured sense of newfound comfort in the water, which made me feel proud.

During the fall of grade thirteen, the student council, in conjunction with the guidance department, organized buses for a field trip to a variety of local universities and colleges in the Greater Toronto area. I went on one fieldtrip visit, and that was because I'd only applied to one university. I was putting all my eggs in one basket, and that was York University's theatre performance program. But the competition was tough, and they were only accepting thirty performance students into their first-year class. Students applied from all over Canada and the United States.

By now I had the confidence to articulate a possibility that I could be gay, and although I had never really explored this part of myself before, I felt the timing of going off to university was perfect. I was quite curious about a new sexual identity in both an intellectual and personal expression of untapped happiness. Moreover, I was happy to discover my classmates and friends welcomed my openness, whether I was straight, bisexual, gay, or otherwise. I felt safe and unjudged in my theatre classes, and I felt safe and secure when I made it my area of focus in university. Most important, I had squared my new personal inclinations and directions with my girlfriend Lynne when we both realized this would be the best time to part ways. My greatest concern was to disappoint her and make her feel in any way unvalued or disrespected.

In response to all these new changes manifesting in my life, I had grown my hair out in a rebellious expression of non-conformity, just like the American Vietnam draft dodgers and hippies I had met as my next-door neighbours in Cabbagetown. I experimented and explored gay-trendy fashions, and I conceptualized how to use more gender-neutral and non-binary fashions to buck conventional thinking and societal expectations. I leveraged non-conventional outdoor items like kimonos as an open-tied and knotted shirt.

By the time convocation arrived, I had built up a unique holding of eclectic clothing and accessories at a moment's notice that would draw attention to me. In preparation for convocation, I whipped together an outfit that consisted of a short kimono I had tied in a knot just above my bellybutton to show off my clear, orange-plastic belt that I threaded through my chestnut-brown, bell-bottom corduroy pants. I custom-dyed my construction boots in an orange-blossom colour with matching shoelaces that reflected the colours in the kimono, and I wore several inexpensive metal bangles on my arms that clanged every time I moved.

In terms of the response from the parents and families sitting in the audience, they were not amused with my sartorial expression, and they let me know their feelings in no uncertain way. I could tell my presence made many of them feel uncomfortable with my non-binary, unconforming style while the other boys conformed by wearing a shirt and tie. The school auditorium broke out in loud whispers and finger-pointing in my direction, while the principal and vice-principal looked at me like they had just seen a ghost!

Everyone seemed in absolute horror that I would choose to come to a school ceremony dressed the way I was. Some of them could not figure out if I was a girl or a boy, as evidenced by the dude sitting next to where I was standing. He had the temerity to ask me for clarification of my gender in a condescending tone. My quick wit and surprising response to his face was, "I am a fucking man, you idiot, so deal with it!" This certainly broke the tension in the room, especially for my classmates who were already feeling anxious about going up on stage. Some of my classmates let out approving giggles at my response, and this strengthened my resolve to march up on the stage with great bravado.

When my name was called, I went up onto the stage to receive my diploma from the vice-principal. He reluctantly lifted his limp hand to give me a pathetic and perfunctory handshake. Meanwhile, the school principal declined to shake my hand and turned his head toward the next student coming up on stage left. When I realized I had been shaded by him, I exited from stage right and under my breath said, *"Fuck him" to my classmates in the wings.* I vigorously tossed my shoulder-length head of Farrah Faucet curls and smiled back toward the stage before I gaily swished my sweet ass off the stage. I held my head high and stretched my neck so long that it would give any Audrey Hepburn wannabe a run for their money! My latent queerness and flamboyance were busting out of the closet right before my eyes, and as I walked out of the auditorium, I knew that no one was ever going to challenge me on my looks or what I wore ever again. I was tired of being invisible, and I was going to do everything in my power to make myself noticed and feel fearless to release myself from the constraints of the rampant gay and lesbian discrimination that was pervasive at the time. Like the Archangel Saint Michael, I used my appearance as both a shield and sword to fight off the demons who castigated homosexuals, and I was fed up with feeling the queer community was considered second class at best.

My earlier dramatic training and the new confidence that I had recently acquired at Central Commerce were peaking at the perfect time. I began to completely transform my outer appearance and reinvent myself from the inside out. I could not be any happier to have my dignity restored as I achieved my life dream of completing high school and move onto higher education with my acceptance into York's theatre performance program. My lifelong ambition and dream were manifested, and although I invited no one to my convocation, I wasn't disappointed with my decision. All that mattered was the new man who looked back at me in the mirror, and I liked what I saw.

By the end of May I turned eighteen and began working as a summer lifeguard at *Riverdale Pool.* This gave me time in the evenings to explore Toronto's numerous gay bars, discos, bathhouses, and bookstores. It was all tremendously exciting, and I welcomed each new adventure as if it were a blessing in my life. In the process, I acquired a small circle of four new gay friends: Frank Amodeo, whom I dated briefly before he went off to chiropractic college in England; his best friend *Kurt Jones*, who became my first Black friend, who was finishing up his fashion studies at Humber College; and then *Robert Murray*, who was Frank's friend from his childhood. At the time, he was just a tad too narcissistic and self-absorbed for me to take a shine to. My fourth friend was an acquaintance and someone I would build a close friendship within my first year of university. That special man was the fabulous *Aerol Ramsey.* He just happened to be entering his final year in theatre performance at York University and because we shared common ground, he would soon become my lucky horseshoe and the most reliable friend on campus, outside the Glucksman twins.

Aerol lived in a shared downtown apartment with two extraordinary creative roommates and outrageously talented gal pals, *Holly,* and *Janis.* On occasion, I would stay the weekend as Aero's guest. The gals were fiercely independent and studying moviemaking at Sheridan College. Not long after their graduation, they moved out to Vancouver and went on to make a well-received documentary called *Hookers on Davie.*

Meanwhile, on weekends, Aerol and I would hang out and party all night at the after-hours *Manatee* disco on St. Joseph Street. But as it was a non-alcoholic club that was colloquially referred to as a milk bar, we would start off a little earlier and have a few beer drafts under the historic clock landmark and queer venue known as the *St. Charles Tavern.*

Back in the early 1970s, the St. Charles clock tower was a beacon to the gay tavern. Facing onto Yonge Street and just north of College Street, it was a simple no-frills tavern with veteran straight waiters who worked there for decades and ran a tight ship. They watched out for the gay patrons and at the slightest possibility of trouble inside or outside, they warned and encouraged patrons to exit out the back. The back alley was like our queer underground railway and took us away from public view and risk of "gay-bashing." It served several gay establishments, including: the *Parkside Tavern* and *Stages,* which was an after-hours club. There was also a small cruising bar called *Dudes,* which was a boutique bar for preppie gay men. The interior included a feature bar design that was laminated with pictures from *Blue Boy* magazine centerfolds, and sex videos played on wall-mounted TV screens. From the various gay venues, my queer compadres and I could walk safely south in the alleyway toward College Street and grab a late-night snack or early breakfast at the queer-friendly and iconic twenty-four-hour Frans Restaurant.

The back lanes were the safest way to travel, especially on Halloween, when throngs of local straights and tourists would head into the downtown core. Out front of the infamous St. Charles facing onto Yonge Street, the drag queens and female impersonators attracted large crowds of curious onlookers and drunks, sprinkled with smaller groups interspersed with suburban hooligans seeking anonymous cover. It was the singular night of the year when the queer community could celebrate our High Holiday and the drag queens would be publicly welcomed and tolerated, even if it was for only one night. But it wasn't without reprisals from a minority of haters and bashers on the lookout for trouble. What would start off as a fun evening would invariably erupt into the taunting and terrorizing of readily accessible drag queens and gay young men like me who were just starting to come to terms with our sexuality and identity in the queer community.

As a single young eighteen-year-old man who had just come out, I can recall standing with the crowd of onlookers congregated on the opposite side of the street to the main entrance to the St. Charles with my back firmly planted up against the wall of the Howard Johnson Hotel. I was one of the many onlookers eager to get a glimpse of the glamorous drag queens making their arrival. Without any provocation, the crowd suddenly erupted, and strangers started randomly pelting eggs and beer cans at anyone with even a whiff of queerness about them. While the regular gay patrons scurried into the club for cover, I was isolated on the opposite side and not so lucky. I got pelted with eggs for simply being alone and assumed gay. I felt tremendously violated, and it triggered all kinds of emotions from when I was bullied and terrorized as a kid. It was at that point I decided to never enter a gay venue directly from Yonge Street again, and I stuck to the discreet access points to the bars from the back lanes.

And that's the hidden logic behind the reason I particularly enjoyed the discreate pop-up queer events like the gay dances at the University of Toronto and the community-sponsored summer barbecues on Toronto's Hanlan's Point. But my favourite and most expensive diversion from the readily visible bars and clubs were the queer boat parties on the Mariposa steamboat paddlewheel around Toronto's harbour. The glamourous boat rides were organized by Toronto's legendary female impersonator Murray (aka Mama Cooper), who performed at straight nightclubs on Yonge Street, and she even had her own after-hours club for a short period of time above the gay-friendly Parkside Tavern. These pop-ups events and boat parties predominantly attracted gay white men and rarely involved public harassment. They were mostly advertised from within the confines of the gay bars and bathhouses. Everyone in my small clique of friends earnestly planned, dressed, and accessorized for these patently inspired, unique paddleboat outings on Lake Ontario; it was a big extravaganza that often-involved copious amounts of drinking and snorting of illegal substances by the affluent, while disco blasted out from high-quality rented commercial speakers strategically located for impact and continuity of sound around the boat. We were always accompanied by a flotilla of allies and supporters honking and whistling-blowing in support. You would have thought we were celebrities by the way we were followed and applauded for nothing more than a smile and a wave.

In advance of the floating summer parties, my four best friends would escort me to Mama Cooper's house on Seaton Street so that I could purchase the boat tickets for the group. You might say it was her way of first-hand screening any new faces who wanted to attend her private boat extravaganza. And as my friends alerted me in advance, if you didn't cut the mustard, you would simply be told the event was sold out. Apparently, I not only cut the mustard when I was introduced to Mama Cooper, I was also commanded to sit on the side of her bed while she dramatically inhaled her cigarette from a long cigarette holder, as if she were starring in Breakfast at Tiffany's. She coquettishly lounged while swaddled in a very luxurious flowing robe, resting on top of an exotic satin bedspread covered in peacocks. She was still wearing her makeup and glamour-length fake nails from the night before.

She reeked of stale perfume and cigarettes, but I found it her very intoxicating, nonetheless. After she was satisfied with my introduction and lap-dog attention, she extended her open hand for my money in exchange for the highly coveted tickets that she procured from what looked to be a large jewellery box on her nightstand table. Afterward, she dismissed me with a peck on the cheek's goodbye.

As we were walking out of her bedroom, her parting words to my group were to remember that the theme of the boat party was the colour white, and if we showed up not wearing white, she said, "Your tickets won't be honoured and there will be no refunds!" There was no one more formidable than this seasoned performer and professional party planner. Mama Cooper was indeed a Toronto original and a brilliant entrepreneur. Afterward, my buddies took me out shopping to investigate novel fashions and bargains in Kensington Market, before heading up to Bloor Street and the affluent boutiques in Yorkville. My new pals would often refer to Yorkville as New York's equivalent to Fifth Avenue. And really, what would I know from Fifth Avenue, already? Well, other than from what I gleaned from Marilyn Monroe's version of Diamonds Are a Girl's Best Friend, which popped into the video cassette inside of my head.

Meanwhile, we would spend the following week on the phone, updating our progress on our white fashion selection for the boat ride. I believe I ended up wearing a pair of white painter's pants, and a tight white T-shirt and baseball cap, accessorized with an armful of metallic bracelets for a hit of sparkle. That was all I could afford on my financial slim-fast diet plan. In my opinion, other than the ass-hugging painter's pants, the gayest part of my ensemble were the clear jelly sandals I purchased from one of the overstock bins in Kensington Market. As I would like to say, my ensemble was "cheap and cheerful." Without question, it was my fit-body and youthful good looks that made me look like a million bucks, or at least the price of a Cartier or a Tiffany watch! Well, for heaven's sake, let's all agree for argument's sake that at least I looked like the economic cost of a new Timex. I mean, who was I kidding with all this pretense back then!

It didn't really matter all that much. We all knew that we had a role to play as undeniable eye candy for the older established queens and party-circuit queens on the boat cruise. Everyone knew our place in the hierarchy of gays, and we used our youth as currency into the cherished and private upscale culture of gay life in downtown Toronto. Often, the boat rides would lead to new acquaintances and invitations, but for the most part we stuck to our own group. Murray Cooper was an iconic star in Toronto's flamboyant queer community, and she was renowned for her flawless make-up and hair. She only wore expensive, glamorous fashions wherever and whenever she performed as a female impersonator. I felt blessed to have made her acquaintance on several occasions and to receive her nod of approval in my early days of coming out in the summer of 1973.

Over that particularly hot and eye-opening summer, I'd blasted my ass out of the proverbial closet and not only became a queer fashionista, but also a queer activist and an ally for a few married men who I knew at the time were still leading double lives and identities. I always recognized that it was our fabulous home-grown drag queens and performers in Toronto who inspired me to become visible and out there for others. And clothing and appearance were my armour that rocked the boat and propelled me forward. It was a time and an age when I felt uber invincible and aspirational. The 1970s were a heady era for Toronto's explosive gay community.

High school lead in You're a Good Man Charlie Brown.
Central Commerce High School

10
OUT AT YORK UNIVERSITY
VANIER CO-ED STUDENT
RESIDENCE, 1973-1974

In late August of 1973, I can recall getting an unexpected call from my sister Janet. It had been a good two or three years since we last saw each other in high school after she gave birth to her daughter, Shauna. She suggested we do something fun from our childhood and said that she would make baby-sitting arrangements so we could have some one-on-one time together. She suggested we meet up at the old familiar Pape Recreation Centre's pool before I started school and moved into residence at York University. As young children living on First Avenue, we had gone there many times. And later, when we were in grade eight, Janet joined a synchronized swimming club and was part of the team selected for competitions that convened at the very same pool. It seemed to be the best place for both of us to meet, as it was a place of happier times and memories that we both shared.

Out of the blue and in between our moments of splashing around in the pool like carefree children, Janet informed me she wanted to take a rest in the shallow end of the pool and asked me to join her. I then discovered the reason she wanted to get together in person. She wanted to tell me face to face about our long-estranged father, whom she recently met up with after so many years apart. Less than a month after meeting him, she found out from a distant cousin that he had just died. He was only fifty, and according to her, he had died from a heart attack that she suspected came from decades of unhappiness and a broken heart, caused by years of personal conflict. I couldn't figure out how she knew all this and how she came to be in contact with him, but it didn't really matter at the time. All I understood was he reached out to her at some point. Then she took off a silver signet ring that he gave her, and she put it on a chain to wear around her neck.

While we were standing in the shallow end, she removed the ring from the chain and gave it to me as a good luck token for when I went off to university. I told her that she was too generous and perhaps she should hang onto it. Although she recalled how our dad had confessed that he had always shown a preference toward her, she firmly believed that it wasn't his intention to make me feel any less important. She maintained that he would approve of her passing his ring on to me as his eldest son. And I told her I loved her for always having a special place in her heart for me, and she would always be my most beloved sister.

My head was swimming with confusion and questions, but it was not the time and place to have a meaningful discussion. After changing and showering, we caught an eastbound streetcar. She was enroute to the subway and then heading northbound to North York where she was currently living with her daughter and boyfriend, Danny Rose. I was enroute to Paul Barnard's house on Albemarle Avenue in Riverdale, where I was currently residing. We attempted to change the topic of our conversation to something a little lighter and we reminisced about the old days. However, neither of us could let go of the topic of our father. Janet continued by saying she believed our dad was a flawed man, but no less or more than anyone else. As she pointed out, "Who were we to judge?" He was our dad, and we both agreed that his life ended far too soon before he'd had an opportunity to redeem himself for not saying goodbye to us so many years ago. I responded by telling her that I felt robbed of an opportunity for him to see me as a grown man. I was finally becoming the person I was meant to be as a gay man and an activist for human rights. I always wanted an opportunity to meet him to tell him how much I loved and missed him. And I wanted so desperately for him to be proud and happy for me as his son.

When I asked Janet if she was happy with the way her life turned out, she avoided the topic of her personal feelings and shrugged her shoulders. In response to the direct question, she said that she missed the carefree days of our early childhood. In the light of the day, I could see her eyes looked vacant and there was no trace of the old twinkle. Just before I got off at Broadview and Gerrard, I looked at Janet and said, "You know, Janet, we never had a chance to say I love you to our father nor to each other." I gave her a brief hug and I whispered these very important words to her for the first time. These would be the prophetic last words that I would say before her unanticipated demise in four months.

Meanwhile, as I looked at my dad's signet pinky ring that fit on my wedding finger, the best thing I could do for myself was to have my surname legally changed to reflect my actual rightful place as his biological son. My surname, "Taylor," has no ancestral connection to me, but I felt I could not drop it, as it was my family's surname. My best option to honour my father and my mother was to use both names, hyphenated; hence, the genesis and rebirth of *Michael Thomas Plasse-Taylor*. And for a second time in a two-year period, I experienced a "coming out" as a rightful descendant of my biological dad, Lucien Plasse. I truly felt for the first time in my life I knew who I was, and I liked myself. It was a long road to travel, and my ongoing inner healing was more important than any degree of higher learning that I was intending to pursue. A simple thing like a name change made my outlook on life optimistic and promising. I finally knew who I was and was proud to step out from the ghost of my dad.

It was the last week in August and just before the Labour Day holiday when I decided to move into Vanier residence at York University. I was singularly inspired and on my way in a Diamond Cab heading north up the Allen Expressway toward the Downsview suburb and the flagship Keele Street Campus of York University. Everything I owned in the world was thrown into the trunk of the cab and packed inside an old thrift-store suitcase and a large black trash bag. As I sat in the car for the long ride up to my destination, I reflected on a couple of adult friends who'd profoundly impacted my aspirational dreams of going to university. Next to me on the back seat was a souvenir laundry sac with *Harvard University* inscribed on it with burgundy-coloured letters. My friend Paul Barnard had brought this inexpensive souvenir back to me from Harvard University's graduate school of architecture and his alma mater that he visited while on one of his recent business trips to Boston, MA.

It may have been just a simple laundry sac and a spontaneous gift from Paul, but for me it was emblematic of a scholarly vessel that was empty and ready to be filled with my own academic dreams or as a receptacle for soiled childhood memories. For a poor boy from the wrong side of the tracks, this symbolic gift was of great magnitude and personal value. I could not help but smirk as I said to myself, "Oh my dear God! What do you think this is that you're clutching at your side, Michael? A family heirloom?" If Paul knew how much drama I made of his gift, he would have said something to the effect of "It's only a laundry sac!"

Life in residence would put me on equal footing with many other freshmen. And it would certainly give me a respite from the short and sometimes chaotic periods when I lived with the Barnard family, first on Carlton Street in Cabbagetown and then on Albemarle Avenue in Riverdale. Their marriage was breaking down in an unpleasant way in front of my eyes and so was my relationship with their family. For a second time in my life, I was being abandoned by a conventional straight family who once claimed that I would be an integral and cherished member forever, but alas it was not meant to be.

And that led me to reflect a bit more on Jan Sheffield, who mentored me through my coming out and helped me decide what electives I should consider taking at York. I was enthralled with her no-nonsense, open attitude about life and the importance of education; after all, this was her professional career as a public-school teacher, and it was her big passion in life. She was a tremendously intelligent person and an omnivorous consumer of books. She seemed to open a new book with every new package of cigarettes, and she was pretty much a chain smoker! She was blessed with the sharpest wit and insight of anyone I had ever known. Her humour reminded me of Dorothy Parker's mantra "you can't teach an old dogma new trick." I could easily imagine Jan sitting around a table, smoking, and drinking at the Algonquin Hotel in New York City. She was of the same ilk, but Canadian, of course, and a tad more introspective.

As the cab crossed the 401 Highway, I reflected on how she was a mature, no-nonsense kind of gal and how much I loved the cadence and crackling of her voice; it was measured and slow with just a touch of a rasp, no doubt due to years of heavy smoking and a fondness for single-malt Scotch at the time. She was my first hero in Toronto's queer community.

When I turned eighteen at the end of May, Jan had called me at Sue and Paul's house and said to come over and spend a little time in the late afternoon with her at her white wood clapboard duplex in the east-end beach neighbourhood. She mentioned, "I have a birthday surprise for you, and I will be taking you out tonight for a drink to celebrate." She seemed to suggest that I should dress less casually but not overdress. And so, I followed her instructions. I showed up in a pair of dockers and a freshly pressed short-sleeved shirt. We spent the afternoon in her duplex, listening to her favourite record by The *Carpenters ad infinitum.* We ate some Chinese take-out and celebrated with a tiny birthday cake that she presented with a solitary candle. She told me to blow it out and make a wish. And I didn't realize how prophetic these words would become later that very night! After the birthday cake, she said, "Let's hit the road." She literally took me by the hand and drove us downtown and parked her small sedan in a lot at Hayden and Young Street. We got out of the parked car and walked a half-block west and turned the corner onto Yonge Street. The next thing I knew, she was opening the door to a very noisy and smoky bar. I looked up at the sign above the door and it said *The Quest.*

As soon as we walked in, there was a security guy standing by a red velvet rope that separated us from a secured staircase leading up to the second level, from where I could hear loud disco music playing. "That's where we are going," Jan said bluntly while pointing up to the second level. Without any response, the bouncer unclipped the velvet rope with an obsequious smile. So up we went, and I followed Jan like a loyal pup on his first walk outside. When I got to the top of the stairs, Jan stood waiting at the threshold to the second-floor bar and together we walked in and sat at a table for two along the north wall toward the front of the room. We were within proximity of a small dance floor that was virtually empty, notwithstanding a handful of attractive guys about my age who were dancing and laughing! As I looked around the room, it occurred to me there were no women other than Jan. I must have looked puzzled. Before I had time to absorb everything around me, Jan had already ordered our drinks and was inhaling her first cigarette, which she had lit from a candle on our table. After she exhaled, she looked directly at me and said, "Do you know where we are? This is a gay bar, and are you okay with that?"

I took one fast look back at the dance floor with the attractive guys having so much fun and I replied, "For sure."

For some unknown reason, I sat with Jan as if I had been there a million times before and took a small sip of the gin and tonic that she had ordered after the waiter scoped me out for my personal identification. I thought to myself, not bad for my first alcoholic drink. At that point I noticed Jan had blown our table's candle out. I looked around at the other tables and it didn't make any sense that some of tables had lit candles while others did not. Without missing a beat, she explained to me that when you were available for companionship, you kept your candle burning. On the other hand, if you were not interested in company, then you blew the candle out. And Jan just blew our candle out, apparently alerting the patrons that we were not interested in company. In my view, we were sitting at a table for two and there was no room for anyone else, so it seemed a bit unnecessary.

Anyhow, the four guys on the dance floor disregarded the apparent "candle code" and came over to ask if I would like to join them on the dance floor. We all looked toward Jan's hawkish eyes, studying the situation. She took a moment sizing them up and then she pulled a tight-lipped smile, nodding her head that it was okay. I had barely found my dancing feet and was feeling the intense heat from the proximity to the other guys and out of nowhere, Jan marched onto the dance floor. Much to my shock, she pushed the guys away who had surrounded me. She snatched me by my arm and said, "Enough for one night, we're out of here."

And before I could explain to her that I had barely started my drink, she hauled my ass so fast out the door, you would have thought the place was on fire. And I guess in a metaphoric sense, Jan was on fire. As we exited the second floor, I glanced back at my dance buddies, who were laughing hysterically.

As a footnote, the following Saturday I went back to the Quest on my own, and sure enough, the same four guys were there. When they came over to greet me, the first thing they said was, "And where's your mother tonight?" It was now their turn to playfully grab my arm as Jan had done previously and they ushered me over to their large table. I noticed their table candle was lit, indicating "the more the merrier."

Throughout the course of my evening with an apparent new group of gay friends at the Quest, there were continuous rounds of drinks and dances while they further educated me about a raft of other gay codes and symbols prevalent at the time. Kurt happened to smoke Menthol Salem cigarettes, and as he demonstrated with his package on the table, when a stranger offers you a cigarette or asks for a light, notice which letter of the word "Salem" is pointed toward you. If the closest letter is the letter "S," it symbolizes the guy is not necessarily looking for a "sadist" but rather a "top." And conversely, the letter "M" suggests the guy is not necessarily looking for a masochist but rather someone to "bottom." All this messaging from a package of innocuous cigarettes, and all I could think to myself *are they kidding me?* I was so naïve and had so much to learn in my early days. Someone else elaborated on what side of my pants I should wear my keys to represent whether I was a top or bottom and what side of my back pockets to place my bandanna in, which came in various symbolic colours representing preferential proclivities. I told my buddies that I preferred wearing my bandannas around my neck, in neutral territory, just like Switzerland.

My new buddies informed me how it was safer to mix pronouns to remain undetected in the company of straight society; everything was about the pronouns "she," "her," and "the girls," and it wasn't just to be camp, as they explained; speaking in codes could save my life in the company of strangers. They gave me examples of gay establishments with everyday common names that wouldn't raise suspicion when you were out in public. For example, if someone said they were heading out to the library, it meant you were headed off to a gay bath house named *The Library*, which was discreetly located off a service lane, adjacent to the old location of the Toronto Humane Society at Wellesley and Yonge Street.

I was reminiscing about a whole new language of recently learned gay vernacular as the cab turned off Keele Street and onto York Boulevard at York University's campus. My final thought before arriving at my dorm was how lucky I was to have had Ian Sheffield as a mentor and friend. She unlocked my proverbial closet door. More importantly, she'd supported my dream of attending university and guided me through the application process and the selection of some of my electives. She intrinsically understood about the joy of learning at a post-secondary-school level, and her infectious enthusiasm for what I was about to embark upon was precisely the assurance and confidence that I needed. She was my trusted wingman when I needed support and encouragement.

I had to laugh to myself as I recalled her parting instructions about the four Royal F's a day earlier, and she cautioned me about future sexual encounters while I was a student:

(1) *Find Him*
(2) *Feed Him*
(3) *Fuck Him*
(4) *Forget Him*

And with that final thought in the cab, I rolled up to the front entrance at Vanier College dormitory and was dropped off feeling like Orphan *Annie*; out of place and fully dressed in a smile. I was enthusiastically ready to fulfill my educational destiny!

When I arrived on the ninth floor and entered one of Canada's first two experimental co-ed floors in 1973, I had to stop for a moment and get my bearings. I noticed a nearby wall-mounted list of rooms and room-mates posted next to the elevators. While I stood there searching for my name, a female dorm mate with her hair wrapped up in a towel, who was wearing a heavy chenille bathrobe, came up and introduced herself as Helicia Glucksman. She asked me to excuse her appearance as she was just returning from a shower in our co-ed bathroom down the hall. She happily volunteered to help me locate my room and identified my new roommate as Sidney (Sid) Clarke. I told her that the name "Sidney" for some reason conjured up an image of a red-haired, nebbish kind of pale, white guy, and she laughed.

In response, she said nothing more than, "Sid is a great guy" and she deferred from describing him until after I had met him. And she then proceeded to escort me down the right-side corridor and back to the very last double dorm room, next to the fire escape. And as I knocked on the door to announce my arrival, Helicia returned to her room, which was situated across from the floor lounge, elevators, and pay-phone booth.

I heard a voice respond, "Come in," and as I opened the door, Sidney got up to come across and shake my hand before returning to his clearly demarcated side of the room. The room was ridiculously clean and organized, with not a thing out of place. It was like he was only visiting, and I could see nothing personal of his on his desk other than the standard dorm-room desk lamp. What I found instantly remarkable about Sidney was he was a beautiful-looking young Black man, and as I later discovered, the singular Black person in the entire Vanier College residence. I expressed that I hoped we would become great friends over time, but Sidney displayed an evident uneasiness about my candid queer identity.

I believe that my opening salvo was something to the effect of "Are you gay? And if not, I hope you have no problem having me as a gay roommate." He was speechless at my audacity, and as his head started to retract back, I tried to make fun of myself. "I mean look at me," I said. I am a theatre performance major, and I couldn't look any gayer than if I was auditioning for my next role at a glory hole in one of the washroom stalls. I am sure that my flamboyant tossing of my hair gave him more than enough of a vivid picture. I could see his struggling poker face start to quiver before me; just enough to register his judgemental disapproval. When I reflect on our first introduction, I could see my appearance had rattled his sheltered, suburban mentality and his Baptist Christian upbringing.

I could tell that he was put off by my introduction, and as a gesture of common courtesy, I suggested we did have something in common; we both appeared to be fashionistas from polar sides of the spectrum. I told him he looked like the promise of an all-Canadian prep-school boy in his khakis, button-down collared shirt in pale blue, argyle socks, and penny loafers that contained two shiny Canadian coppers! Good grief, I thought. Give Sidney a chance. Maybe my experience living with a Black, (closeted) preppy room-mate would take a little more patience and time before he would come to trust me. In the meantime, Sidney would need to relax about my sexuality, sartorial aesthetics, and direct frankness. And as I considered the two of us as viable roommates, I resolved to look at our personality differences as a social experiment in personal courage, with great potential for us to become a dynamic duo of roommates as pre-determined by our residence administration.

However, something told me (like the subtlety of a hammer to the head) that my opening observations about our first meeting was not the icebreaker and impact that I had intended. Once again, I apparently stuck my foot in my mouth as I had done so many times throughout my life. I was never one who subscribed to "think before you speak" because it did not make any sense to me; of course, I thought of all kinds of things in my reservoir of my life experience. I simply did not want to waste time marinating in self-doubt or worrying about how my voice would be received or "appear."

If someone had an issue with my delivery, then the time to speak up was then and there. It took me a long time to find my voice, and I had a lot to say as a proudly open gay man who would no longer accept criticism and discrimination from the careless thoughts and words, nor the actions, of others. Join another circus, not mine. Further, I would no longer feel restrained or restricted from cursing. It was so liberating to feel the power of shouting "Fuck off" to others and "Fuck me" when I was to blame for egregious remarks of profound stupidity. The immediate emotional release from expressing myself became a great new coping mechanism when enough was enough and it was time to walk away. And like a tortoise, it took me eighteen long years to have it sink into my hard shell that I had the right to exist and prosper!

In my optimistic mind, I thought my introductory chat with Sidney was perfectly open and honest. I had intentionally set the tenor of who I was as a gay activist for equality and visibility. I wanted to show him how open and comfortable I was in my smooth Estée Lauder-creamed complexion. Unfortunately, he chose not to engage and acted preoccupied with some random new textbook that he had just opened, based on the crackling book spline. Thank God he was a fine-arts major and not a theatre student, judging by his disappointing performance. As my limited time was now of the essence, I continued putting all my belongings onto my bed to organize. It was at this point that Sidney uttered his last proclamation before shutting down our first meeting. He basically handed me a moral imperative to "Respect his privacy and to stay always on my side of the room," and then he indicated an invisible the line on the floor separating his side from my side of the room. My first impression was that he was the most remarkably uptight person of our generation. I proceeded to unpack, and it occurred to me that I wasn't going to waste any more time on my new roommate for the moment. I simply needed to finish and get outside to clear my head.

I started to unpack my battered thrift-store suitcase, which I am sure horrified Sidney. I removed my photo album and a few books and mementoes from my past, as well as a small, portable electric typewriter and record player that I had purchased from my past two years of savings as a lifeguard.

I placed my personal crap on my desk in full display to Sidney. The last object I took out of my suitcase was a small stuffed koala bear souvenir from my recent affair with Jay, who worked as an assistant manager and receptionist at the Toronto Club Baths on Mutual and Carlton Street. Oh dear, I thought to myself, wait until Sidney asks me about Koala-Jay, as I put the cuddle-bear in the honorary centre of my pillow, where I knew it would put a bee in his bonnet but give me joy and comfort, nonetheless.

Next, I picked up my big black, heavy-duty garbage bag that was filled to the brim with an eclectic variety of clothing and accessories to get me through my first semester. I emptied the entire bag onto my bed and began folding and placing the contents into my designated built-in console of drawers, secreted behind a set of beautifully finished, light- oak-wood closet doors. I quickly hung my light jackets and a heavy old, recycled racoon coat that smelled of mothballs. Meanwhile, I could feel Sidney's eyes burning into the back of my head in judgement and disapproval of what I was dragging into his/our pristine room!

Oh well, I said to myself. Welcome, my dear Sidney, to Liberal Fine Arts at the alleged most progressive student residence in Canada. We were the second-largest Canadian campus of just over 470 acres and there had to be room for diversity, wouldn't you think? After I finished unpacking, I told Sidney that I was going to head out and explore the labyrinth of tunnels connecting many of the campus buildings, particularly those connected to our Vanier residence and the nearby Ross Humanities and Social Science Building. As I began my journey of exploration, it gave me great joy to know that in the dead of winter while everyone was wearing boots and coats, I would be able to travel underground in shorts and coatless!

I had a lot of preparatory boxes to check and uncheck in my campus explorations. The behemoth architectural star on the campus was the Ross Building and the Curtis Lecture Halls that had just been completed in 1968, five years prior to my arrival. My very first class was scheduled in Curtis Lecture Hall "A" with a seating capacity of close to two hundred students, and I knew from the class roster that we had a full class in the large lecture hall. There would be theoretical lectures for the entire class and then we would break down into smaller seminar groups of about twenty or so for intimate discussions on a variety of topical literature from authors such as the German novelist Gunter Grass's 1959 book *The Tin Drum*; the Russian novelist Alexander Solzhenitsyn's *Cancer Ward*; and the Latin American film director Alejandro Jodorowsky's 1970 movie *El Topo*. Frankly, I had no clue who these guys were, but I would quickly find out and become absorbed with their critical and political cultural contributions to society.

Now, let's skip forward to my first shocking and eye-opening class. When I arrived and sat down in the front row, there was no class introduction and absolutely nothing to prepare me for what was about to happen next. The lights went dark and a recessed screen in the ceiling quietly descended. Without any announcement or class introduction, the eye-opening black-and-white movie began. From the opening credits, I could see the film was identified as a propaganda Nazi documentary film entitled *Night and Fog*, which was in limited release, after ten short years, from the Jewish Holocaust. Innocently, I acknowledged to myself that I was completely ignorant about this issue, and I sat back to see what I could learn.

I was so naïve, and I had never met anyone Jewish that I was aware of until I moved into my residence at York University. But here I was being immersed in a film that appeared to be far removed from my experience and history in Canada. As the film progressed, it revealed the unfiltered documentary wartime footage from Auschwitz. The film exposed the horrors of the Nazi ideology and the systematic killing and burning of Jews in ovens! Their intention was to stamp out what they fervently feared as an inferior race. The existential crisis of humanity and the annihilation of an entire race of people was shocking to witness, and I felt for the first time that I was walking into the reality of war and the evils of mankind. It was grotesque, and unlike some of the other students who got up and left, I sat paralyzed and glued to the screen. The unanswered questions racing in my mind were about who, what, where, and why all this could happen, and they could only be answered by watching the entire film.

I will not share all the nuanced atrocities and inhumanity of what I saw in the film, but I will say that I felt completely eviscerated by the time the lights came back up. The humongous lecture room was dead silent, and many in the Humanities class sat in a puddle of our own tears from what we had just witnessed. As the lecture-room lights came up, our class lecturer came out and introduced himself briefly. The class was over, and we were promptly dismissed with a caution for us to follow up in our subsequent seminar class two days later. That was it. And it was certainly more than enough for my very first class in university. While 25% of the class transferred out that very day, I was hooked on Humanities and wanted to know even more, no matter how difficult and challenging this course would be. I had no precognition of the long-term dramatic impact this opening class would have on my life.

As I dragged my skinny ass back through the tunnel to my residence, I felt exhausted and drained. I could not figure how to process the atrocities I just witnessed. My carefully curated sense of identity and the newfound power that I'd recently discovered as a budding gay activist now made me feel comparatively selfish and insignificant. I questioned everything I ever knew about humanity and the existence of God; how in hell could anyone let this horrific Holocaust happen? How come no one condemned these sins against mankind at the get-go? I had never learned about such shocking details and atrocities from the Second World War in school, nor anywhere else, for that matter.

When I got back to the dorm, the first people I saw were Judi Glucksman and her twin, Helicia. They were sitting in their room with their door wide open, as per their daily ritual. When I got off the elevator, they excitedly beckoned me over with wide, open smiles and asked me how my first class went. They had not yet attended their first class and were very curious about what my first university experience was like. In passing, they mentioned that I had just missed their parents, who were returning to New York. I told them I was sorry I didn't have a chance to say goodbye. I had initially commented to the twins about how much I had enjoyed meeting their elegant parents. Specifically, their mother's soulful eyes had really impressed me. I told them, "Your mother is one of the most elegant and beautifully dressed women I've ever seen in Toronto, and although she wore long sleeves while it was still warm outside, she owned the look and appeared cool as a cucumber." As a self-proclaimed little fashionista, I commented to the twins on how much I loved their mother's tasteful camel-coloured long-sleeve jacket and matching skirt with the high-buttoned white blouse underneath. She looked so elegant and refined! She was picture perfect, in my view.

After the opening greetings, I sat down on one of their beds and proceeded with some hesitation to tell them about my first class. Just as I began to mention the shocking Nazi propaganda's film *Night and Fog*, they initially responded by putting their hands over their mouths and gasping as they nestled together in front of me. I knew something was instantly wrong when one of the twins went over and closed the door. The three of us stood, momentarily paralyzed in awkward silence. Simultaneously, they caught their breath and proceeded to painfully confess they had something personal to share about their mother and father who had just departed back to Flushing in Queens, New York.

I was not prepared for Judi when she told me her Jewish family was in the holocaust. She first told me about their Aunt Tobi, who was a survivor and always covered her arms to hide the tattooed ID number she had received as a new prisoner; it painfully served as a reminder to the horrors of the German concentration camps for the Jews. In fact, Judi commented that Aunt Tobi had pulled her friend Lola through the bars when they were screened upon arrival to the camp and separated. That act of fearless courage saved her friend's life. According to the twins, with whom I have remained in contact for close to half a century, their mother was never tattooed because she'd managed to stave off from being sent to a concentration work camp through sheer grit, determination, and chutzpah. For a few years, she remained free, but eventually she was rounded up and sent to a prisoner's camp at Greenberg. Fortunately, they did not tattoo prisoners at this camp. She had volunteered to go to Greenberg when her older sister Genevieve was selected to go, and they could be together and not be separated.

Judi mentioned that she had never seen *Night and Fog* and said, "I don't know how you managed to sit through it." She could tell that it had clearly shaken me to my core, and she apologized that I'd had to learn about the Holocaust in my very first class at York University. On the other hand, she argued that there was no easier way to get an education about Nazi-occupied Germany during World War Two than *Night and Fog-which her family had heard about and lived through.* She recently reminded me over the phone that most people were only too happy to pretend it never happened. Looking back now after witnessing this Nazi propaganda film, I could never unsee the systematic and horrific massacre of six million human lives who just happened to be of Jewish faith. You did not have to be Jewish to appreciate this fact. My only reference to the Jews during World War Two was in high school when I had read The Diary of Anne Frank. I truly never understood the barbaric inhumanity and annihilation of another race, and I couldn't fathom how the world could let this happen. It was the most shocking thing I had ever seen and viscerally experienced. All I could think of while standing in their dorm room was that I hoped the Glucksman twins would have a much less dramatic first class and a happier first impression at York.

Two years after leaving the theatre department at York University, my ongoing love of live theatre exposed me to further educational moments pertinent to the Holocaust and the Nazi persecution of homosexuals to life on the stage. Before heading off to graduate school in New York in 1981, I saw Toronto's production of *BENT,* starring Canadian legend Richard Monette, who I had seen in Toronto's 1973 production of *Hosanna* along with Brent Carver, who would later go on to win a 1993 Tony award for the Broadway production of *Kiss of The Spiderwoman.* The word "Bent" was a pejorative term used for homosexuals and a license for the Nazi persecution of thousands of gay men during the Holocaust. They were branded and identified in the camps with symbolic Nazi pink triangles on the prisoner uniforms, a symbol of reinforced degradation and systematic dehumanization. To this day, I cannot look at the celebratory rainbow pride without imagining the countless Nazi pink triangles from the systematic destruction of our imprisoned queer brothers and sisters. I wish the rainbow flag incorporated a small pink triangle on each stripe of colour to acknowledge the ongoing murder of our queer sisters and brothers. I swore to myself that the memory of our annihilated community members would not ever be forgotten. Anyone can tune into the news or check in on your social media and see that there are still many countries who systematically destroy, torture, and kill homosexuals as a scourge on the earth. It might even be happening in your own neighbourhood at this very moment.

As a life-long gay activist, I am always reminded that the pink triangle symbol has been directly associated with the homosexual pejorative known as "*Bent.*" On the other hand, the symbol assigned to *heterosexual* persons was simply *freedom from persecution,* unless you happened to be a *Jew,* and then the prison uniform was emblazoned with a gold star and a one-way ticket to hell on earth.

My beloved Judi Glucksman recently reminded me in May 2021 that my interest in the Holocaust back in 1973 was remarkably unique at the time. She told me, "No one who was not a survivor, or a child of survivors, ever talked about the Holocaust. It was not part of the curriculum at school and there weren't any TV shows or wide-released movies with such public impact until twenty years later and Spielberg's 1993 movie Schindler's List."

From Judi's experience, the Canadian educational awareness was lacking even in the Toronto Jewish Community back in 1973; "It was as if the Holocaust never happened," she said. Even Judi's husband, Steve, and his Jewish parents, who had all grown up in Canada, had virtually no idea about the systematic persecution of European Jews and the horrors of the Holocaust. As expats from New York City, Judi, and her sister Helicia were shocked by the lack of awareness in Canada when they'd first moved to Toronto and attended York University with me back in 1973. And during a recent telephone call in the spring of 2021, Judi underscored my early awareness and said "So, you, sir, were and are quite unique and wonderful. It's one of the many reasons I love you."

Nothing I had ever gone through, even in my darkest hour of attempted suicide at age fifteen, could ever remotely compare to what the surviving parents and aunt of the Glucksman twins had endured and survived. The Glucksmans' personal biographical account endeared them to me as one of my earliest unprecedented heroes! I also learned a valuable lesson as an open-minded Christian and as a burgeoning gay activist who knows that someone like myself would have surely been imprisoned in Europe if I had been born just a decade earlier.

As I recall, my Humanities class lecturer would later discuss and review other humanitarians such as Solzhenitsyn. When discussing his novel *Cancer Ward*, our professor told us that Solzhenitsyn said something to the effect of "the battle line between good and evil runs through every man." And for many Christians who have grown up in the church (like myself), it resonated with a bible passage on how Joseph said to his brothers, "You meant evil against me, but God used it for good" (Genesis 50:20). I am sure there must have been past occasions in my youth when I fantasized about plotting something positively evil in my imagination to get back at someone who had done me wrong. The great thing about maturity is that you learn to brush the crumbs of bad intentions away. I may be no saint, but I do believe my better angels will always win out! In hindsight, I would argue Alexander Solzhenitsyn's ethos is relevant to every person under dire existential circumstances, regardless of religious affiliation or lack thereof. And this is an awareness forever etched in the back of my mind. Just look at what's happening around the world today. The evils of mankind continue beyond the confines of my immediate world, and the only thing I can do is select the cause and charities worthy of my time and support.

It is fascinating to look at my formative years at York University; my theatre performance major did not have any lasting impact on my future career but my passion and love for live theatre and human rights never diminished. And although my major had not worked for me, the power juggernaut of *that singular course on* post-war problems in modern culture has had such a profound impact on my life. There is no status or personal success in my eventual chosen profession of interior design that compares to the profound impact of that first day of my Humanities class at York University. Everything pales in comparison to the world of humanity or lack thereof.

But I digress. Let me briefly tell you about a happier/awkward highlight and dramatic scenario that transpired in my first two years in York's Theatre School in one simple anecdote. Between 1973-1975, my theatre performance training was all about "ensemble" acting, and no one in the first two years of the program could present individuality and exercise potential star power. Everyone in my class felt as though we were auditioning for a school production of *A Chorus Line*. It was rigorous and physically exhausting and most disappointing, in my opinion.

One of my celebrity instructors was Miss Jill Courtney, who had choreographed Queenie's dance routine in the original movie version of *Fortune and Men's Eyes*. Although I found her charismatic and lovely outside class, inside was a different story. To be perfectly blunt, she had occasions when she could be a little too "queenie" and bitchy herself. She was a veritable taskmaster like no other, in my view. There was no doubt in my mind that she was directly responsible for the department's year-end faculty decision to euphemistically "not invite me back into third year." Oh my God, I thought; I didn't exactly get a failing grade, but my ass had been fired from the performance stream, along with my instigator classmate and friend, James. I held him accountable for their decision and here's why. The studio drama unfolded in one singular improvisation class and when it happened, I knew instantly that it was all over for James and myself. We were the only two visibly open queens in our class, and the two of us thought Professor Jill Courtney would have been a little more empathetic and appreciative of our queer humour and random moments of campiness. She should have known better after her recent Canadian professional experience choreographing the outrageous queens who starred in Fortune and Men's Eyes. Apparently, it was okay to act out on a movie set but not so much in our theatre class. The two of us paid a serious price for our mutual, unbridled queer representation in the early 1970s.

Anyhow, it was an hour-long studio, and for the first half hour, the entire class had to do never-ending *jetés* and other ballet moves to the beat of Jill's tambourine-like drum that she beat relentlessly with her fluffy marshmallow baton. And when I was not jumping fast or high enough to her liking, she would physically punch her corporal baton into my chest while shouting, "Higher, higher, higher!" The only thing I could pull out of my gay young ass to distract myself from her madness was to internally hum Diana Ross's lyrics for "Touch Me in the Morning." Both sets of my lips were clenched tighter than a steel trap, and when I could no longer take it, I thought to myself, oh dear God, get a grip, already! Move on with your dirty-old baton! She must have read my mind because as I was about to say it out loud, she moved on down the line and terrorized the next person on her list.

Following our class warm-up, we continued without taking a break. Drill Sergeant Jill instructed our class to get into a little method acting and use the remaining thirty minutes on our hands and knees by moving around the room like a "unified herd of cows," sauntering around in circles repeatedly until the clock ran out. And, let me tell you, it was not so easy. I was reasonably skinny, with not much padding on my bony knees, and I felt tremendous pain as I gingerly ambled about on all fours. But I followed through like a trouper and got into my bovine character, briefly.

Toward the fifteen-minute mark, my classmate James (my bathhouse operatic buddy on the weekends) "mooed" his chunky-ass bovine hips over my way and whispered in a conspiratorial tone, "Aren't you tired of this bullshit?"

I "mooed" right back, nodding in the affirmative, terrified that "Dictator Jill" would catch me breaking character. So, you can bet my lucky ass I didn't say a word. By this point my eyes were moist and on the verge of tears from the physical assault on my knees. I am positive I looked as though I was on my way to the slaughterhouse! And then another familiar tune, *Donna Donna* by Joan Baez, started to play on a continuous loop in my pathetic mind: "On a wagon bound for market, there's a calf with a mournful eye," etcetera. Give me any given situation, and my jukebox brain accesses any number of associated tunes stored away for my personal amusement. It was my poetic strategy for coping in stressful moments or in celebration of happy times.

Meanwhile, as I pulled ahead of James to blend in with the class herd, I felt him come from behind, and then he jumped on top of me and proceeded to dry hump me, much to the shock and horror of myself and all my other classmates. And of course, "Professor Killer Courtney" unleashed her full wrath of her hell on us. She screamed like an Irish banshee for killing her class, and James responded by saying, "I'm tired of being a fucking cow. I want to be a bull."

The two of us spontaneously erupted into a fit of uncontrollable laughter while the rest of the class gasped. There was evidently nothing funny about this unscripted outbreak to Professor Courtney. She immediately *tommy-drummed* our asses right out of the class. And there you have it, case in point! That pretty much sums up the best and the worst of my two years in theatre performance. We were both gone by the end of the following winter semester! And to be honest, we were both ready to sow our wild seeds and move onto softer greener pastures for our brittle knees.

Meanwhile, back at the dorm, my situation with my roommate Sidney continued devolving, and I was confused as to why. Although he always struck me as a little too conservative for someone his age, his ideological outlook was not offensive to me in any way. Nonetheless, our relationship seemed to be taking on a different tone behind my back. I got word from a few good friends that Sidney was making weird allegations to everybody in our floor lounge. He was speculating that I did not like him because he was Black, and several of my friends present essentially told him he was way off base in playing the race card, especially without any evidence to back up his claims. And they pretty much shut him down, as I understood.

All I could say in response was, "Oh my God! Is he for real spreading these rumours?" Their advice to me was to let it go. No one on our floor supported his contentions and they didn't buy into his cockamamie idea about me having an issue with him being Black. They advanced the opinion that his position to discredit me was because I saw through him at the get go when I directly confronted him with my hypothesis that he was a closeted gay. And by this point, everyone else started to come up with the same conclusion. Which, incidentally, turned out to be true! Apparently, after I eventually moved off campus during my second year at York University, he started cozying up with a couple of lesbian roommates on our floor and he started going downtown with them to a gay fern bar at the Carriage House Hotel. The twins, Judy and Helicia, said I had him pegged from the very first day and it obviously irritated him. Meanwhile, I had to figure out how to stop the malicious rumours that he apparently continued to spread about me. And that's when I recalled the old proverb that "revenge is a dish best served cold," and it gave me pause.

I figured I would touch base with my very close gay and Black friend Aerol Ramsey, who was completing his final year in theatre. We made plans to meet up at the Parkside Tavern on Saturday night. As we shared a tray of draft beers at fifty cents a pop, we hatched a plan to dramatically shift Sidney's mindset and plug a hole in his rumours before things got out of control. We pre-arranged to meet up in my dorm room on Monday afternoon when Sidney would be out for class, and we could secretly choreograph a scripted royal command performance for his personal benefit and edification.

So, there we were the following Monday in my dorm room, waiting for Sidney to return from class. As he entered our dorm, I quickly turned up the sensual and resonant voice of *Barry White* and *The Love Unlimited Orchestra* playing in the background. Meanwhile, Aerol and I pretended we didn't hear him enter the room. As choreographed, Aerol and I sat face to face, with me straddling his legs around my waist while we were passionately sucking face with one another. And how unfortunate it was that we inadvertently got caught in flagrante delicto! I quickly apologized to Sidney for my indiscretion. In response, Sidney muttered something to the effect that he came back to the room to just drop off his course textbook, while pretending not to notice us. He didn't waste a New York City second racing his embarrassed ass out the door on the pretext that he was heading out to the library. Let's just say his previous underhanded shenanigans and gossip about me immediately ceased! Like a true Canadian WASP, I discreetly engineered a successful resolution that finally put the issue to bed, and Sidney was none the wiser for our masterful performance and collaboration.

For the following winter term, I made a transfer to a single dorm room on the same floor after a very shy and reclusive student on our floor suddenly dropped out. His unfortunate loss was my gain in the end. And it worked out best for both Sidney and me. He ended up having the large double room for himself with no question of a replacement roommate. And I was happily situated a few doors south in my new tiny single room with all the psychological peace I could ever desire! As ex-roommates, we remained much more friendly and even started to hang out periodically in the cafeteria or in the floor lounge. By this time, it was clear to me and practically everyone else on the floor that Sidney was in deep denial and still in the closet. He maintained he was just too busy to find the "right girl and time to date."

On a more pressing personal financial matter, I found the additional cost of my new single room had left me unable to secure a suitable meal plan at the dorm residence. My student grants and loans were earmarked exclusively for my studies, and I had no other disposable cash or savings.

About the same time, I had a new friend and confidant named Laura who resided in nearby *Stong College, which* was conveniently connected by tunnel to my *Vanier College* residence. She would pretty much follow me around the campus in our free time, hanging out for coffee and chit-chats. While getting to know her, I found out that Laura had food issues and money insecurities like myself. And once again that old "I Love Lucy" lightbulb went off in my pathetic head and I plotted a creative solution to solve our mutual food insecurities. I suggested in my entrepreneurial mind how we could cleverly relieve some of the excess food from the cafeteria offerings, and Laura, who was just like Lucy's sidekick Ethyl Mertz, went along with my scheme. We both had long, maxi-length winter coats. Mine, of course, was a raggedly old racoon fur that smelled of mothballs, and her coat was a non-descript wool schemata in a faded, checkered pattern.

Anyhow, following my instructions, we both opened the seams in the pocket that emptied down into the bottom lining of our coats. We would show up to the cafeteria at the peak rush hour during lunch, when other students and visitors would overtake the cafeteria in large numbers. Whenever it was this crowded, it was very chaotic for the line servers and cashiers. Our strategy was that Laura, and I would pick up our individual trays in tandem and take turns loading something inexpensive on our trays while the other person turned in close and secretly loaded individual-size bottles of apple juice as well as other container items like wrapped sandwiches and assorted cheeses and yogurts and seamlessly slide them into the bottomless pocket of each other's coats. Our weighted-down coats made us swish as we finished our final test by walking up to the cashier and paying only for a single item on our tray. Initially, we were thrilled to have gotten away with our Robin Hood strategy of stealing from the rich and giving back to the poor. More importantly, we finally had something to eat!

We did this same routine over a period of two weeks or so, and after continually cashing out a singular item, we would then scurry back to my dorm room and close the door. We would load my empty wire clothes hamper with the pilfered survival food and secure it outside the window, pulling the curtains closed. It was cold outside, and the exterior cage of food acted as our jerry-rigged refrigerator. We thought we were so clever and thought we would never be caught! Anyhow, as this continued, the cafeteria ladies became increasingly suspicious of us, so we decided to stop and never return to the cafeteria again. We just couldn't risk being caught and expelled! Instead, we would share inexpensive individual pizza slices found in various locations around the campus, which is pretty much what we both survived on for the entire winter term.

One final very fond memory I have of Laura occurred in the middle of winter. I had shared so many of my personal gay escapades in downtown Toronto that she became curious about the various venues, especially *Club Manatee*, which featured complimentary performances by Toronto's top drag queens, including *Michelle Du Barry* and *The Great Imposters*. My dear friend Laura insisted she wanted to go with me on a few occasions, knowing very well that the after-hours club was for men only. Paging Lucy Ricardo and Ethyl Mertz in the back of my mind, the next scheme I plotted was such a pisser! With Laura's short, cropped hair around the sides and back and with no makeup, which revealed a perceptible light fuzzy moustache, she resembled a short, stocky teenage boy. I figured that since it was winter, she could wear one of my big ski jackets with a maple leaf toque and a pair of bulky male skidoo mitts. We agreed that if she did not speak with her soft, feminine-sounding voice, we stood a chance of successfully sneaking her into the club. She loved the plan and even volunteered to bind her enormous bosom while wearing one of my large plaid shirts over top. The final nuance was a scarf tied around her neck to disguise the fact that she didn't have an Adam's apple. We thought we were so clever and had thought of everything, except for Laura's memory to follow my careful instructions.

Later that week on a Friday night, we tested out our plan. We bused and travelled by subway for close to two hours to downtown. Laura was aware that I would be staying overnight at the men's *Roman's Spa* located on Bay Street, just south of College Street. She had agreed that she would find her own way back to campus at the end of the night and promised to take extra cab money in case it was late, and the subways were closed for the night.

When we entered the Manatee Club, we managed to get by the cashier at the front door and then we turned left to go down a set of steps to the lower level where there was another security checkpoint and coat check. At the foot of the steps, I eagerly shoved the two admission tickets into the hands of the security guard at the entry checkpoint. And from that location, we could see most of the interior, including the go-go boys dressed only in underwear and jock straps, who were dancing on elevated column-mounted pedestals on the first level. From our vantage point, we could also see toward the back of the second level, where there was a repurposed old rowboat for the DJ that protruded out over the dance floor below. Ironically, when I pointed out the go-go boys, Laura and I instantly recognized one of the dancers as a shy dormitory resident who lived one floor below me and never spoke to anyone.

Meanwhile, as we were taking it all in for a moment, Laura had unconsciously unzipped her jacket, and when I turned back to talk to her, I could see that the top three buttons of her shirt had popped open, and she was standing there exhibiting her impressive cleavage. It wasn't hard to ascertain that her boobs had clearly not been bound as we had earlier discussed! I didn't have a chance to whisper for her to button up when out of nowhere the bouncer appeared in our faces. He grabbed both of us by the scruff of our necks and marched us back up the stairs and threw our clenched asses out the door! That experience alone was worth the price of admission as we tumbled in the snow. We stood up, holding onto each other, and roared in laughter! It was like a bad scene from a John Waters movie, and we were cast as the quintessential white trash who found our circumstance all too *divine!*

Outside, it was unbearably cold, and I told Laura that we both needed to get warm. As previously agreed, I was headed over to the bathhouse to secure an inexpensive private roomette, discounted for students who showed a valid identification card. Meanwhile, she decided to cut her losses and hustled her way toward the nearby Wellesley subway entrance, a smidge east of Yonge Street. Since I was going that way, I escorted her to the subway entrance, and it was painfully clear to me that Laura had even fewer financial resources than me. I always had an emergency ten bucks folded and secured inside one of the charge-card slots inside my wallet. I didn't have any charge cards and had all these empty slots to hide my valuable assets, like bus tickets, emergency phone numbers, addresses, and cab money. I offered to give Laura my personal stash for an emergency cab ride, but she declined.

No matter how hungry I was, I never touched that emergency fund. My wallet was my portable file cabinet that stored my emergency resources and contacts whenever I needed to get out of a jam. Laura had no such emergency contingencies, and as we hugged goodbye, she confessed that she would not be able to financially afford to return to York the following September, and she thanked me for one last fond memory. As she entered the subway, I waved at her and I pleaded with her to not give up. It would be a damn loss. She was a humble person, and I could relate to her personal financial struggles. But unlike her, I was determined not to give up on myself. And then I carried my frigid, scrappy ass over to Bay and College Street.

The last bit of my personal accounting and memories at York University relates to the fact that I was financially desperate, and I had no discretionary spending money for food or travel. I shared the same brutal economic reality as Laura, and it lit my internal fuse to start brainstorming a way out. I needed to remain humble and do whatever it took to survive. I had significant experience to draw from a lifetime of poverty and struggle. And I was confident one way or another I would find my way. Clearly, I did not think I was better than everyone, as my mother's voice echoed in the background of my mind. Finally, I reached the front door to the staircase leading up to the second floor of the Roman Sauna, and not a moment too soon. It was one of the most bitter cold nights of the year, and I could begin to feel a little frostbite on my ears.

After I checked in and changed out of my clothes and into a towel, wrapping it around my waist, I headed back to the lounge for a warm coffee and commiserated with the front-door receptionist. In our typical discourse, he happened to mention there was apparently a small and nameless seedy sauna above some shops on Bloor Street that he colloquially referred to as the "Varsity Sauna." The manager of the unknown establishment had called the Roman Sauna to see if there might be someone young and fit and possibly interested in a part-time job that paid cash under the table. I tried not to show any indication of personal interest, but I was screaming inside to pursue that invaluable lead the next morning before I headed back to campus. I didn't sleep a wink and was in pursuit of some tension relief. I was up and down throughout the night with Tom, Dick, and Harry. I had a quick shower in the morning and a courtesy coffee from the receptionist and flew out the door.

Apparently, the Varsity Sauna was adjacent to the University of Toronto's Varsity Stadium, which was a few steps from the St. George's subway station. Although it was still bitterly cold, I needed some air and decided to take the brisk fifteen-minute walk over to the sauna. When I arrived at the written address in my wallet, I entered through an unmarked door from Bloor Street. I proceeded up a dark, musty staircase and arrived on the landing and entrance to a second door with a simple one-word sign that said, "Men's Sauna." Upon entering, I saw an open door to a manager's office a couple metres away. A rotund, middle-aged man was sitting in a cloud of smoke with an ashtray overflowing with cigarette butts. He was quite tawdry-looking but evidently very well-read, based on scores of unorganized books and newspapers strewn about.

We introduced ourselves to each other, and he told me he was looking to pay someone cash under the table who could come clean and disinfect the showers and sauna room and finish off by scrubbing out all the toilets, urinals, and sinks. I was desperate for cash, and I accepted his offer on the spot. I was hired for five bucks an hour for a five-hour overnight shifts a couple times a week. That was a handsome, tax-free sum of $50.00 per week, and it clearly helped me augment my summer savings as a city-paid lifeguard at $1.50 per hour. I was not too proud to do this kind of work, as I had seen my mother do the very same thing to support her kids. If she could only see me now. I was "off my high horse" that she alleged to everyone in my family. But no one had any clue of what it took to survive. It was far from easy juggling school, work, lifeguarding, and domestic grunt work that I shared with no one.

Since I knew there was a good chance that I would not be returning to York University for a third year, I accepted the overnight shift and started immediately. I did what I needed to survive, and I was happy for the money. And everything worked out financially well over the course of my second year at York University. By then I had moved out of residence and was living nearby on Avenue Rd. and Davenport, hitch-hiking to and from the campus.

And then one random day I contracted a severe case of itchy and painful scabies that were lurking about in the old wood sauna. It was then I knew I was in trouble and required medical assistance. The skin trauma was so serious that the doctor injected cortisone into the welts in my armpits and groin. After that horrific ordeal, I looked elsewhere for a job.

And that pretty much sums up my final chapter at York University. It wasn't hard to let go of my life as a struggling student and aspiring actor. The firing of my student ass became a catalyst for eventually re-discovering my passion for interior design. I had a pretty good understanding of what bad design was by this point.

11
ACADEMIC BREAK
TORONTO/QUEBEC CITY/
MONTREAL/TORONTO, 1975-1976

After my dramatic failure from York University's theatre performance program and a heck of a lot of scrubbing toilets along the way, I found myself residing temporarily as a guest of Rose and her brother, Joe Puigmarti. They had the back bedroom available for me for as long as I needed. Rose was one of my old neighbourhood friends in Cabbagetown whom I met back in my old high school, Central Commerce. They lived in a charming three-bedroom house on the dead end of Sackville Street that backed onto the St. James Cemetery. Joe had inherited the family home when their parents retired and moved out to Mississauga, so they weren't dealing with the burden of a mortgage and could afford to have me as their guest. What I liked about their location is that it was just a few blocks from the main intersection of Wellesley and Parliament Street: the main commercial hub. More importantly, it was the closest access to public transit, which I desperately depended on to get around in Toronto.

I spent the weekend in my room, ruminating about my unfortunate work experience with scabies at the closeted Varsity bathhouse where I eked out a little cash under the table. But I spent more time thinking about my very positive experiences as a guest at the other more prominent and commonly known bathhouses south of Bloor Street. This triggered my memories back to York University. The only prior education I had on sexual diversity and human rights came from a women's studies course I had taken in my final semester. At the time I enrolled, I had considered myself a feminist in the cultural resurgence that was led by activist women like authors Gloria Steinem and Germaine Greer, and pop icon Helen Reddy, with her ubiquitous anthem, "I am woman, hear me roar." It was the early 70s, a time before queer studies was even on the radar or acceptable. And because I was personally acquainted with several bisexual women and lesbians who were staunch feminists, I registered for the class. As it turned out, I was the only male-no surprise!

I found it fascinating to discuss the course's seminal 1970 text *Our Bodies, Ourselves,* and the negative impact of societally accepted misogynistic men on the lives of women and their reproductive health. I was already indoctrinated in the fight for women's equality and despaired that there was nothing equivalent for gay men; it reinforced how far the queer community had to go. Nonetheless, I felt the paradigm shift toward the second iteration of the women's liberation movement during the early 1970s. In my own twisted mind, I modified lyrics of Helen Reddy's *"I am Woman, Hear Me Roar"* to "I am queer, hear me roar in numbers too big to ignore!" And in no time, I was marching in protest to the Bathhouse raids in Toronto assuming the mantle of a queer activist.

The problem for me was that as a growing activist for gay rights, I desperately wanted to know more about Canadian queer history and seminal research to support a comparable queer studies program. Where were the courses and programs? Clearly, I was not aware of any available at the time, and I rationalized that it must be because it had only been a short time since same-sex equality had been made lawful in Canada on June 27, 1969. Fortunately, the course professor gave my class a community-based, in-situ research assignment that required community-based interviews from local leaders that advanced the rights of minorities and marginalized groups in the broader Greater Toronto Area (GTA). Through various round-circle class discussions, either the teacher or one of the other students volunteered the name of *Attorney George Hislop.* Apparently, George was a Toronto queer activist and an early defender of human rights. He had a well-established practice on Church Street in the heart of Toronto's Gay Village.

Immediately following this new insight, I contacted George Hislop by phone. There was no secretary answering his phone, as I recall, and he picked up the call on the first ring. Meanwhile, I was thinking to myself that George was doing just a little too much pro-bono work and couldn't afford an office assistant. After I introduced myself as a gay student at York University who was doing research on a class assignment, he immediately extended an invitation to come and interview him. Our interview was very casual and highly informative.

One of the first community and nearby literature resources he pointed me toward was the *Glad Day Bookstore,* which had opened in 1970 as Canada's first queer bookstore and is considered in 2022 to be the oldest LGBTQ+ bookstore worldwide. He gave me a copy of the most recent edition of the *Body Politic,* Canada's first gay magazine, which was published in 1971. In addition, he pointed out the *Hassle-Free Clinic,* which provided anonymous and discreet testing for drugs and socially transmitted disease [STD] that first opened on Yonge Street as a twenty-four-hour, seven-days-a-week clinic. It serviced the queer community and was spearheaded by counsellors from the Rochdale Free Clinic in February of 1973; the very same year I attended York University. I believe this is where I had gone to medically treat my embarrassing scabies issue.

The last thing we talked about were the numerous gay bathhouses, of which I confessed I had extensive personal experience. Remarkably, it turned out that we both knew *Peter Bochove* before he'd become a bathhouse entrepreneur and political activist. I met Peter socially back in the summer of 1973 when we both hung out in the front lounge at Club Toronto's *Bathhouse* on the corner of Carlton and Mutual Street. Peter and I had frequently chatted for hours in the coffee lounge in our towels, drinking copious amounts of complimentary coffee and chain smoking our way to hell. He was always talking about his dream of opening his own bathhouse, which I'd thought was just a pipe dream as I yammered on about starting university.

Just before I left York University, Peter realized his dream and opened his *Richmond Street Emporium* for gay men, which was like no other place in Toronto. His emporium allowed me an escape from the anxiety of not knowing what to do with my future or where to live. And as my mind started to wander in the back bedroom of my friend's. house on Sackville Street, my old penchant for interior design started to kick in.

I visually recalled how his new bathhouse had a central coffee and smoking lounge right inside the front doors and open to a view of a small swimming pool on the far wall. Guests could swim in the pool nude, just as I had done back in grade nine at Jarvis Collegiate. The shower room was exceptionally well designed, with atmospheric, black-tiled walls and floors and a feature glass brick wall into the sink area and main circulation. Guests would walk back and forth as they monitored the hot guys who were showering and soaping up. There were a few regulars who did nothing more than pass back and forth on a continuous loop, and it appeared to Peter that this was money well spent on the interior design.

Peter was a proud proprietor of his remarkable gentlemen's spa, and it was a terrific social-networking platform for gay men, well before the advent of the internet. In addition, he knew what was good for business and how to market young, good-looking influencers in the naked flesh. As a result, I was always encouraged to get a complimentary upgrade from a locker to a roomette whenever he was on the premise. And the fact of the matter is that if Peter had his carton of cigarettes and a fresh pot of coffee, then he wasn't going anywhere, twenty-four/seven. He hung out in the lounge for hours on end with his coffee and newspaper, welcoming everyone from young to old and everyone in between as valued guests.

But I have to say, from first-hand knowledge, Peter was very fond of attracting the city's most beautiful college studs who walked around in shortened towels like we were wearing a terrycloth mini skirt. We were thin and trim and wanted to expose the illusion of longer legs up to our other assets above. Walking the labyrinth of corridors lined with private roomettes was like walking through a game of Snakes and Ladders; you never knew what you were going to find. Sometimes I would find lonely, slithering reptiles seeking out a little body heat and other times I might step into an erotically elevated experience. It was always a fun game of playing the odds; sometimes I would strike it lucky but most times I was there to watch the actions of other players. The bathhouses provided a casino-like atmosphere, with bells and whistles going off all through the night. Even when it was quiet, I could find action going on in the dark corners of the hallways and locker room.

Other than my youth, I had a lot of great senses in my favour: for start-ers, I possessed a visual sense of curiosity about the human smorgasbord. In addition, I had an ear for the wild and wicked, and a touch of kindness and an internal sense of knowing ... what else...? Let me think. Oh yeah, a testosterone-fed ego! Despite all that, I was an introvert who outwardly presented an engaging personality. I was not much of a drinker, nor did I do any drugs at the time. Because of my theatre training, I learned how to respect my body. My physique was at its peak from all my dance and theatre exercises, underscored with years of competitive swimming and lifeguard-ing for the City of Toronto.

As I reminisced and rested in the back guest bedroom at my friend's home on Sackville Street, I considered spending a few nights a week away at the bathhouse once again, as soon as I could find a job and afford to go. I didn't want to give the impression that I was taking advantage of Joe and Rose's kindness and hospitality. I knew they would appreciate my effort to not overstay my welcome. In addition to giving my hosts a little extra privacy, it would provide me an opportunity to meet new friends and make connections within the broader gay community. As a young dude in his prime, there was a pervasive air of heightened sexuality at the bathhouse and an opportunity for promiscuity. However, I found myself happy, for the most part, socializing and catching up on gossip about the latest events and cultural openings going on in Toronto. That said, I was no angel, and I didn't let the occasional opportunity to score with someone of special interest pass me by. But I was considered by the older members as a good old-fashioned cock-tease whose sexual affections couldn't be bought, no matter how hard they tried!

There were always a few interesting and discriminating men with alert minds and good souls who I found most appealing to talk with, regard-less of their looks and age. I wasn't interested in randomly jumping in the sack, and most of my buddies could not understand my lack of appetite for anonymous sex. The trade-off for my reserved libido and discriminating taste paid off. Frequently, my socializing and harmless gossip led to outside invitations to socialize with some of the more discriminating patrons at the bathhouse. Most times, I was too chicken to follow up on the invitations but there were a few times when I did, and I must admit I always had a pleasur-able encounter. In addition to making connections outside, I received invites to numerous dinner parties and group dates to the theatre and concerts. Many of these highly successful men resided in private condos in the luxury *Colonnade* on Bloor Street or in the homes in nearby Yorkville, Rosedale, and Forest Hill and over to the exclusive estates on the Bridal Path. I may have been a struggling young undergraduate, but I was considered great eye candy by many friends and acquaintances, and I always had something novel and youthful to add to their exclusive parties. The only thing I had to take as a host gift was my youth and good looks. Well, that and a wallet with enough cab fare to get home.

Intrinsically, I was a person of good character and integrity with a voracious curiosity about the world that I was beginning to adult in. Moreover, I was always out for a damn-good time. For a brief window, I was regarded as young tender chicken on the private invitation list of older, elite gays in Toronto. On my very first Monday morning at Joe Puigmarti's house, I got up early to head out and find a job. I had showered the night before, so the following morning, I only needed to shave and dress to avoid disturbing Rose and Joe from their sleep in the adjacent bedrooms. Afterward, I tiptoed down the creaking steps and immediately headed out while everyone was sound asleep. I left their home around eight a.m. and my first stop were to head out for a hearty breakfast at the Pancake House located under the *Hudson Bay Centre* at the corner of Bloor and Yonge Street. I knew it would be a cheap and filling meal with unlimited coffee refills and a complimentary newspaper with help-wanted ads for me to peruse. I easily spent over an hour at the pancake house while eating and taking notes about some of the ads.

Afterward, I walked a block over to Bay Street and into Yorkville before the shops opened at 10:00 a.m. I wanted to scout the neighbourhood to refresh myself with the lay of the land. Then I strategized a priority list of where I wanted to go and introduce myself. The main east/west streets in Yorkville were Cumberland and Yorkville, and the main north/south streets were Avenue Road, Hazelton Avenue, and Bay Street. However, as I walked about, what caught my attention was a small, north/south street named Bellair Street. It was on Bellair that I noticed a newly opened men's European underwear and swimsuit specialty shop called *The Yorkviller*, which had opened next to *Be Gay*, which was a longstanding specialty lingerie and swimwear shop for women. Everyone knew the antiquated term "gay" was once understood to describe happy and joyful, but it was now a part of the universal queer narrative and tourists, and locals would often stop out front and take pictures. I soon discovered Be Gay and The Yorkviller were owned by the same European family. James Barrass was the first generation born in Canada and was the proud proprietor of the new men's specialty shop featuring much higher-quality European imports in Toronto at the time.

The Yorkviller was filled with sexy briefs and swimsuits for men, and it was right up my alley. Most certainly, it would be a refreshing change from scrubbing toilets for a living. After checking my reflection in the amber-tinted glass, I leveraged everything I had going for me, walked in, and applied for a sales position. Within twenty-four hours, I received a call back from the proprietor/owner, James, who extended a job offer!

In the beginning, James and his wife, Joanne, worked alongside of me. They were a newly married couple; young, uber-smart, and both graduates from the University of Toronto. We hit it off immediately and it took us no time to bond. After my first two weeks, I received my first paycheque and was able to then put a deposit on my first and last month's rent at the very modest and historic *Ernescliffe Apartments*, located at 477 Sherbourne on the southeast corner of Wellesley Street. It was situated kitty-corner from the Wellesley Hospital where I had my tonsils removed a month later.

At the time, I had only a mattress on the floor and an old trestle table from a thrift store in the kitchen along with two chairs, courtesy of my new boyfriend *Ghislain Gilbert*. We met by chance at a recent spring dance that my friend Stan Griffin had invited me to. The gay dance was hosted by the University of Toronto. All the guys in attendance were doing their best to get Ghislain's attention. He was considered the hottest man at the dance. I figured he was way too fine and out of my league, so I paid him no never-mind. As fate would have it, at some point in the evening he pulled up to the urinal next to me in the downstairs washroom and his first soft hello led to a few dances and drinks upstairs, followed by an invitation back to his house on Parliament Street. In fact, he lived just around the corner from where I grew up on Lancaster Avenue. By morning, he confessed his lust for me and his desire for us to become boyfriends. Ironically, he was the first guy I even considered a promising partner, but I said nothing about my feelings. It was all a little too premature, in my opinion, and I then laughed to myself, thinking, what on earth does he think we are, a pair of nesting lesbians, already?

Ghislain mentioned in his charming French-Canadian accent that he was from Levi, Quebec; just across the river from the Hôtel Frontenac in Quebec City. I discovered over breakfast that he worked as a waiter at the trendy *Toby's Hamburgers* on Bloor Street just a block south from The Yorkviller at the corner of Bellair. So, I made him an offer to show up as a random diner on my lunch hour to cruise him at work, knowing he would break into a self-conscious sweat. He was half-heartedly game for it, so I gently reassured him that I understood he was working, and I would keep everything above board, and no one would be any the wiser.

Anyhow, Ghislain originally helped me find my first apartment which happened to be located a half block from my old high school, Jarvis Collegiate. When he first moved to Toronto, Ghislain resided in my apartment building with his good friend and current roommate, "Cecil," who were living together on Parliament Street adjacent to the old familiar Brewers Retail Store (the beer store). Ghislaine was a tremendously shy and humble soul. He was generous to a fault, and whatever he possessed he shared or gave freely to many of his friends. In addition to offering me a wooden trestle table as a housewarming gift, he gave me a beautiful white French-Canadian *Catalonia bed cover* that was made by his mother and constructed from rolled cotton rags. I was completely dumbfounded as to why he would part with something so valuable with someone he barely knew. His intense pursuit of me led to our fabulous and sexually compatible relationship up until I decided to move to Quebec City.

Ghislain had introduced me to both European and French-Canadian music and records, including: a 1974 record by Quebec's band, *Beau Dommage*; an album by *Les Seguin*; as well as two other European French records from vocalist *Daniella Licari and* Nicole Croisille. *We both thought the music would inspire me to learn how to speak French, or at least have a working knowledge.* Instead of using the records to learn to speak French, we ended up using one memorable song for making out, "*Une Femme Avec Toi by Nicole Croisille.*" All these years later, I still have her on my iPhone playlist. If you feel intrigued to hear it, you can always check out her song on YouTube. It's a classic.

Meanwhile, with all this timely French-Canadian culture he brought into our relationship, it made me question my lack of knowledge about my own French-Canadian roots on my father's side of the family. In late November, an early winter started to set in, and I started to get apprehensive about my future. I knew I wanted to go back to university at some point, and I knew for sure that I wouldn't have anything further to do with a career in the theatre. I cut my losses but what to do next was still an unsolved mystery.

Inspired by Ghislain and my French-Canadian roots, I planned my next adventure and move to Quebec City. As good fortune would have it, James mentioned in passing that he thought we might need some extra help over the Christmas holiday season, and he asked me if I had any friends who might be interested in applying for a position. This was a perfect opportunity to recommend my bookish friend and disco pal, Peter LeRoy. Without hesitation, James hired Peter on the spot. In full disclosure, my friend Peter was privy to the knowledge that I was planning to resign at the end of December, so he knew that the initial part-time position I recommended him for would eventually lead to my full-time management position after I resigned. And this was the best possible resolution to my ethical dilemma of leaving James without a suitable and trustworthy replacement.

Oh, my sweet Jesus, Peter and I had some fun times over the next few months at The Yorkviller. We had plenty of local and international celebrity customers. Our first notorious client was Xavier Hollander, who recently had published her memoir *The Happy Hooker*. It was only the second memoir I had read since I first read *The Diary of Anne Frank*, and I realized that there was something I really liked about the extreme contrast between the two compelling memoirs. Other celebrities followed, including one-time drop-ins by Sonny Bono and Elton John on separate occasions. I specifically recall the details of Elton John, who was accompanied by a personal assistant and carried his European leather-zipped pocketbook. At the time, Elton was flamboyantly dressed in a leather lattice coat constructed and adorned with what appeared to be either ermine or fox fur tails, randomly secured the entire length down to his ankles. After he selected a couple of items that I showed him, he proceeded outside to wait while his personal assistant paid the bill on his behalf. According to Peter, there was speculative gossip in the local gay community that Elton was getting hair-plug transplants in Toronto and there were rumours that he was attending AA meetings. It was all silly gossip, as far as I knew, and as my granny would like to frequently tell me as a child, "loose lips sink ships!" In retrospect, I am sure there was some merit to the speculation that this was the time when he first met his future husband, David Furnish.

The Yorkviller was a tiny shop with a dressing room that was no larger than a broom closet. The sliver of a space was located behind the stair landing leading down to the stockroom. Unless a patron was ultra-thin like the quintessential 1960s model Twiggy, it was next to impossible to undress comfortably in this narrow space. It could not have been more than a foot and a half wide by three feet deep, with just enough room to hang a draw-string curtain. Clients who could squeeze into the space sideways were forced to come out of the space to see themselves in the full-length mirror sandwiched between the change room and the cash register. Of course, this was amusing, at times, and I would gladly assist by swinging open the curtain on their behalf when they were ready to come out, saying, "Ta-da" for dramatic impact. Most clients would prefer not to approach the jigsaw puzzle of a space and opted to take their merchandise home.

One of my most handsome clients was Gaëtan Dugas, who was a French-Canadian flight attendant who happened to come into my shop on a random summer day. Anyhow, he was interested in trying on a hot-pink bikini bathing suit that was featured in our shop window. He was trim and fit and could squeeze into our Barbie and Ken-sized change room. There were just the two of us in the shop and he'd left his convertible silver Mercedes with the hood down parked out in front for me to watch. One of his many wealthy paramours "lent" him the car, and I promised to monitor it while he tried on his European swimsuit from HOM. We hit it off as he camped it up and pranced around the shop like the bottle-blond Adonis that he was. After I packed up his purchase, he passed me a calling card and said, "Call me on Saturday and we'll go out dancing at the Manatee." Anyhow, I followed up with a call and we went out that same weekend. Moreover, we did this periodically over a few months leading up to my first resignation from *The Yorkviller*. He was not sexually interested in me and ditto myself. We were the perfect foils to each other, and we were admired by others on the dance floor.

Years later in November of 1987, when I was in bed with my partner Gary Laswell in New York City, we were watching *60 Minutes on TV, and something caught my immediate attention.* A commentator mentioned that an Air Canada flight attendant had been identified as "Patient Zero" by the Center for Disease Control (CDC) for a Gay Related Immune Disorder (GRID), which was the precursor to acquired immunodeficiency syndrome (AIDS). I will never forget how I jokingly turned to Gary and said that it was probably my friend Gaëtan Dugas. No sooner had I mentioned his name and his picture was put up on the television for the world to see. I was shocked and devastated! Gary and I both looked at each other and said nothing more. Everyone in New York started scapegoating Gaëtan, and I must confess that it was hard to explain that I knew him as a nice guy and one of my favourite dance buddies in Toronto. It just didn't sound like the same guy I knew.

Meanwhile, getting back to my Toronto life in 1975, the calendar starting edging toward the Christmas holidays and New Year's, and I decided to finally hand in my notice, effective December 31. I explained to James that I would be leaving *The Yorkviller* and moving to Quebec to reclaim and celebrate my French-Canadian heritage. I told them that I wasn't sure what I was doing but I felt compelled to go, nonetheless. He seemed to understand and once again told me I could always come back if things didn't work out for me. I explained that I was not sure what I was going to do or where I was going to live but I would figure it out as I went. So, I gave up my apartment after less than a year and moved my trestle table and a couple of chairs for safe keeping back into Joe Puigmarti's house on Sackville Street. I was set to deploy myself for a new adventure in the belle province of Quebec.

On January 1, 1976, I boarded a VIA train early in the morning from Toronto to Quebec City. It was a twelve-hour-trip on a one-way ticket, stopping only to switch trains in Montreal. At the time, it was the coldest place I had ever been in Canada. When I arrived and departed from the Gare du Palais train station, I had no clue where I was or where I was going with my one suitcase. I knew I wanted to stay in the old quarter near the magnificent *Château Frontenac*, and although it was not a particularly large area to cover, it seemed to be all uphill, exacerbated by huge icicles that crashed randomly down from rooftops as they melted under the bright sunlight of the day. Fortunately, a local passerby pointed at me to go out to the middle of the road where it was safer to walk when the roads were empty from vehicular traffic.

As I meandered around, a sign caught my eye in one of the historical old houses: "*Chambre à Louer*," or room to rent. I knocked and used my pitiful French, augmented with a bit of *sign language* by pointing to the window sign *et voila!* I exchanged cash for a temporary roof over my head. I had paid for one full week in advance, with an option to stay longer if I wished. My next objective was to find a job and learn to speak French. Unfortunately, I lasted only the week. I realized I could not survive a winter in Quebec City. The following weekend I booked a train ride back to Montreal and got off to seek my fortune in what was then considered the most bustling city in Canada.

I didn't have to drag my suitcase too far before I discovered another sign that read *"Chambre à Louer"* just a block or two from the central train station at *Place Ville Marie.* I rented a room in a house on nearby Bishop Street that was located just a few doors south of St. Catherine. There were two rooming houses side by side that were owned by the same landlord. Both houses had a roster of crazy young people like me. And as soon as I moved in, I became friends with Jacques, who was a massively handsome gay tenant, along with his best "fag-hag," who was an American expat. All they seemed to do was party all night long at one of the nearby drag bars while I desperately tried to find employment. I had no clue where they got their money from, but one thing for sure, they didn't work for a living. Meanwhile, I applied for everything from construction work to dishwashing at the Old Spaghetti Factory in Old Montreal down by the harbour area. Everywhere I went, I was systematically shut out as an Anglophone, but I caught on quickly and began speaking with an American accent, which made the French-speaking community assume that I was a tourist and garnered me nicer treatment. Who could blame them, and who wasn't motivated by the American dollar?

To pass some time, I would sneak into the back of the French learning lab at Concordia University and place the headphones on my head to fit in with the legally enrolled students. The winter term had just begun so I blended in—that is, until about three weeks into class when the instructor asked me through the headphones who I was. He said he was pretty sure that I was not supposed to be in his class. So, with a pardonnez-*moi,* I ran my little Anglo ass out the back door, never to return! Following that disastrous attempt to find free French-language classes, I went to a multitude of government agencies that were providing free French classes to new immigrants. But once again, as a Canadian citizen and Anglo, I was SOL (shit-out-of-luck).

While mucking about in Old Montreal, I ran into a guy who introduced himself as Giovanni Mowinckel. He was a British expat and owned a small, high-end decorating company called *Colvin Design*. We immediately hit it off, and well, one thing led to another and within a few short weeks, I had moved into his exquisitely designed and furnished apartment, located in an exclusive residence that included a doorman, which was rare in Canada back then. We had a whirlwind romance. He took me on several visits to meet his friends on the American side of Lake Champlain where he skied in the winter months. On other occasions, we went north of Montreal to stay on his lady friend's country estate, which included a barn, a horse stable, a paddock, and a small, self-contained cottage that he purchased next to the manor house. There was a full-time horse trainer who had an apartment built right into the barn and stables, so we did a little riding on the weekends and spent most of the time relaxing. Everything was going perfectly for the first month and according to Giovanni's bigger plan for a long-lasting relationship. But for myself, not so much. I felt stressed and anxious about how quickly our relationship was accelerating, and I wasn't ready to be tied down.

I became acutely sensitive to the fact that I was beginning to feel like a "kept-boy," despite his opinion to the contrary. He maintained that he simply wanted to share his privileged lifestyle with me. The considerable difference in age and status in life revealed an inequality of economic power and contributed to my co-dependence in everything he wanted and could afford to do. But I could not reciprocate. According to him, I was the "missing piece" in his new life in Canada. He confessed that he had recently left London and a complicated personal and business partnership and decided to make a fresh start in Montreal. His personal aspiration was to have *someone* to love and literally be there at his side.

I wanted to tell him that I was not his doting lapdog and muse, but I knew it would be unkind and too blunt. I momentarily sucked up my misgivings and said nothing. Everything we did revolved around his hectic schedule and his professional goals, and I was expected to just be there like some sort of *Stepford Wife*. And that was one comparison that I didn't want to be playing on a loop in my mind! I felt increasingly swallowed up in his world, and I began to see my soul and spirit slipping away. I was tired of waiting around to see what he planned and assumed was the next logical step to cement our relationship. And all I could do was thank sweet Jesus that there was no legal same-sex marriage back then. I am confident I would have been the proverbial "runaway bride!" But in a weird kind of way, I was.

On my birthday at the end of May, while we sat around the dining room table for a celebratory dinner, I skillfully summed up the courage to tell Giovanni that I had a future birthday gift for the two us. When he asked what it was, I told him that I was planning to go back to university and complete my undergraduate degree in interior design. I told him wholeheartedly that I believed this was a gift that would enrich both our lives. He argued that completing my degree wasn't necessary and that he didn't want us to be separated and living in two different provinces. After a sleepless night of deep reflection and frustration, I got up and told him that while he went into his office for the day, I was going to pack my bags and be on my way back to Toronto. There was nothing more to say. After a prolonged moment of silence, Giovanni left and closed the door to a future relationship with me. In my mind, I was thinking as you like! I felt both deflated and exhilarated in knowing that I had made the right call.

On the train ride from Montreal to Toronto, I had several hours to think about whether there was a Canadian university program that offered studies in interior design. What I did know is after spending time with Giovanni, he brought back my childhood memories of my love for interior design. It made me laugh as the train chugged along, and I recalled an old memory from age thirteen that popped into my head. At that age, I was convinced that I should have had the larger front master bedroom with the view overlooking Riverdale Park; this seemed only logical since I was the family member who spent the most time in the sanctuary of a bedroom. Although my mother was exasperated by my creative endeavours and the damage that I had done to the hall walls and hardwood floors, she consented to let me have my way with the move. She stated she had a house to run and agreed that she was an insomniac and required no more than three or four hours of sleep. She said my original bedroom might suit her better as she could more readily monitor who was coming up and down the stairs outside the middle bedroom door. And at age thirteen, I became the unofficial designer for our house and took on the calculated risk of rearranging furniture in some of the other rooms as well.

I had learned early on how to successfully argue my point with facts about how spaces should function, based upon rational observations and alternative layouts to better suit the needs of myself and family. Clearly, I had all the underpinnings and potential for a future in interior design, and now I needed to find out what university would be best suited to complete my undergraduate studies. At that time, Ryerson was a polytechnic institute and I opted to take the advice and consensus of Paul Barnard and Noel Hancock. They both recommended I apply to the *University of Manitoba* (U of M). Since I already had two years of electives and a portfolio of art and self-taught design sketches and detailed drawings, I mailed them off along with an application and two recommendation letters. Before the end of June, I received my acceptance, and I was set to start classes in the fall of 1977.

While waiting for the September start, I resumed my past employment at *The Yorkviller* and stayed initially as a temporary guest with my friend Joe Puigmarti. Shortly thereafter, I moved into my friend Michael Harding's warehouse on Adelaide Street as his guest while I squirrelled money away for my next adventure in Winnipeg. I knew this opportunity was going to change my life in the best way possible, and I couldn't wait to make up for lost time. I spent the summer checking out bookstores and libraries to find everything I could about Winnipeg and the University of Manitoba. When I saw how far the campus was from downtown Winnipeg, I knew in an instant that I needed to apply to live in residence at the university. I had heard stories about the long overnight hours in the studios, and the last thing I wanted to face after something like that was waiting for public transit ride in the sub-zero winter temperatures. Although, as I later discovered, there were heated and enclosed bus shelters. I also found out, much to my chagrin, that they all smelled of piss. On the occasions when I needed to catch a bus, I remained outside in the cold fresh air.

In researching the school's department chair, I discovered *Professor Joan Harland was the* founder of Canada's first program to have a Bachelor of Interior Design degree (BID). She was a role model and trailblazer at a time when women applicants to university were not common. In fact, when she had first applied to study architecture at various schools from across Canada, the only program that accepted her as a female applicant was the University of Manitoba. Clearly, it was one of the best decisions the school could have ever made. She not only made it possible for other females to apply to architecture, but she also established interior design as a recognized profession for the first time in Canada. Apparently, she was one of the original international founders of the Interior Design Educator's Council (IDEC) who created professional educational standards throughout North America.

Being a proud Canadian and having a familiarity with feminism, I couldn't wait to attend the school and make her acquaintance. Most of the famous women that I knew as feminists were mostly American and Australian. I couldn't believe Canada had these remarkable women and trailblazers who went unheralded and simply got on with their life, breaking down a few barriers along the way. With the odd exception and notwithstanding the singular sensation of renowned Canadian author Margaret Atwood, many ground-breaking Canadian women went globally unnoticed.

In an article entitled "Mistake by the Lake (II)," by Allan Fotheringham, he described Toronto as "having the penis-envy of wanting to be New York" in *Maclean's*, April 3, 2000, edition. And as a queer man and an aspirational accredited interior designer, I have to say I subscribe to that theoretical position myself. I mean, phallically speaking, what man wouldn't agree that New York was not just bigger but better, if not the best, right? However, as a fiercely proud Canadian feminist, I asked myself, *does size really matter?* I would argue that when it comes to equitable and critical media support of homegrown women as trailblazers in our Canadian landscape, the disparity between men and women *does* matter. Proportionally speaking, the schism between conventional binary genders is painfully humongous, and this *hurts* me. And let's not discuss the critically important narratives and countless absence of non-binary folks, overlooked since forever already!

I thought I was a strong person with great purpose and integrity, but there were still lessons to be learned and appreciated from the expanding roster of alphabets in the queer community: LBGTQI+ ... and more. And as I fight to remain vital and valuable to others, I am honoured to share my torch with the shining stars from the next generation. Unique people like my neighbour Mark Henderson are individuals who inspire me to realize that age is nothing but a number for those who like to number-crunch, and not for creative types who have the blessing of mind and spirt to sissy-on down the road. Like myself, but in a much more aggressively creative way, Mark is demolishing both queer and straight barriers of rigid, confining stereotypes with the bold courage and resilience to gaily move forward. He just so happens to have the passion, technical skills, and professional talent to back up his innovative "lewks."

12
UNIVERSITY OF MANITOBA
WINNIPEG, MANITOBA, 1977–1982

PREAMBLE: Prior to my last remaining months at York University, I had met the fabulously social and refreshingly eccentric British expat Michael Harding. He was locally renowned by Toronto's artsy cognoscenti for his Sunday-afternoon gatherings that embraced a range of intellectually creative young minds in the theatre as well as other performing arts that embraced music, dance, and comedy in Toronto's rich cultural scene. After the West End in London and New York's Broadway, Toronto's downtown theatre district is considered the third-largest English-speaking theatre district in the world. His invitation described his residence as *The House at Pooh Corner* in honour of the children's book about a series of stories and characters imagined by author A.A. Milne. Michael's grand Victorian house was located on the south side of Elgin Street and just a few houses west of Avenue Road in Toronto's ritzy neighbourhood of Yorkville. His Sunday gatherings were legendary back in early 1970s, and there was a revolving menagerie and hotbed of local artists, actors, writers, and musicians who attended. Whenever I attended, I never knew who I would meet. There were always plenty of spirits and sumptuous charcuterie boards located throughout the first floor. His home was Bohemian in style and incorporated: colourful wood-beaded curtains; plenty of large Moroccan cushions; and colourful, sheer atmospheric fabrics draped in all the windows and archways. There were plenty of whimsical objects and acrylic/oil paintings that dressed the interior walls. I always felt like Sally Bowles on the set of Cabaret whenever I attended one of his functions. The theatrical atmosphere was quintessential divine decadence! And everyone spoke with "darling this" and "darling that." Michael Harding was a veritable first-class European bon vivant and supporter of the arts.

Anyhow, at one of his fabulous Sunday gatherings, I had befriended a gay couple who were compadres of Michael and British ex pats as well. Luis Negin was a well-established local actor, and his life partner Charles Dunlop was a former television and film designer. Louis and I had struck up an immediate friendship, and I'd invited him to my term-end production class for my directorial debut of one small scene from *The Effect of Gamma Rays on Man-in-the-Moon Marigolds*. Luis had a last-minute audition, so he sent his lovely partner Charles on his behalf.

If I am not mistaken, Luis was auditioning at the time for The Actor's Stage Company production of *The Rocky Horror Picture Show*, to premier at Ryerson's Theatre in 1976. And just a month later, after I returned from Montreal, Luis invited me to audition as an extra at Ryerson's old theatre school on Gerrard Street. He mentioned to me that that he would be playing the role of Riff Raff and Brent Carver would be playing Dr. Frank-N-Further.

I foolishly auditioned, knowing very well that the cast of professional actors were celebrated national treasures and I was a theatre drop-out. I knew I had no business being there, but on the behest of Charles and Luis, I went in for the "auditioning experience." When I entered the audition room located on the first floor of the Ryerson Theatre school, the casting director confirmed my name on his clipboard then pointed his finger toward the front of the room and directed me to stand next to the piano accompanist. Without looking up from his notes, the pianist instructed me to nod my head when I was ready. Well, I was evidently not prepared and could barely keep up with the piano accompaniment; my singing did not match the key and cadence of the piano and my confidence rapidly devolved. It became crystal clear to everyone in the room that my aspirational audition had expired. I was pitiful, and thankful that Luis was not present for my audition. And no surprise to anyone, there was no call back from the casting director.

When I eventually attended the sold-out opening-night of *The Rocky Horror Picture Show*, it was clear why the casting director had kicked my tired old ass to the street. There was no room in the show for mediocrity in this stellar Canadian staging of the show!

Meanwhile, by the late Spring of 1977, I had been accepted into the University of Manitoba's Faculty of Architecture and Department of Interior Design. I moved from Cabbagetown to the warehouse district east of Yonge on Adelaide Street, chez Michael Harding. He recently gave up his "*House on Pooh Corner*" in Yorkville and we were now going to share his airy, double-storey, L-shaped loft situated on the southeast corner of Princess and Adelaide Street. Michael slept on the third floor in an open attic that ran east/west, while I slept on the second floor in a north/south wing leading from the top of the stairs that came up from the first-floor warehouse and entrance off Adelaide Street. My private wing ran parallel to Princess Street, so I called it the "Princess Suite." The washroom, kitchen, and living room ran below Michael's private third-floor loft. On the far south end of the second floor, there were two French doors that exited onto a roof patio that faced out to Princess Street, which was continuously lined with a row of parked trucks that ran the full block. Because of our different schedules and the layout of the vast space, Michael and I rarely saw each other. Mind you, I knew when he was home because he always had the record player on when he was home.

Toward the beginning of August, Michael Harding decided to host a Moving Away to Winnipeg Party in my honour. As I recall, the celebration was convened on the most blistering hot sunny day, and you could literally fry an egg on the tarpaper of the patio roof. But that didn't dissuade me from making a grand entrance as the guest of honour. At the time, I was still being asked for my ID in bars to prove I was eighteen, even though at this point I was twenty-four and still considered a "pretty-boy." And I hated being described this way.

I began acting out, and I altered my physical persona to reflect a hyper masculinity in the most dramatic way that I could conjure up, and that was biker-black leathers from head to toe! At the end of May, I used my tax refund and went into Northbound Leather on Yonge Street, located just north of the Wellesley. I walked out of the shop fully dressed as a leather queen from head to toe, and I was thrilled to test out my dramatically changed image. It was the middle of a busy Saturday on Yonge Street, and as I headed southbound toward Adelaide Street, I could see strangers' heads turn, and I started to quietly sing Lou Reed's "Take a Walk on The Wild Side." It played in a repetitive loop for the full twenty-minute walk home. Whenever I had a gay old tune in my head, I knew that I was in my happy place. And although I was not fully conversant and experienced with the queer culture of leather, I was clearly happy with my latest iteration of self-expression and the requisite fashion portal to a marginalized fringe in the gay community.

So, here I was at the onset of my party, powdering my body and sliding into my tight black leathers as the guest of honour. Heading out the set of French doors onto my roof deck, I could see it was packed with familiar guests and several people I had never met before. As anticipated, everyone's jaws dropped when they saw me swaggering out in full-on biker leathers, and they applauded my arrival. The intense heat and humidity made me sweat profusely, and I felt erotically pumped and ready for a damn good party. The truckers who were parked below looked up to the partying noise on the roof patio, and as I walked the line of the roof parapet like a runway, I cruised them openly and unabashedly in front of the party guests. I did not want the truckers to assume I was straight nor perceived as a weak gay man. I wanted to appear tough and challenging. I must admit that even though it was a little over the top and a bit dramatic, I thought to myself, so what, who cares already! It's just clothes! It's just another facet of my curiosity and willingness to dramatically explore outside the box of *conventionally* thinking.

One of the new guests I met at my party was a French-Canadian who introduced himself to me as "*Beau.*" He told me that he came to Toronto each summer from up north of Thunder Bay to "sow his wild oats." He confided that he was a leather queen and that we should arrange to get together and go out partying sometime. And it didn't take more than a quick kiss and a dart of my tongue to ignite our passion. We made an instant date to play long and hard after the other guests left the party, and that was my first attempt at serious leather roleplay, which seemed to meet with Beau's approval and a plea from him for an encore. On our second rendezvous, Beau told me that he had leather friends living in Winnipeg who were currently away on summer vacation at their trailer in the *Spruce Sands* RV trailer park adjacent to Lake Winnipeg. When he learned that I had never been to Manitoba and that there would be no one to greet me in Winnipeg, he confirmed that his leather pals could meet me at the Beaux Arts train station in the historic "Forks" downtown area to welcome me on his behalf.

My first introduction to Manitoba happened two short weeks later when I found myself in a sleeper car on a VIA train to Winnipeg. It was the first prairie province west of Ontario, but because of the Great Lakes that we had to go up and around, it was an overnight ride. While I carried a small, raggedy-ass suitcase to my sleeper car, I had previously checked my large, blue-metal (brass hinged) steam trunk into the train's storage compartment. I purchased the trunk at a local army/navy surplus in Toronto for all my worldly possessions. It was my own way of demonstrating my commitment to remain in Winnipeg until I graduated. There was no plan B; I was not planning to return without a degree in my hand this time.

The train ride out west stopped at every small pit-stop along the way. At one point, I woke up in the darkness to a piercing and extended blast of the train's horn. I had apparently uncovered myself in my sleep, and when I woke up to the startling noise, I discovered the length of my entire body was pressed up against the window, completely naked! When I looked outside, I could vaguely make out station workers with flashlights aimed directly at my window. The shock of my unintended exposure to random strangers threw me out of my bunk, and I recoiled back in complete and utter embarrassment. I couldn't fall back to sleep after that little trauma. When I arrived in downtown Winnipeg the following morning, I felt utterly exhausted from my train ride's ordeal and flashing to the public. My first thought was how fast can I get to the university campus? I desperately needed to strip down and jump into a refreshing shower and then take a long-overdue nap!

Anyhow, the mature gay leather couple that had arranged to welcome me through our friend Beau was parked out in front of the station as planned. I dragged my trunk and suitcase over to their pick-up. One of the guys on the passenger side jumped out and assisted me with loading my belongings into the back of the truck, and I discovered at this point that they had a different itinerary in mind for my first day. It was their weekend off, and as the summer season was short, they thought it would be great to take me out to their trailer park on Lake Winnipeg for the day. They assured me that we would return by late afternoon and that they would get me back to the campus in time for dinner. Meanwhile, I was shoe-horned into the front seat along with the two of them to my left on the passenger's side. They asked a few introductory questions about what I was studying and a little about my background, and then we continued in silence for the remainder of the ninety-minute drive to the RV campground. As I rode in a cloud of second-hand smoke, I contemplated "what the hell is a trailer park?" *Sweet Jesus,* I thought to myself, please get me through this long day! I was so busy pretending to be preoccupied with the view outside my window that I got a crook in my neck. *That certainly reminded me I was avoiding conversation with my hosts and acting a little stuck-up about the generational gap in our ages.*

As we continued toward the gay campsite, the windows of the truck were rolled partially down, and the fresh outside air gave me a second wind for the remainder of the ride. When we arrived at our destination, they parked the pick-up in front of a very modest and dilapidated trailer, which remained locked the entire day. Outside they had a fire pit and three or four rusted, folding aluminum web-frame chairs randomly strewn about. They also had a honking big-ass cooler filled with beers and a few cans of pop. They gathered up the chairs and placed them around the cooler as if it were a coffee table or footstool. And that's where they contentedly parked their plumber butts for the rest of the day. I think they might have brought some sandwiches from Winnipeg, but I just stuck with the potato chips and a can of Coke. I desperately needed the caffeine and sugar to keep myself awake!

Just as I was about to sit and join the old leather fruit loop, they told me I was free to go explore Lake Winnipeg, and I jumped at the opportunity to get away. I grabbed an extra can of Coke, thanked them for their "hospitality," and quickly scurried into the blazing summer heat. I stopped for a moment between the shrubbery and the beach to remove my shirt and tie it around my waist. I took off my shoes and I rolled up my jeans. But as I was doing this, I could feel annoying insect bites around my ankles. I quickly picked up my Coke and continued walking toward the shoreline to dip my ankles into the cool water for relief. The view and the magnificent long beach were breathtaking and virtually empty. I felt the pent-up tension in my tired body aching for a moment to relax by myself. By the time I got to the shoreline, I had viciously smacked myself into a near full-on anxiety attack to remove the constant nits and insect bites. Maybe that's the reason why the beach is deserted, I said to myself. In great haste, I stripped down to a pair of my European LYCRA/nylon underwear that could pass as a swim-suit and I threw myself into the shallow, refreshing, cool water. Afterward, I picked up my belongings and headed back to a shaded area near a few sun-bleached anaemic willowy trees and tall grass. I used my rolled clothes as a towel and pillow, and I decided to take a much-deserved rest now that I was cooled off and feeling refreshed.

Anyhow, I must have spent a good two hours lounging, with intermit-tent trips to the water to cool off. There was a gentle breeze coming off the lake, and it couldn't have been any more idyllic. I was grateful for my host's suggestion to come out for the day and decompress. However, after falling asleep for a brief period, I was awakened from my meditative bliss by an unfamiliar rustling and hissing coming from the direction of the nearby grasses and rocks behind my head. It startled me, and I got up to take a closer inspection. As I brushed away some of the foreground grasses, I gasped at my discovery of a mass of garter snakes. The active, slithering reptiles were fully entangled in a huge orgy, and I jumped back in absolute panic at the sight. Well, wouldn't you know this little wannabe leather boy reverted right back to his former sissy-boy mentality and screamed "Oh shit!"

All I could do was to thank the sweet Lord that no one was around to witness my hysterical outburst. I snatched up my pants and shirt and vigor-ously shook the sand out while terrified that some of those slithering snakes might be hiding within. I was so panicked that I moved in record speed in about the amount of time it would take to start an engine in a car. My pathetic internal motor was on overdrive, and I was happy to head back to the camp without a precious nanosecond to lose!

Within seconds, I was dressed and scrambled back to the campsite sport-ing my metaphoric cool-as-a-cucumber poise and an automatic service smile. My new Winnipeg acquaintances had a very *laissez-faire* attitude when I returned and asked nonchalantly, "How was your walk?" I told them it was beautiful and awe-inspiring and that I'd lost track of the time.

"No problem," they grunted. After sitting down, I joined them for one more can of Coke while they chugged back another brewski for themselves. After we finished our beverages, they packed up and we headed back to Winnipeg. They dropped me off at 150 Dafoe Road in front of the univer-sity's Taché Hall residence for men. The historic building faced onto a beau-tiful verdant quad out front and toward the Red River out back. There were a few hunky residents out front who saw me arrive. They volunteered to help carry my large metal steamer trunk while I carried my old suitcase and an over-the-shoulder messenger bag. As we walked toward the front door of the building, I was clearly appreciative of their volunteer service, and I momentarily turned toward my older chaperones still sitting in the truck. I thanked them one last time and waved them off with a grateful goodbye. They turned on the key to the ignition and roared off.

Thank God for my angel-boy volunteers! They were certainly a welcome sight for my sorry red eyes, and I had no intention of blowing them off just yet. En route to the dormitory check-in, we exchanged names over a small chit chat about where we all hailed from. They assured me they would wait while I registered, and they would help me locate my assigned room on the first floor. A few minutes later, we walked down the hall and arrived at my room, situated steps away from the main entry. I thanked them as I opened the door, and they carried my belongings inside the dorm room. It was clear that my roommate had already moved in, but he was evidentially out. My dorm mates who assisted me welcomed me to Taché Hall and pointed out the direction of the communal showers and washrooms. They said they would probably see me at the cafeteria for dinner in about an hour. The timing was perfect. I was famished, and I had just enough time to finally shower, shit, and shave for the day.

My roommate was there when I returned from my late-afternoon ablutions. He shook my hand and introduced himself as Gary Van Patten. He told me that he was a third-year transfer from Humber College in Toronto, and he was entering into his third year in interior design. How cool was that! I would be living with a potential student mentor as my roommate. By this point, we had established that it was time for dinner, so he offered to chaperone me to the Pembina Hall cafeteria, which connected to Mary Speechly Hall residence for girls. Apparently, this was the cross-roads where the two binary sexes in separate dormitories could socialize and eat.

Over dinner, Gary enlightened me that it was near impossible to remain in the dorm room with all the noise and sophomoric pranks going on. All the young freshmen were hot-blooded and testosterone-driven jocks who apparently went out of control when the sun set. "Welcome to the sequel to *Lord of The Flies*," I said. We both chuckled and admitted we were too old for this kind of crap. He mentioned that he had gone out earlier to visit the architecture building and investigate the interior design studios to organize his desk and locker assignment before classes started on the following Tuesday. He indicated that he would pretty much live and work in the studio and not be around the dorm. The room would be all mine most of the time.

Unfortunately, within my first forty-eight hours of residing at Taché Hall, I was ready to move out, and I began exploring the campus for other residential accommodations. Gary was a great guy and I think we would have hit it off, but I was not prepared to live in the company of crazy town Taché Hall. After two weeks of sleepless nights, I transferred over to University College Residence into a single room. The atmosphere was blissfully quiet and calm. The residence was modern and beautifully designed. Many of the residents were non-jocks and more liberal minded, and I knew instantly it would be a perfect fit. The overall atmosphere was significantly more mature and to my liking.

Soon after moving in, the housing administrator in the provost's office became friendly and chatty with me. And by the end of September, she had invited me for a weekend away at her cottage near Kenora, Ontario, which she shared with her alleged "roommate." When I met her long-time roommate, it was clear they were a lesbian couple in a committed but closeted relationship. This behaviour was so archaic in my view, but I suppose it was the practice of the older generation to avoid homophobia and work discrimination at any cost.

Irene was near retirement, and she was a good forty years my senior. Although the entire weekend was peaceful and lovely, there was never any elaboration of their personal relationship or displays of affection in my presence. Everything they said appeared carefully curated and rehearsed over decades. The story they gave me was that there were only two bedrooms and that they would share one room to let me have the other. Did they think I was a potato that just fell off the farm truck? The chest of drawers in my room was completely empty, apart from a folded extra blanket in the bottom drawer. There was absolutely nothing personal of theirs in the guest bedroom. Meanwhile, I made a point of sharing that I was an open gay activist, but they didn't bite at that. I was hoping it would give them permission to relax and chill out, but my strategy had no discernable impact. They spent the most part of the weekend whispering to each other. And I spent most of the weekend canoeing around the lake in solitude.

University College Residence was a great experience for my first three years. From a design perspective, it was a contemporary, well-designed residence at the time. It was the newest housing addition to the sprawling campus. The residence had a great room that acted as a multi-purpose cafeteria for special event socials and mixers. However, the biggest surprise was just down the hall on the main level, where I accidentally discovered an unidentified and secured room of great historical value next to the provost's office. What very few of the residents or the general campus population knew was there was a private Victorian Room. The room was in great contrast to all the surrounding modern design and architecture. It contained a priceless collection of unique, mid-nineteenth- century Victorian furniture and furnishings donated by Dr. Joseph Doupe, who was the former head of the Department of Psychology. I can't recall the specific reason at the time, but I was invited by my friend Irene, who was the executive assistant to the provost, to attend a private and intimate gathering of upper-school administrators, along with two or three hand-selected student residents from University College.

I was only in there once or twice, but I won't forget what a superb, museum-quality collection it was. This is when I first started to think about design opportunities to inject historical references and whimsy into modern interiors that was apparently being introduced elsewhere as an expression of *post-modernism* that lasted from about 1970-1990. However, back in the interior design department in 1977, our professors never talked about this anti-establishment approach to modern design. It was not even on the radar, and it was something I didn't find out about until I moved to New York to pursue graduate studies at Pratt Institute in 1981. Moreover, it wasn't until much later, in 1995, when I would return from New York to take up my position as a tenure-track professor, when I could then inject a more inclusive and personal concept of modern design.

By that point, it was a little late and overdone, but nonetheless my students were clamoring for an escape from the restrictive founding design principles that needed revisiting for a fresh new approach to creative design thinking. Decorative embellishment and a whimsical nod to historical design was something I subscribed to from the get-go as a student, so it was a great relief when I could finally inject a bit of fresh air to the stale old way of studio design. Vernacular design and cultural "*placemaking*" was finally an acceptable narrative in design discourse and practice. I had waited almost two decades to see the spillover to professional design in Toronto and across Canada. It had been happening in local gay culture and queer interiors and stage design since the 1970s, and specifically in our private world of "gender-fuck drag," going all the way back to Roman antiquity. And it was clearly not on the lips of most heterosexual men. I maintain if it wasn't for drag queens, the world of post-modernism would never have taken off in straight culture, in my opinion. Can I have a little Amen for that?

Naturally, the Faculty of Architecture's ethos conservatively embraced the mid- twentieth-century tenets of modern design that lasted from roughly 1947 to 1957, but for all intents and purposes, the school's philosophical approach to interior design went even further back to the first school of modern design with the Bauhaus School (1919-1933). The German school combined new manufacturing technologies with wood/metal and textile crafts and fashioned them into lighting and furnishings with a gesture toward fine arts in the form of painting and sculpture. These were the guiding principles and the golden rule when I started my studies in 1977. *"Form Follows Function"* and "God Is in the Details" were pretty much the metrics used to evaluate our work. I really couldn't find any faculty who was willing to subscribe to decorative embellishment other that Dr. George Fuller, who had both a bachelor's degree in interior design and PhD in art history. He was eminently qualified to teach with expertise in both studio design and art history and probably the only professor to do so throughout my entire academic career in Canada. He was also the only instructor that I knew that admired the secret *Victorian Room* with its museum-quality Canadian collection at the doorstep to my University College residence. Historical design references were literally still "in the closet."

Beyond honing my observational design skills as a first-year student, the first queer activist thing I did after moving into University College residence was to voluntarily work on campus for the Gays for Equality office in the main University of Manitoba Student Union (UMSU) building on Friday nights from seven to ten. Equality was very much on the forefront of my mind, and this gave me an opportunity to provide service to the local queer community in Winnipeg. However, in all the time I worked there over my first two years, I never had a single faculty member, student, or anyone else from campus drop by the office. Occasionally, campus security would check in but that was about the extent of my visitors.

It didn't matter much, as I was busy working the phone line in the one-person office. I dealt with inquiries and referrals for everyone from pranksters to truckers to queer youth at risk and their concerned parents. Closeted married men were one of the larger groups calling in as a precursor to phone-sex hotlines. And of course, I could only refer them to a marriage counselor and to a very small list of available local bars, private clubs, and a singular gay sauna for men located along north Maine Street. And although there were weak moments when I considered their request to meet, I did not breach that ethical line. Coming from a large city like Toronto, there were so many more resources and services for the gay community, and I must admit there were times on the phone when I felt inadequate with the limited offerings. But it sure was a lot better than having nothing to offer. And it sure was more than enough for me as a focussed student with limited time for personal connections and assignations; I remained vigilant to the "four royal FF's" that I learned from Jan Sheffield back in Toronto.

Winnipeg was all about the gay socials. I had never heard this term in Toronto, but it made perfect sense with the limited public offerings of gay venues and bars. Due to antiquated provincial liquor laws in Manitoba, drinking was restricted to private clubs a lot of the time, outside of hotels, casinos, veteran clubs, and in the privacy of residences where you could host a "social" at your home. Over time, I could clearly understand why creative and ambitious young gays in Winnipeg would eventually leave on a Greyhound bus for either Toronto, Vancouver, or even New York City. A great many queer youths moved away to seek out their fortunes with autonomy from their families and the limitations imposed by their geographic isolation.

Three of these typical gay youth were good friends that I made during my undergraduate time in Winnipeg: the first was Randy Spence, who I briefly dated and who eventually left for NYC about the same time I did; the second was his roommate Garry Evans; and the third was his other roommate Stephen Corbett, who introduced me to the musical soundtrack of A Chorus Line and later moved to Toronto to intern at the Rainbow Room, located in Rosedale and next door to the original Roots store. Sadly, my pal Randy would later succumb to AIDS after returning home to Winnipeg with his human immunodeficiency virus (HIV). The last time I saw Randy in NYC was at the old Greenwich Playhouse at 97 Greenwich Avenue and West 12th. We had run into each other after seeing the 1990 movie Ghost, starring the one and only Whoopi Goldberg, who was brilliant and glued the narrative together. The entire confluence of this movie and our last time together still sends shivers up my spine.

It is true when people say that "Peggers," or people from Winnipeg, are the nicest and friendliest people in Canada. I would subscribe to that in a heartbeat! Not only nice but perhaps due to its geographic isolation, I found Winnipeg to be a hotbed of talent in the performing and visual arts. They had the world-class Royal Winnipeg Ballet Company, which was Canada's touring company at the time and starred the incomparable prima ballerina Evelyn Hart, who originally hailed from Northern Ontario. I would occasionally cross paths with her in Winnipeg's Osborne Village at a local upmarket café and specialty desserts shop. Winnipeg had a fantastic symphony orchestra and a stunningly beautiful concert hall that hosted many international guest artists, including the hilarious all-male drag corps de ballet, *Les Ballets Trockaderos de Monte Carlo!* So, it was always a pay-for-gay passport if you had money. If you could afford to plug into the available wealth of cultural and community-enriching experiences supported mostly by privileged white folk, then you were very blessed and fortunate as a young queer person, particularly during the long, harsh winter months when everyone spent a lot of time indoors.

But even with student discounts and free tickets earmarked for university students, it was a challenge for busy students in the Faculty of Architecture to even find a free night to get out from the rigours of an intense workload of studio-design assignments. I was grateful to live on campus so I could simply walk through a few tunnels and back to my dorm room without having to worry about where I was going to eat from a plethora of food resources and cafeterias on the campus. And because of my self-discipline and schedule, I maintained my weekends free for cultural enrichment in downtown Winnipeg. I was hungry to take advantage of the local performing and visual arts community while I was there. I actively sought out all the discounted and free tickets. I even had my insider connection and friend, Irene, who always alerted me to tickets that had been donated and made available to University College students. There were a couple of good friends from interior design who also lived in my residence and would join in on my excursions periodically. There was the talented Pam Ducker, who was in third year when I was in second year, and then there was the effervescent and bursting-at-the-seams Sue Namath from Vancouver, who was in first year. All three of us had one thing in common that underscored we were all overachievers and highly competitive.

Anytime there was a Halloween social in the Faculty of Architecture, we invariably won best prize for costume design over three consecutive years. And speaking of Halloween, while we were working on our homework assignments, the three of us would listen to the local radio station with an ear for invitations to call in for prizes. I believe I was in third year when I got lucky and won two free tickets to the radio station's Halloween party, which was hosted at the Fort Garry Hotel. Unfortunately, my class buddies weren't available but luckily an exchange graduate student from Germany named Ruth Mueller jumped at the offer to be my guest.

For some bizarre reason it was always a challenge to find a Canadian dormitory resident to go when I had an extra ticket. I started making a point of inviting international students like Ruth Mueller and my lovely friend Misako from Japan. Misako would always dress in her formal kimono garb whenever we went to the Winnipeg Concert Hall. The international students felt very honoured to be my guest and they were always grateful for a culturally enriching Canadian experience and a break from their studies. In return, their enthusiasm opened my eyes up to other cultures and customs around the world and seduced me with the great possibility of travel somewhere in my future. Honestly, I met some fascinating individuals living in the dorm. And of course, many decades later, both Berlin and Tokyo were at the top of my list for travel. I thought they were random choices for my travel, but writing this memoir makes me aware the seeds of my destiny were planted way back in the late 1970s at the University of Manitoba.

Like many North American cities, Winnipeg was designed with a culture of sports in mind. Their sold-out venues and arenas made a great economic impact on the city. Even someone like myself found recreational and competitive swimming something that I really enjoyed and supported. And I couldn't go anywhere better in Canada than Winnipeg's *Pan Am Aquatic Centre* that was completed in 1967. It had two world-class fifty-metre pools, one kid's pool, a dedicated competition-level diving area, two weight rooms, an aerobic studio and places to speed walk or jog. More importantly, the centre enjoyed a stellar reputation for the inhouse clinic for sports injuries and physiotherapy. And in 1979 I became one of the physiotherapy patients. Fortunately, they were able to help me after tearing a ligament while jogging in the underground grotto at the university while vainly trying to retain my young "girlish figure."

Many of these elite health services that I took for granted made me realize for the first time of my white privilege as an undergraduate. However, if you were not a student and happened to be a queer youth-at-risk and marginalized, it was a daily struggle just to keep from falling through the cracks for necessary medical interventions. And it was even more challenging if you happened to be a two-spirited Indigenous person. When I first moved to Winnipeg and went downtown, I was certainly shocked when I encountered the plight and homelessness of innumerable Indigenous persons strung out on Portage and Maine, behind city hall and across from the Winnipeg Concert Hall. Most local white folk seemed inured to their untenable conditions and never talked to me about the issue. I noticed how white folk avoided contact and simply walked over the indigent to get where they were going. It evoked painful memories from my own childhood on Toronto's skid row.

In Winnipeg, I saw very little support from the broader Caucasian community. It was a harsh and stark reminder of what I had experienced from poverty and the plight of the poor. Compound this with the fact that if you were gay and bullied, the chances of you dropping out of school increased proportionately and led frequently to alcohol and substance abuse. And sometimes even to suicide in numbers statistically much higher than their straight counterparts. It was my view as a gay activist that Winnipeg's queer youth-at-risk were not being recognized and addressed adequately back in the late 1970s. However, if you were privileged *and* white, like me, it was much easier to be treated with compassion and care, while marginalized minorities were simply shit out of luck, shunned and disrespected. It was tremendously difficult for me to wrap my head around the disparity.

I had a few gay classmates and friends who felt they'd had no choice but to get the hell out of Winnipeg when they graduated and head out for greener and more gay-friendly pastures. One of these friends was my classmate Roger Zwickel, who headed off to New York City. And the other was my classmate and fourth-year roommate, Andrew Steycek, who headed off to Toronto and worked for the interior designer Morley Winnick. One thing I will say about young Canadian gays from Winnipeg and from across Canada, we were all willing to take risks and make a dramatic move to improve the opportunities and quality of our gay young lives.

My gay sensibility and local activism in Winnipeg were further manifested in my design studio and classes. It wasn't difficult to stick out and be noticed, and I had no intention of blending in. I was about four years older than my peers who'd come directly from high school, and I had no time to waste. I was there (with laser-like focus on the program) to work like I had never worked before, with commitment, passion, and the ambition to be one of the top students. I made sure I integrated queer diversity into everything I did at school: from data gathering and design research to client-needs analysis and programming of spatial requirements through to conceptual design development and final presentation. Wherever I designed an interior, I shoehorned diversity into my work in one way or another, and this was never an issue with Professor Joan Harland. She was one tough bird, and it was hard to get anything past her that wasn't up to her high standards and expectations. However, my philosophical and personal contextual approach was never an issue. She was a woman who confessed she understood discrimination from first-hand knowledge and personal experience, without personal elaboration beyond that.

I was most fortunate to be at the tail-end of her tenure when she eventually retired and passed her baton onto the next generation of educators, moving our profession forward. She was a personal hero of mine, along with Professor Grant Marshall.

There will never be another Joan Harland. She was a walking vault of history and modern design. She was a taskmaster who pushed her students to see critical design elements and principles in every exercise and homework assignment. Her discourse focussed on how design decision-making impacts the psychological wellbeing of the end-user beyond building codes and subjective aesthetics and stylistic trends. When your work did not rise to the level of professional communications that she demanded, she questioned whether you were in the right program, and her disappointment was reflected in your grade and descriptive feedback. Heaven forbids you should submit or do any quick sketching in front of her without compositional layout qualities that demonstrated a variety of line weights and stroking techniques. She did not hesitate to dispatch a student directly to the inhouse architecture library to source out reference examples and bring them back to the studio as a sketching resource. She had no time for "willy-nilly doodling," as she would like to say. Doodling, in her opinion, was a weak substitute for effective communications, even though it was the sketching techniques that many classmates often tried but failed to impress her with. Professor Harland's tutelage on the issue of design sketching was something I carried forward into my own future tenure as a professor and instructor in graphic communications for over two decades.

I was so enamoured by her design leadership by the time I got to the fourth year, I applied and received early written acceptance into Pratt Institute for graduate studies. My research into requisite academic require-ments indicated that all future hires for professors would require a post-graduate or doctoral degree, and I was totally on board with raising the academic threshold of excellence in Canada that was trailing far behind the USA, from what I could ascertain. I set up an appointment to meet up with Joan Harland over lunch, along with the company of Professor Dianne Jackman and Professor Ron Veitch. As I discussed my aspirations and goals, Professor Harland casually mentioned that she had established a scholar-ship for graduate studies in her name and that I should submit an essay about why I thought I was deserving of her inaugural scholarship. And I did just that by the very next day.

I was very honoured and humbled to become the first recipient of the *Joan Harland Scholarship for Graduate Studies* back in 1981. The scholar-ship money was very helpful, but it was the validation and prestige of being Professor Harland's very first nominee that strengthened my resolve for graduate studies in New York. The last thing I would like to mention about my personal achievements as an undergraduate was that although I received a couple of Hudson Bay design awards along the way, I was most honoured to have had two of my projects from second- and third-year studio repre-sented at the annual International Interior Design Exposition (IIDEX) in my home city of Toronto.

My final year of study was the most brilliant experience of my entire four years. It was the first time I was introduced to Professor Grant Marshall, who was the course and year coordinator. I instantly fell in love with my new instructor during my first studio-design critique. I was blessed to be in his section for the project introduction and research assignment, and I challenged him on what I thought was an old-fashioned and myopic view of what defined a married couple. Our class was assigned a mission to find either "a real or theoretical married couple" to use for the purpose of researching the client's functional and aesthetic needs, and the subsequent programming of the spatial area requirements and proximities for anticipated behavioral relationships.

The project brief indicated that our client was planning to retire in Winnipeg and had grown adult children who would come back periodically for visits and had to be accommodated in the space. The retired couple theoretically purchased a large condo that was situated in a Middle Gate triplex in River Heights, which was an exclusive enclave in Winnipeg. The project floorplate combined two smaller apartments into a third-level penthouse in the triplex. In addition, one of the individuals had to have an interest/hobby in art, sculpture, painting, or music The professional retired couple was profiled as reasonably affluent, so the budget was open for consideration and design applications. By this point, I was getting tired of designing for straight clients and told Professor Marshall that I had a couple of wealthy men in mind back in Toronto. They were now retired and fit the client description and they just happened to be gay.

I explained to Professor Marshall that my unconventional couple were essentially married in everyone's eyes at a time when legal marriage in Canada was not an option until much later in July of 2005. I argued that it was time for the changing of the guard about what defined a couple and marriage. I remember Professor Marshall taking a long pause and then saying in this low kind of mumble that he sometimes used when he wanted to say something quietly, "I think that is a great idea." With that, I had his blessing and broke down one more barrier in queer visibility and representation back in 1980.

I found my project was of broader societal importance and felt immense responsibility to do it justice. If the $400 cost wasn't enough for the dramatic reverse-print, white-on-black line drawings of the plans, elevations, and custom millwork, then my perspective interiors showing a naked gay male couple inside a glass-walled shower certainly elevated an eyebrow or two. I insisted on conveying an air of sophistication and elegance for my hypothetical client based upon a gay couple from my social acquaintance with Gildo Polito, the vice-president of the Bank of Rome, who was momentarily residing at the Harbour Castle in Toronto.

The project concluded with an ultra-chic modern interior that was peppered with European paintings and Persian carpets resting on top of Italian black-marble floors. In one of my final atmospheric boards, I included a symbolic client photo of two men who were arm in arm in matching tuxedos, standing in front of their art collection, and holding a glass of champagne. The master bedroom featured an ensuite clad in tempered floor-to-ceiling glass, with a barrier-free glass shower for two. Next to the shower was a white-marble "his-and-his vanity," with one large mirror that reflected into the glass shower enclosure.

I included three perspective viewpoints and line renderings, illuminating the featured open-planning concepts: the first area revealed the large, open entry sitting room, den, and kitchen; a second perspective constructed from a different station point of the same area; and the final perspective taken inside the main bedroom and connecting ensuite. My realistic drawings of nude scale figures were inspired from photographic images from a *Blue Boy* magazine reference. In 1980, my renderings were realistic and shocking to many. However, as my professors noted, my scale figures were essential to the inclusive narrative of my gay client, where sexuality was proudly at the forefront of how they chose to live. Everything about my final presentation was a stylistic gesture toward a gay flair and a sexual narrative, expressed through a splash of atmospherics that included homoerotic art and sculpture. It was my passion project and a truly fitting way to say adieu in my final year. I'd completed a life goal to attend university on my own terms as a gay activist, and I no longer felt a need to prove anything to anyone. Queer was here, and my close classmates and professors were ready to cheer! For many of the homophobic dudes from architecture, not so much. Thinking to myself, I said, "Get with the program, boys!" Although they didn't have the courage and respect to confront me directly, I could hear their goofy-assed snickering amongst themselves in the design studio.

If my memory serves me well, each school term included two six-week projects in the fall semester broken up by a one-week reading in between. Since we had just completed the Penthouse project, our class was asked to meet a week later for the introduction to the second project at the new building site, located at Portage and Maine Street. Our project tenant would occupy an upper floor in the recently opened office tower. We were there to survey a footprint for our next project on corporate design. Professor Grant Marshall was there, buzzing about with Professor Nancy Maruca. At one point as I randomly passed by the two of them, Grant touched me on the shoulder and whispered at my ear, "You did a fantastic project!" Those five simple words piqued my curiosity.

The following week, I showed up early to see the Faculty of Architecture's biannual showcase of work curated and displayed in the centre-space. It was a retrospective of student work from all the departments: environmental studies, architecture, urban planning, landscape, and interior design. Around 8:00 am, I meandered through the labyrinth of hanging interdisciplinary projects while sipping from my thermos of coffee and taking time to scrutinize every detail on each project. And thankfully, with no one around at that ungodly early hour of the day, I could really enjoy the show.

As I navigated through the rows of applied theoretical work and conceptual design development, I discovered at the very end of the student work display my very own capstone penthouse project! I really couldn't believe my eyes. There, in full display with all my in-your-face gay erotic images and queer-focussed design development, was my recent project that allegedly represented the best of the interior design department. And for the benefit of the entire Faculty of Architecture, no less. It was my queer-centric capstone and the most profound work I had ever produced, and I was awarded the most joyful A+ that I had ever received. I had met all my undergraduate educational and personal goals beyond my wildest expectations. And to boot, I met a hell of a lot of inspirational folks in the Winnipeg arts community and the Faculty of Architecture.

1981 Interior Design graduation dance.
The University of Manitoba, Faculty of Architecture.
(Left to right): Andrew's date, my roommate, Andrew, my trans date Garth, and myself.

13
PRATT INSTITUTE
359 WASHINGTON AVE.,
BROOKLYN, NY. 1982-1983

I arrived at LaGuardia Airport in New York about two weeks before the 1981 classes started at Pratt's Graduate School for Interior Design. I was outwardly fearless, even though I had no knowledge of my new where-abouts in Brooklyn. I had never visited Pratt's Campus and I had no clue how to get there other than by taxi of course. I did not know a personal soul or contact in Brooklyn. Although I did have a past acquaintance named Stan Vincent from *Voyage Records* whom I had met at The Yorkviller in Toronto five or six years earlier. Unfortunately, we had lost contact over the past few years, but I'd never forgotten his hospitality when he had invited me to be his guest for a week in Manhattan.

As I rode into Brooklyn from the airport, I reflected on my prior trip to Manhattan years earlier. Stan's hospitality in Manhattan was life-changing, and part of the impetus for why I subsequently applied to Pratt Institute; I wanted to live in New York, and I knew graduate studies would be my passport. As his invited guest at the time, Stan provided me a place to stay at one of his staff's apartments on the Upper West Side. He also generously comped me a Broadway theatre ticket to see the highly acclaimed *On the*

Twentieth Century, starring Madeline Kahn in the title role of Lily Garland at the St. James Theatre on West 44th Street.

After catching the fabulous show, I crossed over to the east side of Broadway and decided to explore my way north, walking toward my Upper West Side accommodation. As I approached 54th Street, I saw a huge crowd waiting outside a marquee that said *Studio 54*, and I had no clue what this was at the time. I stood for a moment on the far side of 54th wearing some trendy fashions that I had picked up earlier on Spring Street in SoHo. I decided to rest my back against a wall on the north side of the street and momentarily observe all the people and commotion. I was very curious as to what the big hullabaloo was all about. Was it another Broadway show, or perhaps a recording studio for celebrity artists?

Within two minutes of propping the wall up, the crowd in front of me suddenly parted and I could see a direct line to a doorman/manager with an imposing bouncer standing outside the front entrance. Both guys were frantically beckoning me to come toward the velvet rope that separated the crowd from the main entrance. The crowd physically pushed me forward, and the next thing I knew, I was being ushered inside to what I subsequently discovered was the infamous and exclusive Studio 54 nightclub. Frequented by many celebrities and other eye candy, I kind of felt awkward by myself and felt out of place. I instantly ran to the bar to down a gin and tonic before heading up to the rows of old theatre seats that stepped up from the main level. About midway up, I reached a landing on the second level and decided that would be a safe place to sit and observe the theatrics and the crowds dancing below. Well, before I knew it, I had to take my first piss for the night, and I could see to the left of me that there was an entrance archway with a sign above indicating "Lounges." I picked up my glass and headed over.

Once I got inside, let's just say that one thing led to another, and I ended up getting high in the men's lounge on the upper level with some incredibly handsome guys who called me over to do a few lines of coke with them. I had only ever done coke once before, and I thought that since there was a big moon face suspended over the dance floor with a coke spoon up its nose, it would be okay to participate. I thanked the guys in appreciation for their welcoming generosity and then I returned to my seat for a moment. I could see from above that everyone was over-the-top high on the dancefloor, and I wanted the appearance of fitting in.

I won't bother you with the specific nuances and cast of who's who and what I did in my remaining time, but as soon as I polished off my drink, I got up the courage to go down to the dancefloor without a dance partner. I joined in with the other people who were randomly moving about and dancing without partners. At one point when I looked up, I realized that I was dancing next to two or three of the Village People, who were wearing their performance drag from their album cover. As I personally recall, Studio 54 was indeed a hedonistic experience back at the time in 1977. That was four long years ago and one undergraduate degree before I now found myself in 1981, riding in a cab from LaGuardia airport into Brooklyn to start a new chapter in my life.

As I snapped back to reality inside the cab, I could see we were heading out of Queens and entering deeper into Brooklyn, enroute to the closest YMCA to Pratt Institute. I decided it would be best to head there first to see if I could rent a cheap room for a day or two to get my bearings. I knew that once I could establish a temporary place to rest, I could investigate a more permanent option for my living quarters. Like the proverbial fish out of water, I immediately recognized that I was going from a comparatively small pond in Toronto to the behemoth ocean of New York City, consisting of five large boroughs that seemed to effortlessly blend in together, including: the Bronx; Manhattan; Brooklyn; Queens; and Staten Island. My African American driver eventually shuttled me to a rather dilapidated-looking YMCA inside what once appeared to be a rather impressive historical multi-storey red-brick building, circa 1905. It was located at the corner of Bedford and Monroe Street in a run-down minority neighbourhood that looked like it had seen much better days! After I paid the driver, he informed me he would take a cigarette break and hang outside for a bit to see if I would be okay.

When I went inside, it was quite noisy, with voices and sounds reverberating from the high ceilings and hard surfaces; even just schlepping across the tiled floor with my heavy bags caused enough echoing to draw people's attention to me. There were a handful of young Black guys loitering on the feature staircase and checking out everyone who was coming and going.

When I walked into the double-storey lobby, I could see their eyes were clocking my every move as if to suggest, "What the hell are you doing here?" I was too preoccupied with the urgency of my situation, and I paid their stares no never-mind. I hustled my tired Canadian lard-butt over to the reception counter like I knew what I was doing, and I pleaded with an older gentleman that stood behind the counter for somewhere to leave my bags after I found out there were no available rooms for him to rent. I explained I had come directly from the airport, and I was a visiting student from Canada. I assured him that I didn't know where else to go and I wanted to find a temporary place to leave my bags in the nearby vicinity of the Clinton Hill Campus for Pratt.

He smiled and nodded like he understood and mentioned that this place was probably not the best place for a "white boy." And honestly, I was so green and naïve that I had no clue what he meant. Clearly, I was out of my element, and everything was a little overwhelming to me. Perhaps, I was a bit naïve and knew nothing about all the unspoken rules regarding where Black people lived and where white people lived, and so I pleaded with him to understand my predicament. I expressed all I wanted to do was to live somewhere cheap, regardless of the neighbourhood. Anyhow, his avuncular response was that I could temporarily secure my bags behind the counter with him, but his shift would be over in three hours and if I did not return by then, he could not guarantee my bags' safety. I understood and slipped him a few *singles* for his trouble; I promised I would return before the end of his shift.

Outside, I managed to grab the very same cab that had taken me from the airport. The driver had the motor idling with his window rolled down while he was finishing his menthol cigarette. He laughed and said he hadn't thought I would be in there long—and he was right! On the way over to Pratt, he informed me I had been lucky to catch him because cabs don't come into certain areas of Brooklyn and that's when he explained about *Gypsy Cabs,* or illegal private cars that serviced more of the high-risk neighbourhoods in the Bronx, Harlem, and parts of Brooklyn; exactly the kind of area where I was coming from at the YMCA.

So, as we pulled up to the campus, the driver made it abundantly clear that as a white newcomer from Canada, I was lucky he'd waited, and he cleverly manipulated me for an even larger tip. I left him another five dollars for his trouble and thanked him for his generosity toward me. Welcome to New York, I thought to myself. I'm not in Kansas anymore. Welcome to Oz (Brooklyn), *Dorothy!*

When the driver let me off at the main gates at Pratt on the corner of Dekalb Avenue and Hall Street, it took me a few minutes to figure out where the interior design studios and the office of the registrar were situated on the map. At the top of my list, and with no time to waste, I needed to find the

Office of International Affairs (OAI) and apprise the staff of my immediate crisis with a request for their assistance to secure a campus location where I could stay, temporarily. Anyhow, I must have been wandering aimlessly about the campus for twenty minutes, but it felt like an hour. I continually stopped strangers to ask where the OIA office was located. And everyone kept telling me I had to cross "the field" and I would find the office on the north side, inside the East Building, which could be accessed from inside a small courtyard surrounded by three buildings that included the Main Building, South Hall, and the East Building where the OIA was located.

Arriving fresh from the Canadian prairies just a few months back, I thought I had a pretty good idea of what a field was. After two- or three-times asking strangers where the damn field was, they all pointed toward the exact same place, to what I would describe as a wide boulevard of grass about the width of a four-lane street; it was not what your typical Canadian would refer to as a field. In fact, most North American universities would refer to it as a *campus rectangular quad, and even that would be generous*. However, *the field* was a part of Brooklyn and Pratt Institute's lexicon. It was all a matter of relative perspective and vernacular placemaking in one of the most densely populated neighbourhoods in Fort Greene, Brooklyn. And across the field/boulevard I marched! I entered through a small court-yard that took me to the East Building courtyard's access to the *Office of International Affairs*. The best scenario the senior administrator could do was to set me up temporarily in the married graduate-student residence. I was told that I could share the apartment for a couple of nights with two other foreign students like myself. Clearly, I was desperate and very appreciative of Pratt's emergency accommodation. I had a mission, and I wasted no time. I needed to find something more permanent, immediately.

After expressing my sincere gratitude to the OIA, I quickly went across the campus to do a fast check of my temporary accommodations. Following the staff's written instructions and armed with a subway map, I made my way back to the YMCA from the closest subway at the corner of Washington Avenue and Lafayette Street. Upon my arrival, I entered the YMCA and was relieved to see the same reception clerk who had promised to watch over my luggage. And by the look on his face, I could see he was relieved to see me before his shift ended. I really wanted to hug the dear man, but I thanked him with a monetary tip instead, noting to myself the currency of showing appreciation in the United

States was through tipping—almost for everything and anyone who provided the most nominal courtesy! Normally, a hug or a handshake would suffice back home in Toronto. Anyhow, I retrieved my bags and headed back to the subway for another adventure back to the campus.

Alone and awkwardly loaded with my luggage, I must have looked out of place, judging from the skeptical subway passenger faces. I was the only white person in the crowded car, and it was my first time that I can ever recall feeling like a visible minority. I now had an inkling about what it felt like to have the shoe on the other foot. I felt all eyes staring with a sense of suspicion and felt like I probably didn't belong there. I couldn't imagine how marginalized minorities faced this kind of scrutiny every day. It occurred to me that my initial anxiety was ridiculous, and as I exhaled, I relaxed into the remainder of the ride. I was thankful for the lesson and gift of being outside my normal reality. Coming from a predominantly white population in downtown Toronto, I had never quite experienced something like this.

After arriving back to the campus, I dropped my bags off at the married grad residence and headed out to knock on neighbourhood doors and investigate accommodations on my own. But before I did this, I noticed a greasy Greek diner that I recall noting as the *Pratt Diner* located on Hall Street, directly across from the campus. By this point, I was exhausted and hungry, so I went inside. I sat on one of the bar stools at the front counter and waited a few minutes for the petite, but very butch waitress covered in tattoos who the patrons and staff referred to as "*Jeanie.*"

When I sat down and raised my hand to wave her over, she shouted back to me, "I'll get to you when I get to you," and that shut me up and made me spin around on my stool in public humiliation! Anyhow, everything worked out well, as it gave me a few minutes to scope out what the other folks were eating. When Jeanie eventually worked herself to the other side of the counter and barked out, "What will you have?" I ordered what most of the patrons seemed to be ordering: a gyro with a side of fries. It was my first time tasting a gyro, and it was insanely delicious and fragrant. I knew this place would become my favourite budget-friendly lunch venue in the neighbourhood.

After I finished my meal, I passed by Mike's Diner at the corner of Hall and DeKalb and continued walking west past Pratt's Arts Supplies, which I noted for later reference. When I reached Washington Avenue, I proceeded north toward Myrtle Avenue and passed a row of gorgeous, well-kept brownstones that I knew would be out of my budget. I then backtracked along Washington Avenue toward the corner of Lafayette Street where I had gone earlier to catch the subway. On the near corner was a large Baptist church with a set of open red doors, and I could hear the choir singing in full throttle; it was fabulous, and I really was tempted to stop and enter but I was on a mission! On the far side of the lights was the familiar subway entrance. And just a few doors down from the subway, I noticed a couple of dilapidated-looking wooden homes built in the Federal style, which I soon discovered were the only two Federal-style wood houses in all of Brooklyn. The creaking wooden front steps at 359 Washington looked like you would fall through them if you did not step on the right spot, and the windows were covered with roller blinds and some old, faded, crocheted lace, aged as though they'd been dipped in a pot of old tea. I thought to myself, well this looks very budget-friendly and perfect for me! I walked up and audaciously knocked on the door's inset window and waited, half expecting some elderly person to open the door.

When the door opened, a very scholarly looking white, middle-aged guy sporting a small pair of gold wireframe glasses and wearing a wrinkled white shirt and vest stood before me in his gabardine grey flannels and sock feet. He looked as though I had just woken him from a nap. When I explained that I had just arrived from Canada and was trying to find an inexpensive place in the neighbourhood to live, he invited me in for a chat in his front parlour, which was dark and poorly lit with filtered light through the windows. From the inside, I could see the windows were dressed in multiple layers of curtains and blinds. The interior atmosphere and lighting were positively out of a Dickens novel, and in my twisted logic, I thought I was standing before Miss Havisham from Great Expectations. He turned on a lamp so we could see better, and he invited me to take a seat on his dusty old vintage chesterfield. He sheepishly introduced himself as Bruce Bushey.

About ten minutes into our conversation, he informed me that he was originally from Boston and had recently moved to New York City to do non-profit legal work for the Ford Foundation. He informed me that he had purchased this historical Federal-style house and admitted that it was in great disrepair and in dire need of renovation at some point in the future. And he mentioned that it never occurred to him that his house was ready for any long-term guests. However, once he discovered I was an aspiring interior designer and enrolled in graduate studies around the corner at Pratt

Institute, he was curious to know what I thought about the potential of his home, and we found common ground.

Following our preliminary chat, he gave me a tour of the three floors. The first floor had a typical layout of a very long and wide front parlour and interconnecting dining room. Both rooms were anchored with a greyish white, marble fireplace as the central focus, and at the end of the entrance corridor, there was a large kitchen with a triple- locked and heavily secured back door leading out to an overground and littered backyard not suitable for use. The second floor was essentially Bruce's private domain; it contained an interconnecting set of private rooms off the corridor, which acted as the master suite for himself and his partner *Brian*, who would stay over on weekends. The entire house had only one bathroom, situated outside his bedroom suite and located at the far end of the hall off the top of the stairs. We then moved up to the third floor, which housed two very large and unoccupied bedrooms and a small storage room located at the far end of the stairs. The best feature of the bedroom facing onto Washington Avenue was the unique historical *eyebrow windows* that you could see when you looked up from the street. The back bedroom featured larger rect-angular-paned windows that faced out to the yard and onto some abandoned burnt-out buildings that appeared to be occupied by squatters between other habitable and functioning low-rise apartments.

In my mind, I had put two and two together and realized that of all the doors in New York to blindly knock on, the odds were one in ten million that it would be the private residence of another gay man. At the end of the house tour, Bruce said that he would talk with his partner Brian and that I could drop by sometime the next day to confirm whether he might be able to rent me out a room on his third floor.

The next morning, following a quick breakfast at the *Pratt Diner*, I headed back to 359 Washington Avenue and Bruce welcomed me inside with a deli-cate handshake and his verbal consent to allow me to move in. He was not sure what to charge me, and what he'd settled on was embarrassingly low and perfect for me: just $50 a week. Not only that, but he also mentioned that his partner Brian was out at this very moment buying a new adjustable draft-ing desk and chair for my room! I was blown away by his kind nature and unexpected generosity. I could not believe my good fortune and felt like I had a guardian angel watching out for me. A few hours later, I returned with my luggage. Brian arrived back at the house, and I was introduced to him.

Nowadays, Brian might be described as a young Denzel Washington, with sparkling eyes and the most beautiful smile. When he opened his mouth, I was instantly knocked over by his dazzling white teeth that would put any toothpaste commercial and model to shame. Further, I found myself a home in Brooklyn with an interracial gay couple. I couldn't have written a better script if I tried. I swear it pays not to over-plan and research. Sometimes, it just paid to fly by the seat of my pants and think outside the box.

I soon discovered my neighbourhood vacillated between classic New York brownstones interspersed with several private schools and some small apartment buildings out back of the house with a large tenement housing project out front and one block over. The dominant population of the community was Black, with pockets of nearby shared flats of white and foreign exchange students. We were all economically challenged as a shared common denominator. I guess you could say we were all in the same economically stressed boat, for the most part. In a peculiar kind of way, my dodgy neighbourhood of Fort Greene was very familiar to my Cabbagetown memories and life on Skid Row in Toronto. A neighbourhood of contrast and contradiction on the cusp of gentrification.

Later at the Pratt Diner I met *Chris Clarke* (aka Crystal Barbie) who told me about that poor Irish descendant like us grew up on the rougher streets up in the Bronx, and like myself, he was now at Pratt studying fine arts. He lived nearby, just one block down the street from me. We would become even closer when we discovered that he knew Gary Laswell (aka Dolores), who I met and began dating in early October after stopping in for a drink in the West Village at *Boots and Saddles* on Christopher Street. Ironically, Gary's best friend was John Byington (aka Spring), the man who Crystal Barbie was dating. Small world in a big city—who would have thought!

When I enrolled for my classes at Pratt, I received transfer credits for several electives from both the University of Manitoba and York University. Even still, I was trying to figure out how to expedite my studies, as I knew my money would be short. So, I walked into the office of the Graduate Interiors Program and initially registered with the chair, Harold Leeds, for a full load of courses, minus the courses I was exempted from. Afterward, I walked into a second office and registered for another set of electives spread over two semesters. No one in the two separate offices was aware that I had just registered to take the equivalent of two semesters in one term.

Afterward, I went over to pay my tuition with the official school registrar, William (Bill) Novak, who was at a special registration centre temporarily set up in the phys-ed building at the far end of the "field." Bill smiled at me with a wink and a nod, and when he discovered I had just arrived from Canada he told me he would like to take me out for coffee later.

When he looked at my department-approved courses, he mentioned I had accidentally registered for too many scheduled classes in one term. I explained to him that I could handle it and that I could not afford to stay any longer than necessary to complete my required course work before starting my thesis. So, he made an exception for me, and I was now set to complete all my coursework excluding studio in one semester. By the end of the first term, when I showed Harold my full year of completed coursework after just one term with well-above-average grades, he looked like I had dropped a house on him! He had no choice but to let me proceed with my thesis in the second semester, and I could tell he was not amused. Permission was granted, and he assigned himself and architect Martha as my chief advisors.

Meanwhile, the registrar, Bill Novak, who had originally taken me out for coffee sometime in the first week of classes, continued asking me out for lunches and we found ourselves developing a good friendship.

Throughout both terms I would get to know Bill and his partner, Norman McArthur, who was a house manager for the nearby Brooklyn Academy of Music (BAM). They both lived in a beautiful Prospect Park brownstone with a magnificent back yard. The perimeter of the yard was tastefully landscaped with a variety of lush vegetation and there was a footpath that went over a tiny stream that led to a koi pond. In the centre of the yard there was a stone patio for outdoor dining, with ambient twinkling lights that were integrated into the tree branches and surrounding landscaping. It really was reminiscent of a miniature model of *Tavern on the Green* in Central Park. Both men were gracious hosts with fascinating stories and experiences to share. They seemed to love mentoring me with their wealth of cultural knowledge and interest in local art, music, and theatre. I was all in, hook, line, and sinker! At the risk of getting Bill in trouble for fraternizing with the students, I kept our weekly rituals and relationship confidential from my other classmates.

In addition to inviting me as a regular guest for lunch at some of the quiet gems and restaurants that were favoured by the local cognoscenti around Clinton Hill, both Bill and I shared a love of Broadway. So, when Norman was busy working at BAM, Bill would take me as his theatre companion to Broadway for matinee performances when he could escape for "an extended long lunch," as he would tell his staff. One of the first shows that Bill took me to see was the recently premiered musical *NINE*, and we both absolutely loved the show! We left the theatre singing the catchy tune *"Be Italian,"* the very same song that Fergie from the Black-Eyed Peas would sing decades later in the movie version starring Daniel Day-Lewis.

Toward the end of my last semester at Pratt, I wrapped up my thesis report and my final design proposal for a hypothetical hearing-impaired group habitat located in Toronto and entitled The High Centre. As part of my research on whimsical post-modern atmospherics, I decided to head over to Manhattan and visit the 1979 post-modern SUNAR furniture showroom on Park Avenue, designed by Canadian Michael Graves. Inside the showroom, I struck up a conversation with the sales manager, Gil Weatherly. At some point in our conversation, he asked me what my plans were after graduation, and I mentioned that I would love to take advantage of my visa opportunity to work for a year, but with the slow recovery from an economic recession, it was impossible to get a foot in the door. He mentioned that he had just come from Swanke Hayden Connell Architects up the street and that he had talked with Richard Carlson, who was the partner in charge of the Interiors Department. He told me it wouldn't hurt me to give him a call, and he offered me a courtesy phone in his office. I called the reception at Swanke, and when the receptionist asked how she could redirect my call, I told her that it was a personal call for Richard Carlson. I was then transferred to his executive assistant. When she answered, I mentioned that a good friend of Richard's had suggested I come in for a personal visit, and she set me up with an appointment. That was how I got my foot in the back door that eventually led to an employment offer.

I recall mentioning to Bill that I was to be interviewed the following week for at position at *Swanke Hayden Connell Architects* in Midtown Manhattan at 450 Park Avenue. As a graduation present, Bill insisted that he was going to dress me from head toe as if I were Joe from *Sunset Boulevard* and he was my Norma Desmond, lavishing outrageously kind gifts to transform me into the semblance of a more professional image. He whisked me off to Brooks Brothers in Midtown Manhattan and insisted I dress for Upper East Side success, gifting me a camel-coloured trench coat, grey flannels, and a pale-blue prima cotton button-down preppie shirt with a coordinating tie in diagonal stripes to complement a new dark-navy gabardine jacket. I was flushed with how much he lavished on me. And lest I forget, he also purchased me a pair of dress shoes, considering I only owned sneakers and construction boots. He was truly a one-of-a-kind gentleman from the old school of gay patronage and support.

Honestly, I was speechless from his generosity and friendship at the time. He'd made an indelible place in my heart. I had never asked or expected anything other than his friendship, and I felt a little remorse that I couldn't have been equally as generous to him in my youthful past. No question he felt sad that nobody was coming from my family to celebrate my graduation, so he remarked that he wanted to step in and honour my achievement as part of his gay family of friends. By this point I was kind of used to being a *lone wolf.*

The day of my interview at Swanke there had been a major snowstorm that shut down Manhattan. Meanwhile, another friend of mine, *Margaret,* who had been my first boss at WZMH Architects in Toronto, alerted me a few weeks earlier that she was coming to New York to celebrate the completion of my graduate degree in Interior Design. I offered to host her in the spare bedroom next to me in my Brooklyn residence, after I cleared it with my landlord Bruce. I was so excited to see her that I procured tickets for us to see the amazing Betty Buckley star in the Broadway musical of *Cats.* And if my memory serves me well, we had to walk over the Brooklyn Bridge, as traffic was at a complete stop because of the blizzard conditions.

Margaret emphasized that she was there to champion my scholarly success. However, I had gotten quite used to being my own best company and expected nothing from others when it came to acknowledging my personal accomplishments. The attention made me feel quite self-conscious, but I appreciated it, nonetheless. Margaret had a big heart and wanted to make a big deal over my academic success and flew in from British Columbia! And I must admit, she made me feel quite honoured in a way I had not felt since my grade-eight graduation performance as Charlie Brown. She was another life anchor who believed in me and was a remarkable soul in my life journey.

She stayed by my side as we went to my interview on Park Avenue. Margaret was a great distraction, but I was also a little embarrassed by the fact that it was only an interview and that I might not get a job offer. In the reception lounge, Margaret waited as I was dispatched to my interview with the partner, Richard (Dick) Carlson. En route to see him, I began to feel a little anxious and nauseated. Mr. Carlson's office was located on an executive floor higher up, and I was asked to sit on a two-seater leather sofa adjacent to his office. In front of me there were highly reflective and tinted windows. Honestly, at the time I simply thought I was sitting adjacent to mirrors to visually enhance the space.

When Mr. Carlson came to his doorway and beckoned me in, I could instantly see that he had a clear view out to the sofa where I was sitting. I'm sure I could feel beads of sweat forming on my forehead. Anyhow, after a pleasantly formal handshake and introduction, he asked to look at my portfolio, contained in a small 8.5" X 11" book format. Without a word, he picked it up and flipped through the pages like you would a paperback novel from beginning to end. Without saying a word, he turned to the last page of my portfolio where I had included a watercolour, I had done on Fire Island the previous summer. I don't know why it was there, to be quite honest, and it was obviously very gay, with the image of the men on the beach wearing sexy swimsuits and suntanning in front of the sand dunes and the boardwalk behind. For a moment, I felt a little self-conscious from the silence. When he finally looked up at me, Mr. Carlson said something to me that I'll always remember.

"Michael," he said. "I have met and interviewed a lot of people over the years, and I must tell you this is the first time I can recall anyone who has shown me something more than design strengths and technical abilities in their portfolio of work." He informed me that I was the first person to convey an "artistic biography" of who I represented as an individual, and not simply what I could do for his company. And he seemed surprisingly impressed as he told me to expect a call from Claudia, who was the head of the human resources department. "I am going to ask her to specifically create a position for you, and I want to welcome you in advance to our company, young man!"

I was apoplectic as I shook his hand and mumbled my appreciation, thanking him for the opportunity to work at Swanke.

In a haze, I rode the elevator back down to Margaret, who was waiting in the main public reception area. I walked over and collapsed in the leather lounge chair next to her. She whispered to me, "How did it go?"

It took me a moment as I choked back my stress-released tears, and then I told her, "I think I just landed a job in one of the top architectural firms in Manhattan." We both stood up and she gave me one of the best bearhugs I had ever received in my life!

Sure enough, two days later, I followed up with a phone call made from Mike's corner diner at Hall Street and DeKalb Avenue. When I was put through to *Claudia Moore,* she said to me, "Well, you must have done something to impress Mr. Carlson because we are not hiring, but he insisted on making an exception for you, so let's get you in here to discuss the offer and set up all the necessary paperwork, ASAP." And the offer was accepted, signed, and sealed within the week! My professional career in Manhattan was about to start.

Manhattan View *from Brooklyn Heights*

My Brooklyn Home *at 359 Washington Ave.*

Lunch on Christopher Street *with my Pratt Institute friend Sandy Winter.*

14

SWANKE

The Interior Design Department at Swanke Hayden Connell Architects occupied several floors in their flagship 450 Park Avenue location in Midtown Manhattan. Swanke was extremely busy, with over 300 employees working around the clock. My very first interior design assignment in the Interiors Department was to provide some planning and design development for an executive suite at *Prudential Bache* down on Wall Street and overlooking the Brooklyn Bridge. In addition, the senior designer for the project asked me to custom design some high-end executive office furniture. I was handed a design precedent he had done when he worked at Gwathmey Siegel & Associates. I was instructed to do a higher-end knock-off of his original and uninspired design. I speculated that perhaps this was the reason he was now working at Swanke. I became bored with his design ethos and disenchanted with his fly-by-the-seat-of-his-pants leadership style.

You name it and I volunteered to do anything to avoid the tedium of sitting at my board under his twitchy old eye, the whiff of his arrogance in the air. On many occasions, I would head a couple floors down to the newly installed beta test site for Calcomp Computers, consisting of ten CADD stations in an open bullpen with a secured, temperature-controlled room for the electrostatic ink-pen-plotter machine. The new technology and scale of the projects they were working on was staggering at the time, and I was enthralled and fascinated. I spent time chatting up the CADD director, who erroneously thought I was a new architect hire. I dropped by daily for about a week, before and after my normal workday and frequently on my lunch and coffee breaks. At one point, the CADD director asked me if I would like to be trained, as he was just about to send a small group of four over for a week of training in New Jersey. I said yes, and with Richard Carlson's blessing, I quit the conventional Interiors Department and old-fashion drafting boards to join the architectural CADD team at Swanke.

There was a short but very intensive week of training and plenty of homework that kept me occupied in the evenings. At the end of the week, I went from being a trainee to an alleged CADD expert armed with a massively thick white instructional manual for troubleshooting, and it contained everything I could possibly require as my personal working reference. I was then dispatched back to Swanke and purportedly ready to operate on CADD with minimal supervision and guidance. As a secondary back-up, I had a twenty-four-hour toll-free number for support in California, but the team I worked with enthusiastically problem-solved and collaborated daily. We pretty much handled all our troubleshooting inhouse.

There were three shifts on CADD: the first was a typical 9 to 5/ Monday-Friday; the second shift that I joined operated from 11:00 a.m. to 11:00 p.m./ Monday-Wednesday and a half-day on Thursday; and the third shift worked from 12:00 p.m. to 2:00 a.m./Friday-Sunday. The first project I was asked to jump in and assist with was the behemoth 1 million square foot interiors project, from the total 2.2 million gross square feet available in the new *American Express Headquarters* situated in Battery Park. The building was managed by the international property development firm of Toronto-based Olympia & York and was the largest commission the company had on its roster at the time. In addition to the base building drawings and interior layouts, I worked in tandem with Knoll on new customized furniture standards for the private executive offices, partition walls, and the open-office furniture systems for American Express.

I would always arrive to work fifteen minutes early to review whatever progress had been made on the earlier shift and before the 11:00 a.m. pass-off.

The scope and magnitude of the project was precedent-setting and required immense attention to detail and accuracy. Once I acclimated to the strengths and weaknesses of the CADD operators from the other shifts, I had a much better concept of what to expect. It could be there might be little to no progress, and other times there would be extensive progress. Many of us were working on more than one project concurrently, and each project was considered a priority. CADD designers and operators required the highest level of time management. As my dear old friend Jan Sheffield from Toronto would say, "Busy hands are happy hands!" And she was right, there was no time to be idle and act bored.

The shift that I was detailed to was comprised of six colleagues under the age of thirty-five. We all worked in deafening silence and wore headphones that were plugged into our *Sony Walkman* cassettes. As a company perk at the end of each night, I would charge back my dinner to an expense account and receive a chit for a limousine home. Although some of my colleagues preferred to eat at their workstation, Gina, Cynthia, and I would physically take a respite from our workstations and head over to a few private tables and lounge chairs situated by the east wall of windows and overlooking the evening skyline onto Park Avenue. As a small group, we agreed we needed a moment to socially relax and gossip about the latest goings-on around the office and in our personal lives.

Gina was a fashionable, gregarious Hispanic colleague who was proud of her heritage and food; she introduced my virgin Canadian tastebuds to plantain maduros, which were fried sweet, caramelized plantains with a custardy interior. They were so addictive that I regularly ordered them as a side to anything I ordered for take-out. Gina was one of these colleagues that always wore a heartfelt smile, and she had a wicked sense of humour to boot. She reminded me of my Glucksman twins from my dorm days back at York University. Occasionally, we would socialize outside the office with our mutual gay friend and colleague, Tony Law. I found my tribe in a firm of 300 employees, and they just so happened to work alongside me or closely nearby. What a blessing that was.

On the opposite side of the spectrum, my other regular dinner companion was the enigmatic and shy Cynthia Shubert, who always dressed conservatively in Laura Ashley dresses in small floral prints. She didn't really reflect the stylish way most designers dressed but this is what made her unique and stand out.

She wore minimal to no make-up and brushed her natural blonde hair into a ponytail. Sometimes she would let her hair down and brush it back like she had just stepped out of a TV commercial for Breck shampoo. However, as I discovered in the wee hours of a random morning during a cab ride home from a club, I saw an entirely other side to Cynthia quite by accident. My car had stopped at a red light in her Chelsea neighbourhood. When I looked out my window I saw "Miss Cynthia" walking home in spandex leggings, heels, and a flirty top like she was Olivia Newton John from the 1978 movie Grease. And much to my surprise, she was wearing heavy make-up and smoking a Winston Light cigarette.

Who would have imagined there was a dazzling side to this preppy young lady from work? Anyhow, with my arm hanging out the open window and dangling a *Winston* cigarette of my own, I made a shout-out to Cynthia for her to come over for a second, which caught her off guard. We had just enough time to exchange comments that we both were returning from a night out. She was cordial and wasted no time in requesting a "tiny favour" to keep this part of her personal life private from the office. Unfazed, I told her that it was no big deal. And as the light turned green, I mentioned that I hoped she had a fun night out and not to worry! "See you at work," I said.

Cynthia was rumoured to be from a family of wealth and privilege; she was allegedly connected to the famous *Shubert Theatre* family and was purported to have been hired through her family connections, which made perfect sense to me. After all, it was only her and I who were not architects or architectural technicians working in the CADD department. From that point on, Cynthia and I grew a little closer and shared a conspiratorial wink as other colleagues would chit-chat about their weekend escapades. Her response was always something innocuous like she went to a movie or a family visit to Connecticut; nothing provocative or too revealing. And I would smile back at her as if I didn't know any better.

At some random point, Cynthia and I ended up connecting on separate personal visits up to Toronto. I was up for a three-day visit to renew my visa while Cynthia was up for a one-week vacation to see her sister and brother-in-law. As I recall, I believe he may have recently been relocated as a chief executive officer for *Texaco Gas*. Out of mutual boredom and curiosity during our stay in the great white north, she invited me to cab-ride up to where she was staying for lunch. Her sister and brother-in-law's grand house were located at the end of a verdant street of mansions. It was a revealing confirmation and glimpse into Cynthia's privileged lifestyle and background. Moreover, it was interesting to see how the multi-generational elite live with a retinue of household staff that caters to their whims and needs! This was their everyday reality. Up to then, I had no evidence of the rumours circulating around the office of her "rich family." She was always very humble and modest at work in her dressed-down kind of Little House on The Prairie attire and unpretentious comportment.

After the long weekend, I returned to Manhattan and resumed my corporate design life at Swanke. Shortly thereafter, while standing next to the office receptionist, I inadvertently discovered the numerical key-pad code for the telephone intercom that she used to blast out periodic announcements to the entire office. Later that night when everyone was gone for the day (precluding the CADD team), I decided to test out the amplification code by holding the headphones to my Sony Walkman close to the receiver. My new favourite song at the time was *It's Raining Men* by the Weather Girls. After I giddily punched in the intercom code, the song blasted throughout the floors. I didn't half-expect it to work quite so well! Anyhow, everyone who was in the office roared in laughter, which broke down the typical office monotony for a fleeting moment. I only did it that one time and never again; I knew I could pass it off as a one-time accident and I sure as hell was not going to risk losing my job over a disco tune.

However, later that same week there was an even more egregious and unprofessional situation that involved my poor judgement. It happened when I was working late in the CADD department, sometime after eight o'clock on the Wednesday night. I was working at the CADD station farthest away from the windows and adjacent to the main interior circulation corridor, just outside the main reception. My desk was near a large conference room earmarked exclusively for the partners and their VIP clients. Earlier in the day and before the room was cleaned, a few of us had gone into the conference room to rummage around for leftover food and alcoholic beverages. Afterward, we came back with a stash of various goodies and a few beers and stuffed them into our personal filing cabinets until everyone had left for the day.

It was after 8:00mp.m. and the last day of my weekly shift, so I figured I could get a bit "swacked." I took a bump of coke that was offered to me from another colleague in the washroom. I had completely forgotten that an hour earlier I had also popped a prescribed *Didrex* diet pill and chased it down with a cold bottle of Heineken. "Dr. Didrex" was recommended to me by my best friend Randy McGee (Doll). Neither of us were obese nor even overweight. We used the pills for an occasional energy boost as required. And as "Dr. Didrex" was an unscrupulous and notorious doctor, and we knew of his reputation for pushing pills for profit from his Upper East Side office at Third and 71.st We both knew the prescription for the pills would be ridiculously easy to secure but challenging to get filled. Most pharmacists were aware of this doctor's scam business of pushing pills.

Anyone who knew me then and knows me now understands that I am an early morning person. I knew in advance on that Wednesday night shift that I was going out after work to a new after-hours gay club in Chelsea, featuring a new mural by artist Keith Haring. Clearly, I needed options other than coffee to make it through the long night ahead. I couldn't survive without bringing along some pills from Dr. Didrex.

Meanwhile, I was at my CADD station, buzzing higher than a kite and trying hard to focus on my screen monitor. I had my feet propped up on the desk return, gulping a beer and incessantly rubbing my blurry eyes. I was so intensely focussed on the monitor that I thought I was starting to hallucinate! On top of the wireframe images of the floorplate displayed on the screen, I swear I could see an apparition of a well-groomed gentleman standing inside my computer! And that's when I said to myself, "OMG! that's it; I am cutting myself off! No more booze and pills nor any other recreational pharmaceuticals at work, ever again!" Anyhow, before I could grasp the reality of the situation, I felt someone tapping my right shoulder from behind. As I removed my headphones and turned back to look, I realized instantly that it was clearly not a hallucination! In fact, the reflected image in my monitor was the partner, *Richard Carlson*, standing behind me. I thought to myself, *okay*, this is a moment of reckoning and I am about to be fired!

But then Mr. Carlson surprised me when he quietly leaned in and said, "Michael, I need your help in the large conference room, so pull yourself together, put on your jacket and come in and join me." Like a bat out of hell, I sobered up and ran off to the nearest washroom, threw cold water on my face, and slapped myself silly to wake up. I straightened out my disheveled clothes, put on my tie that was stored inside the filing cabinet, returned to my desk, and grabbed my blazer from the back of my chair. With my split-second transformation, I cautiously marched off to the conference room without any knowledge of what to expect. Surely, he would have called me to his office if he was going to fire me?

I had totally not anticipated that Mr. Carlson apparently assumed I spoke French, from my bilingual last name, and he knew that I was from Canada, a country world-renowned for its Anglophone and Francophone citizens. When I cautiously entered the room, I instantly saw that it was packed with French-speaking delegates from Paris who had flown in to meet about the progress of the renovation of *The Statue of Liberty* project, which we had just started to be transferred onto CADD. For a brief second, I was so caught off guard that I had to stop myself from checking to make sure my pant zipper was pulled up; I didn't know where to look with my eyes nor what to do with my hands, so I just clutched them in front of my groin like a complete and utter fool.

Mr. Carlson tried to explain to everyone that the interpreter had not shown up, and since the French delegates were not conversant in English, he hoped that one of his international staff members from Canada could fill in as an ad hoc interpreter. And then he introduced me and asked me up to the podium. I thought, oh, my sweet Jesus, I am so screwed! While trying to think fast on my feet, one of the lead delegates started a running dissertation in French with his surrounding colleagues, and I suspect it was not flattering comments that they were saying about me! Given the lukewarm reception, I assessed the drama unfolding and raised my upheld hand to gesture for silence. I told our guests in rudimentary French and with accompanying dramatic gestures that I was con-versant in *Quebecois* and found it challenging to follow in their quickly spoken Parisian French (which was a big fat lie).

Mercifully, at just that precise moment, wouldn't you just know the tardy interpreter walked into the conference room like my guardian angel, ready to extricate me from Dante Alighieri's Inferno and the Gates of Hell! My immedi-ate thought was to fall on my knees and kiss his feet in gratitude, but I thought it would be wiser not to encourage my penchant for the dramatic. I realized that I had already experienced enough drama for one day! So, I "merci'd and au revoir'd" my sweating testicles out of the conference room as fast as my feet would allow and headed back to my station with my proverbial devil's tail tucked between my legs.

Ironically, the following week I ran into Mr. Carlson, and he thanked me for my emergency assistance with the French delegates. He invited me to stop by his office later in the day. I discovered he considered my design talent and interpersonal skills could be more effectively exploited by working part-time with him on marketing interior design job proposals and competitions and that this could lead to a promotion to senior interior if everything worked out. I was truly flabbergasted. I had no educational background or expertise in marketing but evidentially he saw a "spark" in me and wanted to mentor me in a new area, working alongside of him. He suggested I take a few weeks to wean myself off CADD and allow time for the department manager to recruit and train a suitable replacement for me. I was elated! I had desperately missed designing, and I missed engaging with clients directly. He asked me to be discreet and to keep this discussion between us for the moment, as he further developed and strategized the details about how this would all unfold.

It was hard to believe that within the first six months, I had moved from a position of junior obscurity in a sea of employees to potentially working directly with the partner who oversaw all the interior designers. And as a visa-sponsored Canadian, I was a foreigner to boot! Not only did I avert a disaster that night, courtesy of my theatre background, but I'd also garnered the favourable attention of Mr. Carlson. My future at Swanke looked very promising, and I was moving exponentially up the corporate ladder through sheer luck and good fortune. I was a quick study and in the right place at the right time.

And guess what else I did: I stopped drinking and consuming energy-enhancing drugs at work, no surprise there! I had too much invested with my career on the line, and I was elated to be returning to the normal nine-to-five-day shift. My natural adrenaline was pumped as I quietly went about my day-to-day business in the CADD department, sporting a grin from ear to ear.

A week later I received a call from my old friend and nationally acclaimed interior designer, Bob Ledingham, from Vancouver, Canada. We had originally met when I was a fourth-year student at the University of Manitoba three years earlier when he had been invited to give a guest lecture in our *professional development* class. After the class, we met up for a drink and hooked up for a one-night stand in his room at Winnipeg's *NorthStar Inn*. Anyhow, he was currently in New York on business, and he wanted to know if he could take me out to dinner on Saturday night. And the following Tuesday, Bob planned on getting two tickets for the new Broadway show *Lena Horne – the Lady and the Legend*. Of course, I jumped at his kind offers. In reciprocation, I asked if he had any time to drop by Swanke for a personal tour, as I knew he would be curious about the architectural Calcomp computers beta-test site at Swanke.

It was never Bob's personality to be animated or overconfident in his personal interactions, but he quickly responded with, "I would love to!"

The following mid-afternoon, Bob showed up to my office and I met him out in the main reception area where I was dressed in my typical navy blazer, khaki pants, and a fresh, sparkling-white shirt that was accented with an avant-garde graphic tie I'd recently picked up for a budget-friendly price at Century 21 on 9 East Broadway in the financial district of Manhattan. Now Bob, on the other hand, was always impeccably and expensively dressed albeit a tad conservative. He conveyed a regal air about him in his everyday natural comportment; his standard look consisted of a French double-breasted jacket in dark navy in a mid-weight European gaberdine fabric. He wore ecru-coloured gaberdine dress pants and tasseled loafers. The pièce de résistance is that he carried a European leather-zipped pocketbook that my male colleagues referred to as his "man-purse." They did not realize that their Canadian neighbours to the north and British expats had acclimated to this European trend years earlier. Many heads in the office followed us around with their eyes as I shepherded Bob throughout three floors of the office.

As I proceeded to show Bob around, I am pretty sure that some of the folks were beginning to speculate about some allegations about behind-the-scenes manoeuvres of Mr. Carlson and an emerging new role for myself. All I could think is that someone in the CADD department must have let the cat out of the bag that I would be shortly leaving the department. Certainly, I had made my closest colleagues know that I would be returning sometime back to the drawing boards in the interior design department. But no one, including myself, understood any of the details as to when and where this would happen. And now everyone was seeing me tour the office with what many suspected was a new client.

I walked around with authority and a whiff of mystery. Throughout our walkabout, nobody stopped to ask where I was going or who I was with; everyone smiled when I opened the doors to various conference and meeting rooms to peek inside. I was so very new that only a few people outside the CADD department recognized me. I assume the onlookers thought Bob must be important and not merely one of the typical showroom vendors who would drop by and hock their latest furnishing and textiles to the interior designers and architects.

My best friend at Swanke and one of my all-time favourite people was a former classmate from Pratt. Maureen Cornwell was the only employee who was aware of Bob Ledingham as my friend and understood the reason he was touring the office was simply personal. On the previous day I had mentioned to her in confidence that Bob Leadingham was someone important in my recent past and a fellow alumnus from the University of Manitoba. I made her aware that he was regarded as a national interior design treasure in Canada. I considered him an instant friend from the moment I first slept with him at his hotel room, when he euphemistically baptized me into his personal world with a spritz from his signature scent, Eau Sauvage. We continued to cross paths and build on our friendship. His impending visit to Swanke was a testament to our curious and mutual admiration.

He'd never lost his connections from the University of Manitoba and frequently he sat on external advisory boards. Many of the faculty invited Bob as a perennial guest to a variety of classes, including *Professional Practice*. He was a friend to many of the tenured faculty and particularly fond of Professor Grant Marshall.

Due to Bob's mature age and public persona, I always thought he might be a tad stuffy. However, I soon discovered I couldn't discount his shy nature and how well he responded to my occasional subversive personality. It was almost as though he vicariously drooled over my peccadillos and seemingly accidental blessings of good luck. During our tour around my office, I quietly requested his confidence as I updated him on some of the private negotiations that were happening with one of the partners and myself. In response, Bob chuckled and said he agreed that I had "endless horseshoes up my ass," as many other of our mutual acquaintances have always suggested. And being the quick-witted fool I could sometimes be, I humorously responded by saying, "Well, you know, Bob, a pretty young girl has got to do what a girl must do in order to climb out of the dark gutters from her past." And on that note, Bob and I mutually decided to take a quick washroom break before we wet our pants in a fit of laughter.

As we entered the restroom, I checked under the stalls to see if the washroom was empty, and we were free to talk. There were company eyes and ears everywhere, and through my CADD colleagues, I learned it was best to always check. As Bob pulled up to the urinal alongside of me, I decided I needed to put an exclamation point on my previous outside remark by quietly singing, "I don't really think I need the reasons why I won't succeed, I haven't started…"

in tribute to Patti LuPone from *Evita*. With my unexpected outburst into song, I noticed that Bob had clearly peed a few drops onto his pristine pants! He quickly took out his hanky to wipe his watering eyes from his stifled laughter. I thought to myself, *Bingo*! Michael, you got him to break character! Afterward, we parted with huge grins on both our faces and confirmed our plan to meet up the following Saturday night in the "Big Apple."

Saturday came quickly, and I met up with him at the *Plaza Hotel,* where he was residing as a guest. His suite overlooked Central Park, and as we stood admiring the spectacular view, he mentioned that he had made early dinner reservations at *Sardis* on West 44th and Broadway. So, after a quick cocktail in the room, we headed out and walked just a few short blocks south to the famous Manhattan landmark and restaurant. It was a little over the top in every best conceivable way, and it was like stepping back into Russian history.

Afterward, we decided we were going to continue our night out. I promised Bob that I would take him to the legendary and exclusively gay club The Saint, which served as an elite entertainment venue from the constant drumbeat of queer marginalization and workplace discrimination outside. Beforehand, we both wanted to change our clothes into something more casual. Bob went back to his hotel to change into a pair of blue jeans and a polo shirt and sporting tasseled loafers and a light fall jacket. I went home to the West Village to dress down in something more serviceable and fitting for *The Saint*: blue jeans, a t-shirt, and my signature bandanna rolled and tied around my neck.

Bob met up with me at my Barrow Street apartment so we could have one final cocktail before we headed out. In addition, it gave Bob an opportunity to check out my West Village digs, which he had expressed great curiosity and interest in seeing. Afterward, we walked up Christopher Street so I could hit the Citibank ATM at Sheridan Square. Bob stood by looking at an Andy Warhol lithograph of Marsha P. Johnson in the shop window next to the bank. I made a mental note to talk about Miss Marsha at the club. But first, we had to grab the empty cab that was stopped at the corner on a red light. Once inside the car, I requested the driver take us over to the East Village and drop us off at *The Saint*; no address was necessary. This was the ultimate gay disco and private members club frequented by hot, privileged gay white boys with disposable income who were looking to party hard and dance all night. It made Studio 54 look like an old veteran's club in comparison.

The club had a circular dance floor under a planetarium-like dome. In the centre of the floor there was an incredible technological hydraulic structural base that housed a phenomenally large and heavy steel capsule, punctuated with pin-point laser lights that shot out as it spun around. Meanwhile, there was another scaffolding-type structure that housed spinning rotating lights with interchangeable coloured gels. The technological wizardry at the centre of the dance floor base would mechanically rise very slowly to the underside top of a planetarium scrim, above. If you didn't want to dance and only wanted to observe members, you could ascend one of the two circular stairs outside the dance floor that flanked the edges of the dome. At the top of the stairs, there was a viewing gallery above the dome, and you could look down below like saintly angels looking down to earth. It was a voyeuristic trip to the heavens above. Behind the gallery were several remaining rows of original seats from the nosebleed section of the original Filmore Theatre; the very last place where one of my favourite singers, Janis Joplin, last performed in New York City.

The old East Side *Fillmore Theatre* had been converted into this mega-technological and architectural phenom. *The Saint* opened in 1980 and was conveniently located just around the corner from New York's swankiest bath-house, *St. Marks*, where I had periodically crashed in Manhattan when I had lived in Brooklyn as a student. I think Bob's eyes almost fell out of his head as we checked our light jackets at one of the several automated coat checks (like you would see at a dry cleaner); this was where guests who were not members were screened and checked in. Members, on the other hand, had their own private locker room at the back of the house and up a flight of stairs; this ensured privacy and shelter of the members personal stashes of recreational party favours and a place to store a fresh change of clothes (for the end of the night). Membership came with privileges! And discretion was the biggest privilege of all.

Many of us who were not private members would strip down right at the non-member check-in and change into whatever dance drag and accessories we'd brought. Most of us wore blue jeans and went shirtless, with our t-shirts tucked into the back of our belts. But then there were those special-event nights with themes like "the *Black party*" (mostly leather), Fetish parties, and the Fire Island *White parties* (which often required a knapsack and a change of clothes to store at the coat check). However, tonight with Bob in tow, it was just a typical Saturday night at *The Saint,* without any recreational accoutrements.

For the first couple of years of operation, guests would enter the first-floor lounge and find a dramatic long ramp and runway, so you could model your ass up to the back industrial stairs, which then led up to the planetarium dome for dancing. There were several stacked modular, carpet-wrapped cubes that you could rest or pass out on. The surrounding main-floor lounges allowed perfect visual access to all the new arrivals entering the ramp. The bars were adorned with spectacular flower arrangements rivaling any of the glorious arrangements at the *Four Seasons Hotel,* and probably costing just as much, if not more. I am sure The Saint had connections to many of Manhattan's most talented "flower fairies," as we lovingly referred to back in the day.

Meanwhile, up on the next level, New York's finest gym bunnies danced shirtless, showing off their pumped-up bodies. Everyone was high as a kite except for me and Bob, and they were ready to pull shade in a heartbeat if we were not on the right side of their altered state of reality and radar. On the dance floor, the "A list men" were beyond spectacular with their million-dollar physiques, while other meth'd-out, skinny-assed queens performed as the most amazingly talented fan dancers around the periphery of the dance floor. And somewhere in between was a mass of gorgeous men dancing under the influence of party favours and poppers. A few of the elite with access could be found openly chomping down on ethyl-chloride-soaked rags. Invariably, random dancers like myself would be invited to chew down on the rag with them. And once you tasted the impact of "ethyl," it was hard to go back to sniffing poppers. Oh my God, biting down on those rags was a liquid freeze on the lips and an-out-of-body experience. "Memories, like the corners of my mind, twisted coloured memories of the world we left behind…" Snap! And I'm back. Anyhow, back in the day, I lived to defy the rules outside work; I was reasonably attractive, and whenever I went to The Saint, complete strangers would drop party favours into my hand or place them directly into my mouth through a kiss on the lips and the slip of their tongue. It was all very high-risk, I suppose, but it was heavenly ecstasy, regardless.

Tonight, I was the tour guide for Bob Ledingham and so I stuck to cold beer…well, that is, until after he left! As usual, the serious party boys I recognized danced nearby with their dilated pupils, while rubbing continuously at their dried-out eyes. As I explained to Bob, my personal clique always carried a small bottle of Visine as a prophylactic in our jean's coin pocket. Every time we hit the washroom; we would routinely refresh our eyes on our way out.

My personal clique consisted of my best friend *Randy McGee* (aka "Doll," from Birmingham, Alabama) and *Chris Clark* (aka "Crystal Barbie," from the Bronx) and myself, who Randy referred to as either "Miss Thang" or "Aunty M"—whichever name captured his mood at the time. And just like Aunty M from the Wizard of Oz, on any given night at The Saint, I took it upon myself to corral everyone and made sure we got home safely. Which normally meant everyone came back to my place for a group chill-down under my watchful supervision.

Another honorary member of our group was the legendry Stonewall queen *Miss Marsha P. Johnson,* who we would occasionally hang out with in the village bars but more frequently inside Randy's apartment. I referred to the Andy Warhol lithograph of Miss Marsha Johnson that Bob had been looking at earlier while I was at the ATM. I explained to Bob that although Miss Marsha was homeless, she frequently found shelter and slept on the Path Subway connection at the foot of Christopher Street. Sometimes, she would crash for a few hours at the apartment of my best friend "Doll," who lived on Christopher Street. She christened his matchbook-size apartment as the "Doll Bar," which also served as the name of Randy's hair salon. Inside his ground-floor apartment, Randy showcased a spectacular, mint collection of Barbie dolls in their original boxes. Miss Marsha often said that both she and Randy were "living dolls." And just like the collectible Barbies, Miss Marsha commented that "we were pretty dolls to be admired but never played with."

And of course, that's how we came up with the nickname for our friend Chris Clarke, aka "Crystal Barbie." No one messed with her Irish trigger-hair temper. On many occasions when we planned on going out for the evening, invariably we would get so "swacked" on booze and drugs while listening to tapes of music made by my boyfriend Tony Mason, who was a DJ at Kamikaze, that we never made it out. And that was fine, as Miss Marsha preferred the hospitality and comfort at the Doll Bar. For everything she had been through in her iconic life, she always remained a humble and dignified lady of the house. We all loved her and knew she was always safe inside Randy's Christopher Street apartment.

Working in an elite profession that was rife with snobbism, my friend Bob was entertained by the notion that Randy was my very best gay buddy in NYC. I shared with Bob that her favourite expression when she could never remember someone's name was "Hey, honey, how's it going?" This was Miss

Marsha's classic greeting, as well as that of my roommate Brad Wright! And when Randy caught her passing by his apartment, he would frequently pull her inside to do her hair/wigs and give her accessories and clothing that he would randomly buy to gift her. Randy said, "It's our duty to do whatever we can for the legendary West Village ambassador and national American treasure." And I couldn't agree more with him! She was the very first homeless person that I considered a friend, and I think this was just too much information for Bob to absorb. I believe Bob was not steeped in the history of the Stonewall riots until I mentioned it.

Meanwhile, I told Bob about the fact that Miss Marsha had inspired Randy and a bunch of his A-list of clients and friends to dress up as high-couture bag ladies for my Halloween party. The costumes were made from plastic bags from different shops. Randy was Miss Salvation Army, and there was also a Miss Tower Records, and a few others as I recall from the old photographs of my party.

While a few of us couldn't stich a bitch to save a life, we did our own thing. Chris Clarke did his Crystal Barbie "lewk," and I dressed up as Patsy Cline, who was both Randy's and my favourite singer at the time. Every year, I hosted a Halloween party at my apartment on Barrow Street, and when I decided the party was over and it was time to move onto The Saint, I didn't hesitate to unplug the music and turn on all the lights, saying "Time to pack up your hot rollers and leave, girls!" And Bob finally agreed that my Halloween party was something he would like to have seen.

Anyhow, the night was getting late for Bob, and he decided he would leave and cab back up to his hotel while I could hang out and wait for my friends to arrive. I walked him back to the coat check and we kissed goodbye. And then, as he walked out, I realized that I should have been more considerate and offered him some of my Visine for his blurry eyes.

I remained at *The Saint* and danced a little on my own for a bit longer and eventually met up with Doll and Crystal Barbie somewhere around two in the morning at our normal spot near the DJ booth. We partied on Randy's pharmaceuticals and closed the damn place down at noon the following day, as we frequently did! Habitually, around six a.m. or so, we would usually do a hit of "Special K" (ketamine), and Randy would turn us all into veritable Gumby and Pokey play toys as our bodies began to feel like flexible modelling clay. In anticipation of the known impact, we strategically sat at the foot of the stairs on the original grand staircase at the front of the house, blacking in and out of consciousness and oblivious to the passage of hours on end. When we regained functional consciousness, we would then head back for our favourite part of the night on the dance floor. The time for "sleaze-*down*" music finally arrived, and that's what we lived for to end our night at The Saint.

And then we would proceed to drag our skinny-ass butts around the emptying floor, shuffling to the slow rhythms and tunes while holding onto each other like a daisy chain. To most of the crowd, it signalled time to leave, but for a few of us diehards, this is what we'd waited all night for...a musical lull that would chill down our temperature and prepare us for a ride home around noon. Later, at home, I would order in our recovery breakfast from the nearby Hudson Diner, and we would listen to some personal sleaze-down mixes from DJ Tony Mason, pop a Valium and then Randy would sober up enough to walk a block over to his nearby apartment and crash for the day.

In my opinion, those were the absolute best days to be gay in NYC—back in the early, carefree 1980s, which was on the cusp of the AIDS explosion and the radical decimation of the queer community. Unfortunately, within the decade, I found myself as sole survivor from my inner circle of intimate partners and friends who prematurely died, and only the laughter from their ghosts remains with me. Eventually, I lost all my long and short-term intimate boyfriends, including *Gary Laswell* from York Institute; *Tony Mason*; Dr. Doug from Beth Israel's psychiatric department; and *Tony Esposito* from Fire Island and resident of Bensonhurst in Brooklyn. All these beautiful men cannot ever be erased, and I honour their lives whenever I have an opportunity to mention their names. My next inner ring of my closest clique of friends was decimated as well, including first and foremost, the irreverent and most beloved friend of mine, Randy McGee (Doll Bar); my dear friend Chris Clarke (Crystal Barbie); and the awkwardly shy Livio Silvestri from York Institute. And there were scores of tertiary friends and acquaintants that perished as well. Feeling numb with pain, I caught myself crying out and thinking to myself, Who the hell were all the homophobic people and Bible-thumpers from my past who said gay men like me couldn't love? Piss on all of them!

And I would be remiss to exclude Gary Laswell's roommate, Robert Rohacek (aka Roe) who had earned a small corner in my heart. Back in the early days of my relationship with Gary, Roe had no privacy in Gary's shared one-bedroom apartment on Horatio Street, which was located on the border of Chelsea. Especially when I was around. And I was clearly always around, seven days a week, which in turn forced Roe to hang out at his friends or to go partying to escape Gary and me constantly making out. There were times when it was unavoidable and the three of us would fall asleep in the same bed, and let's just say that Roe and I did not find it copacetic, to say the least. To some degree, I knew that Gary and I were responsible for Robert's promiscuity when he sought out alternative places to sleep, but it didn't really seem to faze Gary. He wanted me there every night, even though I had my own apartment on Barrow Street a few blocks south.

Let's us say that Roe wasn't enamoured with me. Regardless, he hired me for my very first design project when I was finishing up as a grad student at Pratt. He thought I could use the cash and add a little American work experience under my belt. And off we went in his convertible BMW to the Ethan Allen Headquarters in Danbury, Connecticut. We had club music playing in the car, the rooftop was down, and there was a crisp spring breeze blowing through our hair. It was a marvelous, carefree ride, and it was the first time I got to spend some one-on-one time with him, and I found that I quite liked him. We spent a mad day of sorting through Robert's photographic archives, determining what to keep and what to throw out. It wasn't particularly interesting and noteworthy, but I could tell Robert felt great relief for the assistance. The thing that most stands out in my mind is that Ethan Allen had one of the first robots I ever saw. If I am not mistaken, Roe called the robot Hazel in honour of the 1961 sitcom of the same name. Hazel would drop by several times throughout the day, picking up and delivering mail to the various cubicles and workstations. Hazel was decades ahead of her time. Today, we can find many robotic cousins of Hazel delivering take-out in Toronto and other cities around the globe.

En route back to Manhattan, I could almost imagine myself riding in my own convertible and flipping around the tri-state area. By the time I arrived back at my West Village apartment, I heard rumours from my best friend Randy about a new "gay disease" beginning to spread like wildfire in our community. A year later, Robert Rohacek was the first of our beloved inner circle to pass from this new gay-related immune deficiency, first identified as GRID. And it was scary and hard on all his friends, but none more so than for my partner Gary. We were both speechless and couldn't breach the sacredness of his monumental loss through words. And there would be more to quickly follow.

The fear and uncertainty of who would be next led many of us to make suicide pacts that would appear as "accidental" overdoses back in those early days! At one point, I had a short-term roommate who was a pharmacist; we both secured enough Placidyls, methaqualone, and Valiums to ensure our own intentional demise and control of our destiny. Plenty of gay men were doing this in the early day of the epidemic. This was the reality of New York gays that friends, family, and straight allies never saw.

There was a neighbour in my same apartment complex who I met tangentially through a mutual friend. According to my friend, he was one of a handful of his closest friends who were invited on an all-expense paid, two-week cruise over to Europe on the pretext it was a birthday gift to himself. Toward the end of the cruise, his cabin mate returned late to the suite and found my neighbour on the bathroom floor, dead from an overdose. He had left a note apologizing to his friends, stating he didn't want anyone to see him deteriorate and suffer and he wanted them to remember him as a beautiful man who adored his close friends and as someone who always knew when it was time to exit a great party. When he shared this news, I couldn't help but say what a remarkable friend he lost and that he would never be forgotten by the lives he touched. I barely knew this man, but he impacted how I might consider preparing for my own final departure one day.

At one point, I was internally screaming with so much unrelenting pain and guilt, I lost my own way for a brief period and sought out anonymous and promiscuous sex to accelerate the inevitable and to control my destiny. I couldn't fathom a future without my friends and loved ones. Nor did I want to end up like my friends who spent their last days intubated and in a medically induced coma. Remarkably, through some miraculous divine intervention, I continued to test negative, and it finally hit me that perhaps there was a greater unknown purpose for me to live, and my momentary phase of reckless behaviour ceased once and for all, despite severe melancholia. On the other hand, I joked to my friends that maybe acid, and not blood, ran through my veins. Who knows why some of us avoided the scourge of HIV and AIDS? Everyone who I had been intimate with had succumbed to death, and it just didn't make any sense.

Even my beloved roommate Brad Wright (aka Stripe) tested positive shortly after coming out, and I felt he had been so robbed. He did not get to enjoy those carefree days when gay men only worried about treatable and curable STDs. He was understandably pissed off and became an activist with ACT-UP and later Queer Nation (in response to the escalation of anti-gay violence). I loved Stripe, and he channeled his rage into something he could be proud of. He certainly made a difference in my life, and I eagerly joined in solidarity with the continuous Christopher Street sit-ins and protests. In my eyes, our queer community of demonstrators represented the real saints in the world, and it was okay with me that we fell from grace in the judgemental eye of the public. Our lives were at stake, and we had to stand up and fight back with civil disobedience. Our metaphoric weapons were locked and loaded to mobilize attention for medical research and medicinal interventions from the National Institute of Health (NIH) and the Center for Disease Control (CDC).

But in my youth as a vibrant gay man in his early thirties, my heart was buried with their sweet souls, and my personal zest for life has never fully recovered. The massive loss and impact on my spirit was a significant milestone in my life; I mechanically functioned but desired nothing, especially not any further intimate gay relationships and friendships. I was cooked! My work became my replacement partner and my only source of joy and fulfillment. Especially when I professionally transitioned into the world of academia, and I had an opportunity to focus less on myself and more onto others.

Christmas chez-moi *with neighbour Joan Fontana and Doll (seated)*

Sunday morning hangover *with Doll after Saturday night at The Saint*

Fire Island in the Pines *sketch (Watercolour for portfolio)*

Fire Island July 4 Holiday *Tea Dance (Cherry Grove)*

NEW YORK CITY HALLOWEEN CHEZ MOI-1984

Miss Salvation Army (Doll)   *Miss Tower Records*

MICHAEL PLASSE-TAYLOR

THE NEW YORK BAG LADIES
inspired by our beloved Miss Marsha P. Johnson

Miss Footlocker and Crystal-Barbie

15
PARTISAN POLITICS
OTTAWA, ONTARIO, 1984-1986

I was leaving NYC to move back to Toronto and start the legal paperwork and sponsorship for a new work visa under my boyfriend Gary's newly acquired private business school in Manhattan. He'd recently moved his small, co-partnered private business school out of Brooklyn Heights and expanded into a much larger facility in Manhattan, adjacent to Union Square Park at 16th Street and Broadway. The school was rapidly expanding in the Manhattan location, and he wanted me to come back to do the design renovations and explore the possibility of implementing a program that would tap into the deaf community as a potential market. And on a more personal note, he didn't want to see our passionate relationship end. He was prepared to sponsor me as his interior designer and business educational consultant for the Deaf.

I had learned a little American Sign Language (ASL) from a beginner's course I had taken at New York University (NYU) and followed it up with an intermediate level at the New York Society for The Deaf on 14th Street as part of my thesis research in a second language I was investigating and exploring a proposed community-based centre and interior design concept for a HIGH CENTRE (Hearing-Impaired Group Habitat) to be hypothetically located in an existing building on Yonge Street in downtown Toronto. And this intrigued Gary; he saw a business opportunity to tap into New York's *Office of Vocational Services* and stream hearing-impaired clients into his growing business. So, part of his visa sponsorship and contractual obligation was that I would set up a program for the hearing-impaired at York Institute. Although I felt woefully unqualified, I recognized that his offer lent gravitas to the sponsorship and would allow me to return to the man and the home I most loved in the world-New York City.

In order not to lose my apartment while I was away for the year, I arranged with my roommate Brad to take care of the entire rent by sub-letting my room in my absence. He wasn't thrilled to see me go but was happy that I would eventually return within the year. There were so many dear friends that I knew I was going to truly miss when I left. Meanwhile, I packed a suitcase and headed out to LaGuardia and boarded an Air Canada flight bound for Toronto.

When I arrived, I took a cab to my friend Joe Puigmarti, who resided on Sackville Street in Cabbagetown. He extended an invitation to stay as his guest during my interim stay. In addition, I resumed my previous employment at *The Yorkviller*. I could easily have passed the year in Toronto doing my old job and residing with my friends; however, I did not want to miss a year of building my professional resume after such an incredible start in Manhattan. Fortunately, I arrived back in Canada with a letter of recommendation from Richard Carlson at Swanke Hayden Connell Architects.

Within the first month of resuming my old job in Yorkville, my good friend and dance partner Peter LeRoy, who also spent a year or two working at *The Yorkviller* three or four years earlier, was visiting his sister in Toronto and decided to pop into the shop. He heard I was back in town, and he wanted to know if I was available for lunch at the nearby Flo's Diner. Along with the blessing of my other dear friend and current manager, Robert Pehlke, we headed off to the diner to get caught up. Over lunch, I discovered that Peter had just taken a government job in Ottawa after completing his graduate degree in Library Sciences at Dalhousie University in Halifax, Nova Scotia. My dear friend was a prolific reader and a great intellect; he could always be seen carrying a book and took any opportunity to read. While he was content to fill any voids in social settings with reading, I chose to fill in the gaps with observational musings and local gay gossip.

Over lunch, we reminisced about our good old days with a lot of nods of oh yeahs, fueled by recollections of our outrageous comings and goings. Peter might have appeared reserved and soft spoken, but when he looked directly at me with his magnificent green eyes and long lashes, it was impossible to avert my eyes from his intense focus. When Peter and I were together in Toronto, he would always let his reserved guard down. The two of us were simpatico about never discussing our sexual conquests and pro-clivities, which most gay men consumed as a queer pastime as part of the Boomer generation.

Peter delicately ate his salad and I munched down on my big old fat, greasy cheeseburger. While in between bites of his salad, Peter gave a nuanced account of our long history of going out every Saturday night to the Maygay, below the historic clock beacon at the *St. Charles Tavern*. He confessed how much he missed our good times and our coveted ritual of getting together before heading out for the night. In anticipation of heading out, we would preen our gay-ass feathers while taking a hit of poppers, dance around with unabashed joy and sing out like a bunch of unbridled choir girls. Mostly to the gay anthems of the Pointer Sisters. It seemed so long ago but to Peter it felt like yesterday.

After engaging for just over an hour, Peter advanced an intriguing prop-osition while we were waiting for the cheque. He suggested that I should submit my resume to the *Office of Public Works* in Ottawa to see if there were any government interior design positions available. He knew that the election for leader of the opposition Conservative Party was coming up, and the word on the street was that there would soon be a changing of the guard from the Liberal to Conservative party. As Peter indicated, if this was truly the political ethos, there would be many government employee departures, as well as new replacements, heading into Ottawa. This meant there would be a notable demand for numerous administrative and management hires to fill the historical government buildings and a few of the modern office towers located in the bilingual capital in Ottawa and over the bridge in Hull, Quebec.

Over lunch, Peter confessed that he was a little lonely living as a new resi-dent in Ottawa, and he thought it would be like the old days if I could secure a job and spend the year *chez lui*. We could split the rent, and I could con-tribute a weekly allowance for groceries from the ByWard Market while he would do all the cooking and preparation of our daily brown-bag lunches. "How would that be?" he enquired.

My quick-witted response was, "It will be like living in a hotel's bridal suite—without the sex." We would be roommates, like an unofficially married gay couple! Peter was certainly laying out a most tempting proposition and a compelling argument for me to seek employment in my professional area. He insisted that since I was one of the very few Canadians with a graduate degree in Interior Design from the renowned Pratt Institute that he was confident my elevated academic qualifications would help me stand out. Boy, he had a damn good pitch!

Anyhow, within forty-eight hours of returning to Ottawa, Peter called me with the specific address of the Interiors Department and the manager's name: *Mrs. Marilyn Donoghue.* I discovered she was a fellow graduate from the University of Manitoba. As I did not know anything about Ottawa, I appreciated this information. With Peter's comments in mind, I wasted no time in getting my curriculum vitae off to her, along with a reference letter from Grant Marshall, whom I found out she highly respected. Well, it must have been only a week later that I received a direct phone call at The Yorkviller, asking me if I would like to fly from Toronto's downtown island airport to Ottawa for a job interview at Public Works Canada, courtesy of the taxpayers of Canada. Hell yes! I said to myself but instead I chose to say, "It would be my pleasure, thank you." And a few days later my wings took flight!

The initial interview with Marilyn Donoghue was held in the Esplanade Laurier Building (O'Connor Street Tower) on the top floor. The other Bank Street tower was closer to where I would soon live on Slater Street. Both identical twin towers were clad in white Carrara marble and complemented the materials and finishes of an interconnected two-storey shopping mall. The new sleek, modern office towers strongly contrasted with the weathered and gloomy historical buildings on Parliament Hill and included the *Supreme Court of Canada* and the *Langevin Block.* The Interior Design office for *Public Works Canada* had plenty of natural light, with a single row of individually panelled workstation walls facing outside to the iconic setting of Parliament Hill.

It struck me that my first impression of the gloomy office reception area was rather disappointing. The interior space was a dull, dark, and drab windowless space located close to the elevator core washrooms and fire stairs. The reception area might as well have been in the adjacent (secured) dead-file storage room, as far as I was concerned. It certainly did not look like any design effort or money had gone into it. Meanwhile, the lighting and interior finishes in the adjacent washroom had more aesthetic appeal, in comparison. And if truth be told, I have been known to get a lot of personal business taken care of in washrooms, in my day. Thank you very much.

Nonetheless, at the far west end of the panel-enclosed workstations was Marilyn Donoghue's designated work area. We met, and although I felt a little overdressed, the interview was amiable and pleasant. Within ten minutes or so of her scanning my resume and bobbing her head up and down like a chirping bird, she offered me a position in her department and informed me that she would get the paperwork submitted and approved by the chain of command, which she assured me would not take too long. Before we said goodbye, she walked me through her office, stopping and introducing me to her staff, who were sequestered behind their high-panelled work cubicles. Honestly, the place was not buzzing at all. In fact, it felt a little like a morgue, with all the design- ers silently working, and I was quite surprised to see there were actual project designers sitting behind those high panels at their workstations! I'd thought everyone was out from all the deafening silence. I realized then that I would be wearing my Sony Walkman and earphones to provide white noise and soothing background music!

In the interim, we bade each other goodbye, and she told me that she looked forward to having me come on board. Immediately, I ran back to Peter's apartment on Slater Street to tell him the good news. It was now his turn to respond, and shaking his head, he said, "Let me have one or two of those lucky horseshoes that you hoard up your ass!" We concluded our conversation by confirming our agreed-upon living arrangements and then I returned to Toronto to pack and give my notice to James Barrass at *The Yorkviller*.

Initially, when I started working, I was located two cubicles away from Marilyn and sat next to my colleague Julia. It seemed everyone was located based on a decisive pecking-order from top to bottom, as I would later find out.

The first couple of small projects I was assigned to as the project designer involved working with outside professional interior design consultants.

I was also placed on a much larger project for the offices of *The National Canadian Postal Services Headquarters* in Ottawa, and it looked like it needed to be completed in a time-sensitive manner before the current year budget and timeline ran out with the new changing of the guard. There was a complete set of working design drawings that I had to review, revise, and comment on before signing them off for approval, and I knew I would have to come in and work over the weekend just to get caught up.

Anyhow, I happily went into the office the following Saturday. And before I knew it, I was sitting entirely alone in the office and without warning, the main office phone began to ring and ring. The only person who could be calling on a weekend was my roommate Peter, and I thought, oh, he must be calling me about lunch or dinner plans. And so, I picked up the phone to answer.

Surprisingly, it was not Peter, but it was someone familiar sounding who was asking to leave a message for Marilyn Donoghue regarding the official residence for the newly appointed Prime Minister *Brian Mulroney* at 24 Sussex Drive. At the exact same time, we both suddenly said, *"Do I know you?"* And then it clicked—this was my old boyfriend from Montreal. Giovanni Mowinckel was on the other end of the line. Giovanni was ecstatic and happy to be reacquainted with me and my new project-management position at Public Works Canada. As he spoke, it was clear that he was exasperated by not having had any of his calls returned from Marilyn Donoghue, and right then and there he said, "Can you come over to 24 Sussex Drive? I am here with Mila Mulroney, and we need your help."

I was gobsmacked and said, "Excuse me, did I hear you, correctly? Are we talking about the wife of our new prime minister?"

And he chuckled as he replied, "That is correct."

Without a moment's hesitation, I said, "Of course! If Mrs. Mulroney and you could give me thirty minutes to tie a few things up, I'll be right over."

He replied, "We'll be waiting. Your name will be left at the security gate kiosk."

At that point, I ran back to my nearby apartment to change into a jacket and tie and rapidly alerted Peter about what was happening, saying that I would fill him in on the details later. I left him standing there wide-eyed and scratching his head while I scratched my big old lard-ass, hoping another lucky horseshoe would fall out. I was going to need all the luck and good fortune I could get to retain my cool, professional demeanor!

I cabbed over to 24 Sussex in about ten minutes with great excitement and anticipation. En route in the car, I took some measured breaths to calm my ass down. After checking in at the security gate, an RCMP guard escorted me to the front door, opened it, and followed me into a central foyer. Mrs. Mulroney and Giovanni came out of the front parlour to the right of the grand lobby and winding staircase. We made our introductions; Giovanni gave me a peck on the cheek and Mrs. Mulroney extended her hand. She asked me to call her "*Mila*," and with that cue, the security detail stepped away and left the three of us to our meeting and personal walk about at 24 Sussex.

As they started to show me around the mansion, Mila confided how challenging it was for her when they were leaders of the opposition and living at the official residence at Stornoway Mansion. She claimed that it was near impossible to get any calls returned from my office at Public Works, and then out of the blue, Mila turned and asked me if I was partisan to any political party. And I could honestly say that although I normally voted as a Liberal, I felt it was time for a change, and I voted for her husband as head of the Conservative Party in Canada.

My news brought a smile to both of their faces, and I felt obliged to tell Mila that I was not a political person by nature and that I was just grateful for the opportunity to help in any way that I could as a gatekeeper and project design manager who was representing *Public Works Canada*. As Mila led us both around the ground level, Giovanni took an opportunity of a brief second to whisper in my ear that my response to Mila would bode well for me, as I would be vetted by a long-time friend of the Mulroney's, *Mr. Fred Doucet. Incidentally, I would discover from my roommate Peter that he was known as the "hatchet-man" in their inner circle. And my response was, "Oh Fuck me, what have I gotten myself into, now?"*

Meanwhile, as Mila forged ahead, I took out a pad and paper to take notes. As we walked throughout the mansion, both Mila and Giovanni started making observations and recommendations for necessary design renovations, noting there was an official budget of $95,000 earmarked and approved from Public Works to spend on renovations, which for back then did not seem like a hell of a lot of money for all the necessary upgrades. If there were any potential overcharges, I was to alert both Mila and Giovanni immediately. One way or another they would find a way to get all the priority renovations executed, with no additional cost to the taxpayers.

Apparently, they had "many friends" who were willing to reach into their own pockets and donate "small gifts and services" in kind. Meanwhile, I was thinking to myself, *wow, who was this army of friends and where could I find myself one?* I could barely afford an apartment of my own as I made obscenely large monthly payments on my $26,000 of student loans with compounded interest. And then it occurred to me, clearly, that I have had my fair share of generous and kind friends, *silly man! But they were all small players in comparison to the wealthy political engine at their disposal.*

As we continued up the grand foyer staircase, I have to say that I found Mila Mulroney very disarming with her engaging smile and compelling chit-chat about how she wanted the upper family floors to function. The top floor would function as the children's and staff bedrooms. The second floor would be programmed with the master bedroom, located on the far side of the great staircase at the front of the house. As we entered the main bedroom, I noted that most of the work would be cosmetic, and I asked Mrs. Mulroney why there were two landlines on the bedside tables. Mila mentioned the black phone was for personal use and the red one was for a direct link to the President of the United States, in case of any global catastrophes or possibility of a nuclear war.

And after her response to my dumb-ass question, I said, "Holy mackerel, who wouldn't have problems getting a good night sleep with one of those hot phones next to the bedside!" On that note, we headed into a miserably outdated ensuite that required a complete overhaul. This ensuite would be dedicated for Mila and led into an interconnecting private back hall that was just wide enough for me to design a row of custom-designed closets and millwork to store her personal clothing, shoes, and accessories. At the opposite end of the internal corridor was a second bedroom and ensuite that would be dedicated to her husband's exclusive use.

As we entered his private suite, Mila locked arms with me and we walked in together like old comrades. The bedroom was handsomely appointed with a gorgeous French-Canadian armoire and a lovely antique wood bedframe and headboard. Simultaneously, we both sat side by side and bounced on the bed to see what kind of condition it was in. I noted that it required nothing more than perhaps a new mattress replacement. At this point, I figured my hair and clothes must either smell like smoke, or perhaps Mila was in close enough proximity to see the pack of Player's Light cigarettes sticking out of the inside pocket of my jacket. Regardless, she casually asked if she could have a cigarette. Apparently, she used to be a smoker in the old days, and nobody knew she liked to have an occasional "puff." I was happy to indulge her and join in, as well as Giovanni, who pulled out a package of imported Dunhill cigarettes.

To reassure her, I mentioned that I was trying to stop smoking myself. After a few relaxing puffs, I realized that we must have looked like we were a gaggle of high school girls hiding in the bathroom stalls. When we finished our cigarette, we stood up and headed toward Brian's ensuite to flush the evidence of our private smoke at 24 Sussex Drive.

Once inside Mr. Brian Mulroney's washroom, I was flabbergasted to discover the 1920s seafoam-green bathroom fixtures were still in mint condition. Other than needing some new paint on the ceiling, door, and window trim, Mrs. Mulroney said his bathroom was functionally fine. And just as we were about to head out and tour the remainder of the back guest bedrooms and family living quarters, she said, "Wait a moment! I'm not sure if the bathtub is big enough for Brian." At which point, she stepped into the tub in her high brown-leather boots and mid-calf plaid skirt and proceeded to shimmy herself down, holding onto the sides of the tub. After a moment she said, "Okay, it looks like the tub size will be fine!" At that specific moment I fell in love with Mila's unpretentious practicality and her hands-on approach to managing her family's domestic wellbeing. She was marvellous in how she put me at complete ease. And I thought to myself that she was going to be delightfully refreshing as Canada's unofficial American version of a "First Lady," as well as a remarkable support to her husband, who was the newly elected Prime Minister of Canada. I didn't really care for politics but I sure the hell liked and respected her as a brilliant human being.

After the unexpected weekend invitation to 24 Sussex Drive, I returned to my desk first thing on Monday morning. I asked the receptionist where I might find Marilyn, and for some unknown reason, no one seemed to know where Marilyn was. I thought that as the receptionist and Marilyn's administrative assistant, she would surely know her schedule. So, I discreetly mentioned that I needed to speak with Marilyn as soon as she came in, and she took my message down.

It must have been around 11:30 that morning when Marilyn came into my cubicle area, white as a ghost. I smiled and said hello. Marilyn did not smile back. Instead, she came over in a measured manner and placed a huge project file on my desk. With a vacant expression, she muttered, "This file and project are now your responsibility and yours exclusively." Evidently, she had mysteriously been requested by an undisclosed person to not have any further involvement with the official residences and offices of the prime minister, which had previously been exclusively under her purview.

I looked up at her with a stunned expression on my face and a pit in my stomach; something must have happened to her behind the political scenes and the machinations of the newly installed Conservative government. I wanted so desperately to explain what had happened and tell her I was sorry for anything I might have done unintentionally to hurt her over the weekend. And what I quickly learned is that my naïve strategic decisions had consequences on others. I had no intention to insert myself into the chain of command, and the decision to do so was not mine. Who would have thought I could create such a blistering drama from picking up an innocent phone call at work!

When I looked up from the file on my desk, Marilyn had retreated to her desk and then she left for home and checked out sick for a good part of the week. I was now becoming indoctrinated into the underbelly of politics, and I was unfortunately caught up in it. I felt incredibly sad and conflicted for Marilyn; she was the person who'd graciously hired me and brought me to Ottawa, and I felt great empathy for her. No doubt she had much regret about her decision to hire me, and I can't say I would blame her for feeling that way toward me. But I grew up on the Gospel of Janis Joplin, who sang "Get it While You Can, cause it ain't going to be there when you wake up."

And I heeded her sage words, as I got some unbelievable opportunities. As well as working on the design of the official residences at 24 Sussex and Harrington Lake, I was now commissioned to design the Prime Minister's Offices (PMO) in the historic Centre Block capital buildings, as well as in the Langevin Building directly across the street. Added to this, I was asked by Fred Doucet to design his personal office and to design a distinctly separate executive suite for Mila and her executive personal assistant/friend, Bonnie Brownlee. Without question, I had more than enough of a full plate, working for the highest-profile clients in Canada. I was humbled by their confidence and faith in my role as their personal, government-appointed interior designer and project manager. It was one of the most tremendously exciting highlights in my professional career. I met some extraordinary people, and I must admit the time went by far too fast.

Eventually, after my work was done in Ottawa, I returned to New York City and began my contractual and sponsorship obligations to York Institute. Out of the blue, I received an unanticipated phone call from a journalist for the *Globe and Mail, Stevie Cameron*. She was doing some background research on a book she was writing and digging around for some dirt on the cost of the design renovations at 24 Sussex Drive and the PMO, and I responded that due to client confidentiality, I honestly had nothing to say on that subject matter. As indicated, "I knew nothing from dirt, already." And my blunt response ended the call abruptly and that was that.

Afterward, I called Ottawa and got put through to Bonnie Brownlee, who then put me directly in touch with Mila Mulroney. I shared what had just transpired. Both Mila and Bonnie were grateful for the call and thanked me for the heads-up and for my continuing loyalty to their family. I always treated them with the highest respect, and in return, I remained in their good graces for several years, receiving annual Christmas cards and birthday greetings. Which just goes to prove that I could fundamentally agree with the Liberal Party and still be loyal and maintain a good friendship with the leading members of the Conservative Party.

In 1989, the very same Stevie Cameron published her first book, called *Ottawa Inside Out,* which was a scathing rebuke of the Mulroney government at that time. While living in New York, I knew nothing about the book until I got a phone call from my favourite professor and chair of the Interior Design program at the University of Manitoba. My old buddy and mentor Professor Grant Marshall had devoured the book with a granular inspection for mention of my name. According to Grant, there was a buzz in the Canadian interior design ethos that I was mentioned in the book as the project designer responsible for the interior design and budget. The great news is that I came out clean as a whistle; ergo the reputation of the university and the Faculty of Architecture felt vindicated and honoured that one of their graduates was true to the most ethical and moral standards—just as we had been educated in the Department of Interior Design.

So, although I was in New York, my name was circulating across Canada and people were reading the book that some say put Stevie Cameron on the map. Her highly regarded book led to a guest-host spot with the *Canadian Broadcasting Corporation* (CBC) program *The Fifth Estate* for about a year, before she returned to the *Globe and Mail* as a freelance columnist and writer in 1991.

Department of Public Works (DPW)

16
HOME AGAIN IN NYC!
141 BARROW STREET, NEW YORK, 1986–1988

After a very exciting and politically sensitive year in Ottawa, I eagerly antic-ipated my return to New York City, armed with an H-1B non-immigrant visa under the umbrella of *Specialty Consultants*. I was permitted legal exclusive employment with my new sponsor (and boyfriend Gary) at the York Institute, in the Union Square district of Manhattan. It was the only viable option for me to return as a Canadian national and non-immigrant. Fortunately, I retained my original two-bedroom apartment on Barrow Street under the supervision of my old roommate Brad Wright, aka Stripe. Before my return, Stripe gave notice to his friend who had occupied my bedroom. Clearly, it was a huge relief and comfort to slide right back into my old apartment and neighbourhood in the West Village.

Meanwhile, Gary Laswell and I had anticipated picking up where we previously left off from our prior monogamous relationship. However, many of our friends in our inner circle were becoming sick and starting to die from complications due to AIDS, including Gary's roommate, Robert (Roe), who had died just weeks before my return. This left Gary a very changed man, and he became acutely cognisant of his own mortality. He no longer felt invincible and began to bury himself in his new enterprise, spending less time on our intimate relationship and not prioritizing it.

From the onset, it was unspoken that the AIDS epidemic was at our doorstep. Gary didn't like it one bit when I insisted that our old habits of unprotected sex had to stop, moving forward. And I started to feel like he was now considering me no more than his H1-B visa sponsored employee and feared for our relationship on a rocky road to an uncertain future. Immediately, I sensed that not only had our romance ended, but my contractual obligations at York Institute would also sooner or later be bookended. And then I would be walking on quicksand without a sponsor for God knows how long.

Previously, Gary's persona was typically joyful and happy, but now he wore only a service smile to get whatever he wanted. My friend Cynthia and I knew from personal experience that if you crossed him in any critical or personal manner, as we once had, it would be disastrous.

On one of our weekend trips to his East Hampton house, he started to spiral down from overdrinking and excessive drugs. Cynthia and I tried to intervene by taking his car keys away in the parking lot at The Swamp nightclub. He refused to come back with us, and he headed back into the club. Meanwhile, Cynthia and I drove his Mercedes back to his East Hampton home and waited. The next morning, it was apparent that someone must have offered him a ride back to his house. When he entered, he exploded and told us to get our things and to "get the hell out." He then dropped our asses off at the nearby East Hampton train station faster than a New York City second. We learned a lesson: that even as his closest friends, his personal life decisions were not up for debate. This was his modus operandi, and all his close friends cautiously adapted to his nature. I knew that everything intrinsically changed in him with the advent of the AIDS pandemic, and unfortunately it wasn't for the better.

After we spent the first week trying to reconnect, I knew Gary was preoccupied and certainly not into the new safe-sex policy I insisted upon. So, I decided to spend less time with him and more time at home, reflecting on the decision I had made to return.

Before AIDS, I thought back to how beautiful our relationship had started out-- prior to moving to Ottawa. I can recall on several occasions when the two of us were partying and his emotional guard-rails would come down, revealing a little more about his history. The one thing that really struck me was that his father never approved of homosexuals, and this forced Gary as a young man to stay in the closet. He learned from an early age to mimic his father's stoic expression and to bury his emotions behind a mask, portraying a mischievous smile and a hearty laugh, just like his dad. And in my view, he had inherited his father's need to dominate others and cleverly manipulate every situation to his advantage. If truth be told, I recognized a little of that idiosyncratic behaviour in myself. Gary and I were in some ways very similar and compatible. We were birds of a feather and flocked together intimately, and attitudinally.

Like myself, his family's perception and rejection of his masculinity left Gary no other choice but to move away. I believe his first steppingstone on his eventual path to NYC started when he accepted a teaching position in Akron, Ohio. After a year or so, he was armed with modest savings and some foundational teaching experience adequate to springboard off to the Big Apple, arguably the largest city and gay epicenter in North America. Gary would rarely mention his family to anyone, except to say that he'd grown up hearing from everyone that his father was held in high esteem and that he considered himself a stellar example of *a man's man*. On the other hand, everyone in his family had considered closeted homosexuals like us to be deviants. In my heart, I knew he wanted to prove to his family that he was also a "man's man." And at the time, that meant acting tough and never showing his cards.

We both knew back in 1981 that we were vibrant gay men of the *Boomer* generation who had previously shared the prevailing discriminatory and hateful ethos of rampant discrimination. Neither Gary nor I came from families where we quite measured up. When we'd first met on a Sunday in the West Village at *Boots and Saddles* on Christopher Street, we instantly connected on a sexual level and intuitively sensed that there was more of us in common to explore. He pursued me vigorously and relentlessly. Back then, he wanted me at his apartment when he returned home from his teaching job at a nearby private school. He even gave me an apartment key so I could come and go as I pleased, which I am sure was not something his roommate Robert was too pleased with. I remember thinking at the time it was a little odd, but then again, this was New York, and everything moved at an accelerated pace. I just accepted his key and his demand for attention as the cultural norm for gays in New York.

And before I knew it, we were in an intensely committed monogamous relationship, within the first three months of meeting. I kind of just got swept up in the whole thing, as a relationship was something I likewise valued and coveted, albeit not so fast. We kept a small circle of our own individual friends who would periodically intersect. Both of us became co-dependant overnight. We were kindred birds of a feather; symbolically, he represented a powerful *American eagle* as a cultural icon, and I represented the *Canadian loon* who happened to stop one random day and drink from his pond and never left.

In the beginning, we had nothing to prove and everything to gain by filling mutual voids from our past. We were outcasts who found solace in each other as both partners and as members in a broader family of queer friends and allies. We embraced the power of the term "queer" as an umbrella for a broader alphabet. And we transformed a pejorative term and threw it back at the face of society so everyone would be reminded of the ubiquitous hatred of queer people. Our community and tribe would not sweep the culpability and ongoing discrimination of the broader society under the proverbial carpet, nor erase it from history. No question about it. We were proud to say that we were "Queer as Fuck!"

I thought about New York City's historical landmark Stonewall protest for civil rights at Sheridan Square two decades before I moved to New York. Back then, I discovered that it was commonplace for men in New York and surrounding areas to remain the closet for safety. Only the West Village bars, such as *Julius, Marie's Crisis,* and the landmark *Stonewall Inn*, provided a refuge and an opportunity for gays and non-binary folk to meet. However, the double-life ethos was eventually blasted wide open to the public on June 28, 1969, with the *Stonewall Inn* riots. At the time, homosexual acts were illegal in every state (except Illinois), and it was commonly known by queer activists that most gay bars in NYC back in the day were owned and operated by the mafia. Many of the bar patrons at the time were targeted and often blackmailed and forced to pay a ransom to protect their identity. Many gay men led a double life as married men; single men tried to pass as *straight;* and many beautiful drag queens tried to pass as women when walking outside the safety of the gay village. No one took their safety for granted. Not in the United States, not in Canada, nor anywhere else around the world, for that matter.

Although many patrons at the Stonewall Inn were white, there was progressive acceptance and a welcomed increase in diversity particularly from the Black and Latino communities in New York City. As marginalized minorities, they would play a pivotal role in fighting for equality and gay rights, quite literally at the drop of a hat pin. It was so inspirational that many of the *Stonewall Inn* patrons were self-identified activist drags queens and people of colour, like *Marsha P. Johnson* and *Sylvia Revera*. They were at the forefront as two of the first visible queer activists who, according to Miss Marsha, said: "We're not going to take this shit anymore!" When I first moved to New York city, Marsha was already a friend of our mutual dear friend and expat from Birmingham, Alabama, Randy McGee (Doll). He introduced her to me as "Miss Marsha," and that was the way I always addressed her and introduced her to others from that point on.

I recall one of our very first personal interactions on Christopher Street. During a random early Saturday morning after Randy and I had been shopping at the Union Square Farmer's Market, we ran into Miss Marsha enroute back to our nearby apartments. We met up with her in front of a shop next to the Citibank ATM on Christopher Street, just a hair west of Sheridan Square. Coincidentally, the shop window had the coveted lithograph of her portrait done by Andy Warhol and it was for sale, just spitting distance from where the *Stonewall riots* took place. I remember thinking at the time that I wished I had the money to purchase the lithograph. Meanwhile, *Miss Marsha* recounted to us how she ran outside the Stonewall Inn when it was raided, along with all the other patrons. She and a few others revolted by throwing beer bottles at the police in protest, and it made us feel proud to hear about her remarkable courage and strength. On the other hand, Randy and I felt hurt and ashamed to hear how all white folk took off and disappeared like rats on a sinking ship as they blended in with all the white passersby.

At the end of our spontaneous exchange, we snatched her up and took Miss Marsha back to Randy's Doll Bar apartment/salon for a little cockapoo-mixed drink of Jack Daniels and Coke, as well as a little hairdo courtesy of my beloved friend Doll. Randy always served his clients and friends a little cockapoo, and *Miss Marsha* was always considered a guest of honour. Welcome to the world of Doll Bar!

Conversely, my recollection of the last time I saw Miss Marsha alive was years later in 1991, when we quite by accident met up at *The Eagle* just before I moved back to Canada. I had walked into the bar a little too early and ordered a drink at the far end of the bar. As my eyes adjusted to the dark, I noticed a familiar-looking silhouette sitting at the opposite end, close to the front door. Suddenly, the quietness of the bar was punctuated with, "Hey, honey, you want to buy a pretty girl a drink? And I realized, instantly it was the voice of Miss Marsha as she waved me over to a stool next to her side. She complained that she got kicked off the Path train and had not slept all night and had nothing to eat. As she sat at the bar, she said, "I paid my fare, and they shaded me and kicked me off the train!"

All I could do was discreetly slide her a handful of crumpled bills from my pocket and agree with her that the New Jersey transit authority was a real dick! As I turned to the bartender and ordered her a drink, I thought to myself that although Miss Marsha Johnson was homeless, she had not lost her mind from surviving a brutally tough life on the cold streets of NYC. Ironically, she expressed the streets were the place she felt knowledgeable and most at home. Miss Marsha and I toasted our drinks in honour of our mutual friendship with our beloved friend Doll. We enjoyed a few laughs before I had to say goodbye. That was my very fond and last recollection of seeing her alive.

Meanwhile, back to the time when I was working for Gary's private school, I acknowledged that he was either oblivious to my relationship with Miss Marsha and Doll or he simply couldn't care. I found out in my last remaining year in NYC the truth about his biases and his true feelings about other races. He considered all minorities "gutter trash," as he was fond of saying. I knew for a fact that he was not attracted to Black men, but I had no idea he was not a fan of Jewish men either. Toward the end of our relation-ship, I asked him a pointed question. "What drew you to me at *Boots and Saddles* on Christopher Street back in 1981?"

His unanticipated response to me was, "I was attracted to you because you're a WASP just like me." I had a visceral response to what I heard, and I wanted to go puke. I had loved and committed myself to this very gregari-ous and interesting man for several years, but the charade was up when he finally confessed to me what he really thought about other gay men who were not of the same ilk. In that one singular moment, I lost my respect for Gary, and I was done. My remaining time working for *York Institute* was going to be a big personal challenge; I felt trapped and betrayed. And it was time to seek legal counsel, as our personal relationship quickly unravelled, and I needed to get out.

Meanwhile, the cosmetic renovation at York went off as planned and was paid for by the building management. The baseline budget to upgrade the facility allowed only for economical black-vinyl-composite floor tiles, paint, and that was about it. The school absorbed the cost for my custom millwork in the reception area and the student recruitment intake cubicles, as well two larger cubicles in the adjacent financial-aid office. Frankly, it was a disappointing waste of time and talent, but it was my primary requirement under my work visa status. In less than a month, I went from designing for the Prime Minister of Canada to shopping and foraging for knock-off bargains in the outside stalls on 14th Street in Lower Manhattan.

The most interesting part of my tenure at York Institute was the second part of my contractual obligation to Gary Laswell. It involved my collaboration with Dr. Shirley Munioz, who was a hired as a temporary in-house consultant and curriculum specialist from Columbia University. The area we collaborated on was the curriculum and pedagogical preparations for the recruitment of deaf students and the operational logistics for hiring deaf teachers and interpreters who operated in American Sign Language. We would be the first private business school in NYC to integrate deaf learners with a full-time deaf instructor and interpreters, and I worked hard to garner support from deaf caseworkers associated with the Office of Vocational Rehabilitation in New York.

What saved my sanity and kept me focussed away from the rapid schism developing between Gary and me was my position as Program Coordinator for the Deaf. This new challenge buoyed me up. I was beginning to network and recruit deaf students, and I had just hired a deaf teacher who would guide me through the process, particularly with the recruitment of applicants from Vocational Services. From a networking perspective, I had a personal relationship with a key prominent deaf family in New York: the Hlibok family.

I had first met and had a mini affair with Bruce Hlibok on Fire Island around 1982 while Gary and I were in the beginning stages of our relationship. He was born deaf and one of three other deaf siblings, two boys and one girl, from deaf parents. The entire family was recognized as trailblazers throughout the United States. His father was instrumental in setting up the

Bell Telephone's first deaf-relay service in North America. Bruce himself was an accomplished actor and playwright, his sister was the first deaf ballerina, and his brother Steven and was the first deaf stockbroker in New York. Bruce mentioned in passing that his brother Stephen was in fact looking for a change of work and a new career direction.

I first met Bruce Hlibok during my first semester at Pratt Institute. Out of curiosity and as if I wasn't busy enough, I had registered for a course in *American Sign Language* at NYU. On one of my community walkabouts after class, I saw Bruce on Christopher Street, standing outside Li-Lac Chocolates; I heard this was Manhattan's oldest chocolate house, and I wanted to check it out. Bruce was standing out front, signing with another deaf friend on break from inside. I couldn't help but notice how cute he was. As I passed by to enter the shop, I caught them checking me out and signing that they thought I was cute, and I suspected they were "friends of Dorothy." As I literally brushed by them to enter, I signed "hello," and they asked me if I was deaf. I signed back that I was a hearing person.

In a nutshell, I purchased my chocolates from his friend, who happened to be the chocolatier, and when I went back outside, Bruce was waiting for me and started signing very slowly to me. The next thing I knew, I was invited back to his apartment for a drink. And before I finished the drink, I found myself between his bedsheets and we were planning a weekend away on my first trip to Fire Island the following weekend. Later, when we arrived at the Carousel Guest House, Bruce registered the two of us into a downstairs room with a fitting queen-sized bed. The hosts were aware in advance that Bruce was deaf because he had booked the reservation through Bell's deaf-relay system. When we arrived, everyone assumed we were both deaf. Bruce asked me to play along so I could interpret if there were any comments about us from the staff and guests. Let's just say that we kept the light on throughout the night so we could communicate and play. I learned more sign language in two days than I had over the past semester at NYU.

A few weeks later, Bruce awarded me a deaf "sign-name," which as he explained only someone from the deaf community can culturally assign to you. He slowly took his three middle fingers and tapped the centre of his chest to indicate my name with the letter M for Michael. When I asked what this symbol meant, he explained what it meant, and I thought to myself, Holy cow, Michael from the heart. How beautiful was that! I was honoured to receive such a sweet bestowed deaf sign-name, and this was how he introduced me to his friends and family. The sign symbol for my name indicated that I was accepted into their community as an outsider. In mid-summer, Bruce invited me as part of his inner circle of deaf friends to see the much-acclaimed Broadway production of *Children of a Lesser God*, starring Phyllis Frelich, who then went on to win a Tony award.

Sadly, I much later found out that Bruce died in 1995, a few short years after I returned to Toronto. He was only thirty-four when he died from complications of pneumonia caused by AIDS. His family subsequently created an endowment in his honour at *Gallaudet College for the Deaf*—as it was called back then. It was through my early association with Bruce that I first became familiar with his younger brother Stephen, who had recently graduated from *Gallaudet* when I was working for Gary at York Institute.

So, to make a long story short, I hired Stephen as the most ideally qualified deaf candidate to help me with networking and recruiting applicants from New York City's Office of Vocational Rehabilitation. Despite objections from non-deaf educational experts in the community who did not believe I was qualified to research and study the deaf community; I forged ahead and got the program rolling in Manhattan with the invaluable assistance from Stephen Hlibok. And isn't it interesting when someone tells you that you cannot do something how you find a way? It was my modus operandi.

A year later, the deaf community in Manhattan, unbeknownst to me, submitted my name to Mayor Ed Koch for recognition of my contribution to educating and training deaf individuals in a range of courses and programs at York Institute. Subsequently, I was contacted by the mayor's office to attend an honorary ceremony at City Hall, where I received a handshake and a citation from Mayor Kotch. This was truly an unexpected and undeserved recognition, in my opinion. I was hardly an expert. Far from it, in fact. But I must say, when I look back now, I thank not only New York's deaf community but also my boyfriend Gary Laswell for this amazing and challenging work opportunity at his private business school.

Meanwhile, after the program got rolling and I had fulfilled my visa work agreement and contractual obligations to York Institute, Gary had no clue as to what to do with me. His solution was to have me manage the office of financial aid for the remainder of my service under his employment. This was not something that I signed up for nor particularly enjoyed or felt comfortable doing, as I explained to my personal attorney. She was exploring all the options available to protect me so that I could remain in New York. In addition, she was aware that I could lose my job and sponsorship any day. I recall mentioning my predicament to my dear old friend Lynne Burke when she came for a visit to New York, accompanied by a close friend from London, Ontario. Their visit was a momentary and much welcomed diversion from the personal brouhaha surrounding me.

Not too long after her visit, Gary called me into his office and essentially fired me, leaving me in an awkward situation and in legal jeopardy. Without wasting any time, I contacted my immigration attorney, and she got the ball rolling for my temporary approval to remain in New York. Meanwhile, I continued to look for employment and sponsorship in my professional field. It was a relief to put the chapter of Gary and York Institute behind me. Our partnership had run its course, and I was moving on. I resolved to never mix business and pleasure again!

To celebrate the unknown road ahead and to give myself an overdue break from the lingering possibility of having to return to Canada, I planned a much-needed vacation out to Fire Island. I decided to contact my dear friend Robert Pehlke from The Yorkviller in Toronto and invite him along as my guest. Two years earlier when my relationship with Gary was at its peak, Robert joined me as my Canadian guest to Gary's house in East Hampton. What started out as a fun night out with dancing and drinking at The Swamp turned into a crazy, drug-fuelled weekend with Gary's gay socialites and Manhattan cognoscenti, partying as non-stop at his home. My only sanity was Robert who stood by and commiserated with me while Gary chose to ignore the marginalized two Canadians— Robert and me. No number of partying-pharmaceuticals could dull my pain, nor did I want it to.

I knew I couldn't change the Hampton's debacle, but I wanted to make up for that regrettable experience. And so, I later called Robert after his return to Toronto, and I invited him out to Fire Island as my guest at the Carousel Guest House. Robert indicated he had always wanted to vacation there at some point, and we agreed that there was no time better than the present. Only God knows how much time I had before I had to leave, so it was now or never to share my vacation with Robert. The chance of Robert visiting on his own initiative was slim, and I wanted him to witness this piece of paradise with someone who simply adored both the contrasting magic and madness of The Grove and the snooty calm and elegance of The Pines. It was the best of all worlds. And it was now go-time and Robert jumped at the surprise invitation.

I booked us a room at the Carousel Guest House in Cherry Grove. And that is when we first met Tony Esposito at The Monster on my very first day. Robert and I were nursing our Long Island iced teas, and we couldn't help but notice a very handsome and shy man standing alone at the other end of the empty dance floor. There was only a handful of people at the time, and shy Tony caught my eye immediately. Robert encouraged me to go over and say hello, and I followed up. I looked at him directly from a safe distance and when our eyes locked, I went over and introduced myself.

Shortly after a round of introductions, the three of us began dancing together and the other men who were standing around followed us onto the dancefloor. As time went on, I think Robert got a little bored with my intense focus on Tony, and he politely excused himself, returning to the guest house for a rest. Meanwhile, Tony and I headed out to the beach to sit and talk for a bit. Before we knew it, the sun and temperature were beginning to lower, and I offered to go back to my guest house to get a blanket so we could watch the magnificent sunset together. The age-old conundrum of "is he a friend or someone I wanted to fuck" was something I needed to explore. I returned moments later, and we ended up falling asleep on the beach, but not before I discovered he was leaving in the morning to return to his home in Bensonhurst, Brooklyn. We mutually expressed a desire to meet with each other in the city and we exchanged numbers before he departed on the first boat the following day.

I escorted Robert for an occasional daytrip through the infamous Meat Rack where some of the horny old goats were getting it on in the woods, and then we moved onto our destination to The Pines for an upmarket change of scenery. During the week, I took Robert for a morning hike to the Sunken Forest. Other than that, I pretty much sequestered myself to the beach or inside our Canada Room at the guest house to nurse my severe sunburn. We had a great time relaxing, but I was clearly preoccupied with the thought of Tony. I was so bummed when he left that I had little concept of how Robert spent the remaining two or three days primarily on his own. I have no clue as to what trouble, if any, he may or may not have been up to. All I know is Tony distracted me from the pain of breaking up with Gary. And Robert fully understood my distraction.

After we returned to Manhattan, Robert and I spent a couple more days in my West Village apartment before he had to return to Canada. We laughed about how whenever we were together, something always magically happened, and I was beginning to think he was right! While Robert was staying with me, I received a call with news that I scored an interview for a senior interior design position at SCR Architects on East 61st Street. I was so thrilled that I took Robert out to an old speakeasy, originating back to 1922. It was called Chumley's and was located one block from my apartment on Bedford and Barrow Street. I had so much to celebrate and be grateful for, including Robert's company, a new job prospect, and a new boyfriend from Bensonhurst. I was optimistic about my future in New York and felt the happiest I had been in the past two years.

After Robert departed from New York, Tony and I became an item, and we established up front that safe sex was a priority; we were surrounded by dying friends and we discussed a monogamous and loyal relationship that was mutually compatible. Meanwhile, I knew that I had tested negative for HIV, but Tony never disclosed his status. I told him if we were vigilant about playing safe, I had no problem falling in love with him. And over the next three or four weeks, Tony and I would escape on weekends to his Fire Island house.

Our relationship deepened over the next nine months while I was working at my new job at SCR. By the following spring, an unanticipated tragedy unfolded that required me to detach from Tony for a few weeks.

I noticed I hadn't seen my roommate, David, for a couple of weeks, and I never thought anything of it. He always kept his bedroom door closed, while I preferred to keep mine open during the day. No big deal, we had different schedules and different lives. And then one day, I received a random call from his ex-lover who was calling to check in on him. When I explained he was always busy and apparently out a lot, Jack insisted I open his bedroom door while he had me on the phone. When I opened the door to his room, all I could see was a mountain of liquor bottles. When my eyes eventually focussed on the dark room, I could see David passed out in his underwear on top of the bed and my heart leapt out of my body.

I jumped on the bed to see if he was alive and he was, thankfully. Jack then instructed me to drag him into the shower and to stay with him until he could make it to my apartment. About an hour later, Jack arrived and took over. Later, all three of us sat down in the living room to review what had happened, and Jack explained that David was an alcoholic and that he was a member of Al-Anon. Apparently this was something that never occurred me to consider when I first interviewed David as a roommate. As David sat back in silence, Jack explained that David had a long history of falling on and off the wagon. Frankly, I was in a little bit of shock myself. I told them both that I had no idea how serious an issue this could be, not only for the two of them but also for myself and the safety of my apartment. David was a chain smoker, and I didn't want to come home to find my home up in smoke one day. I then gave him two months' notice to find a new place to live. And they agreed it was probably for the best.

Meanwhile, as I had explained to Tony, I required some dedicated time to find a new roommate and take care of everything involved with advertising in the Village Voice, screening applicants and setting up interviews. Coincidentally, when I mentioned this to my colleague David Fleck at work, he mentioned he had a gay friend who was a flight attendant with North Star Air and currently searching for a place to live in Manhattan. They were planning to meet up for drinks at Julius on West 10th and he invited me along to meet Brad Wright. By the end of our drinks, I was taking Brad to my nearby apartment so he could check it out, and voilà, just like that, I had a new roommate and a new personal friendship. In no time, we discovered that we shared much more with our mutual love of queer literature and activism. Better yet, he had no personal issues with alcohol or substance abuse. And as a bonus, he would be out of town frequently as a flight attendant. So, what's not to love, already?

Now that I had secured a roommate, I took the first opportunity to take a later train out to Sayville, Long Island, to grab the last boat to Cherry Grove. As I wanted to surprise Tony, I called my friend Patsy from the Carousel Guest House to help set up a plan. She volunteered to book me a complimentary first night, which would afford us some quiet time together and strategize the final details. I arrived quite late and anticipated going to bed shortly. However, we ended up reminiscing into the early morning hours after Patsy had checked me into the Canada Room off the kitchen patio deck. She had previously christened this room in my honour.

Patsy was a devout practicing Catholic and embraced the challenge of operating her deceased brother's gay guest house as she had promised him before his passing. She lived in Deer Park, Long Island, and never spent any significant time in The Grove, previously. She had no personal friends that I knew of, nor made any other personal connections with her house guests that was quite as special as ours. I was happy to spend some quality time with Patsy after all her guests had been checked in and all her chores were done for the day.

We recalled memories of how we originally met and how we seemed to just click at the beginning over a random continental breakfast that she had prepared for her Carousel guests. She was surprised when I offered to assist her with setting up and clearing up afterward. It had been no big deal, as I saw she was the sole staff on the premises, and she was running around like a chicken with her head cut off. Somehow, one of our first conversations was about her faith in God and public service. Perhaps it was because I had confessed to her that I had given up on God and religion after the tragic loss of my beloved sister, and she appeared empathetic and non-judgemental.

We both shared a spiritual connection with each other regardless. And she surprised herself when she first met Tony after I had brought him back to the guest house for her to meet. At the time, she felt somewhat protective of me and so she decided to invite us for a private homemade dinner so she could check Tony out for herself. By the end of the meal, she told us that she saw the mutual love growing in our hearts for one another. She noted it was the first time she took a much overdue break for herself, and we spent a good few hours together; the time simply flew by.

I revealed to her over our dinner that I was originally smitten with her honest charm and warmth. Before I could control my big old mouth, there I was inviting her to my place in Manhattan over the upcoming Christmas holidays, months away. We laughed as we both remembered Tony's retractor neck and wide eye-rolling, as if to say this isn't the kind of thing New Yorkers do at a casual first meeting. I couldn't care less what he thought back then. At some point, I confessed to her that I only half-expected her to take me up on the invitation, but God love her, she eventually showed up and kept her word.

On a more personal note, I told her that she kind of reminded me of my sister, Rosemary, who I had lost touch with over the years. And when I mentioned this to Patsy, toward the end of our catching up, I got shivers up my arms when she confessed that I likewise reminded her of her deceased brother, Michael. She saw very similar qualities in our "life-of-the-party" personalities. Neither of us realized just how safe and trusting we had become with each other over a relatively short period of time. Patsy jiggled my hand and assured me that it was now time to end the night and retire to our separate rooms. And off I went with great relief. I was exhausted.

The following day, Patsy was already up preparing the continental breakfast for the house guests, as expected. Afterward, we embraced goodbye before I headed out to make my surprise visit to Tony. On my way out the door, Patsy handed me something, pushed me out, and reminded me to say hello to Tony and to pass on her fond regards. Tony's house was just around the corner and faced out onto the bayside, toward Sayville Long Island. As was my custom, I tried to walk in without knocking but the door was surprisingly locked. I knocked softly and waited with great anticipation while holding a couple balloons that Patsy had proffered me to take along as part of the surprise. A moment later the door opened and a strange woman that I had never seen at The Grove opened the door. Without introducing myself, I asked, "Is Tony home?"

She looked at me with shock and enquired, "Are you a member of Tony's family?"

"Well, you could say that" I answered. "After all, I am his boyfriend and all his family viewed me as part of their family."

And then she said something that struck me like a deadly bullet to my heart. She quietly said, "Tony passed away less than forty-eight hours ago during an emergency visit to the hospital close to his apartment in Bensonhurst." According to this woman, Tony was with his best friend Rodger at the time. And Rodger, of course, was his roommate/shareholder on Fire Island. I recognized who she was talking about, and a tidal wave of fog quickly engulfed my mind. As she continued with the nuanced knowledge she magically possessed, she explained to me that Tony had informed Rodger in his last moment of life that he was not to notify his mother nor myself of his last fight for his life, which was due to AIDS complications.

I walked along the beach aimlessly toward the "sunken forest" on the ocean side of the island and then collapsed on a dune for heaven knows how long before returning to the Carousel House without my balloons.

I honestly can't recall the circumstances of how I got back to Manhattan the following day; it is a total blank in my memory. What I do know is that other than my West Village roommate *Stripe*, no one else knew about the sudden death of my partner. Between Tony's shocking death from AIDS, coupled with the subsequent suicide of my brother later in the same week, I was gutted, emotional, and unsure what to do next. I felt I had nowhere to go other than possibly going back to Canada, realizing it was too impossible to process all this continuous, non-stop loss of lives. I found myself reverting to my childhood way of keeping my emotions to myself and feeling massively inarticulate.

17
SPONSORSHIP
SCR ARCHITECTS ON THE
UPPER EAST SIDE, 1988-1991

Meanwhile, I started work at SCR on the Upper East Side. One of my first projects as a senior interior designer was for the advertising agency of *Kallir, Philipps, Ross, Inc.*, whose new home would consist of 120,000 sq. ft. in the ongoing conversion of an old east-side bus depot. Part of the building had been recently programmed for the end-user functional and client spatial requirements by the architects and project managers from SRC while the project was in the very preliminary construction phase of the project. As an introduction to my new project, I was authorized to go down and do a fundamental site and building inspection of the progress to date. To my horror, as I methodically inspected every floor with my roll of drawings of as-built conditions, I came across a structural anomaly not indicated on the demolition floor plans and notes. This structural oddity interfered with the total usable area on one of the floors, which had been already fully programmed and planned within every available square inch of the floorplate. It was approximately a 600-square-foot rectangular mass, and it couldn't be missed—even at a distance! And yet this anomaly was something the project architect had apparently missed in his earlier onsite inspection of the as-built conditions and programming of the building.

Of course, I had my measuring tape and a notebook, so I quickly sketched and dimensioned the slab on the existing roll of blueprints in my hand and brought my mark-ups back to the partners attention at SCR. Clearly, the structural floor anomaly would be costly to remove, reconstruct, and seamlessly align with the existing concrete floor; it had clearly been overlooked and not budgeted within the existing 10 percent budgeting contingency. I was fearful that it would eat into the entire interiors budget for furnishings, finishes, fixtures, and equipment. After alerting the partners of my findings, we immediately scheduled a return visit, and I chaperoned the key project partner back to the site so he could see the damage for himself. It was determined at that point that the project contract did not have the budget to structurally remove it. And this was a major problem for the company. It would not only eat up the entire budget allocated for the interiors, but it would also cost the firm significant out of pocket money.

The project partner was marginally consoled by the fact that I had caught this serious and costly omission. Upon our visit, we were alone on the empty cavernous floor and at liberty to speak in the echo chamber. After confirming the anomaly for himself, my boss swore out in frustration how he entrusted his well-paid architects and how they had completely *fucked up*. As a result, he thanked me for my professional observation of the oversight and welcomed me into his inner circle and the trusted confidence of his associate partners, who thanked me for my time-sensitive discovery.

I responded that it had been just pure luck, thanks to the recent project management skills that I'd honed while working for *Public Works Canada*. It was all a matter of professional attention to detail and timing. But he was not buying my modesty; his face was crimson red, and I suspected someone was going to possibly lose their job, or at the very least be seriously reprimanded.

On the project site, the two of us troubleshooted the best-and-worst-case scenarios and feasible solutions. I was asked if I could integrate the slab and make it work while keeping this omission between the two us. I agreed that I would turn the physical constraints into a design asset for all stakeholders. What else could I say, as he was my new visa work sponsor, and I was more than happy to comply with his wishes. I suggested perhaps I could zone the executive offices and workstations on the raised platform as a status symbol, but I would need his promise and guarantee for some immediate revisions to the construction working drawings. And I suggested he could raise the ceiling to the full underside of the floor slab above. This could potentially give us the required code clearance to walk freely on the raised concrete slab. I suggested that he have his engineers reprogram the working drawings so that all the proposed new HVAC and electrical conduits would be circumvented as much as possible above the area. As his newly assigned senior interior designer and acting project manager, I could make it look like I'd always intended to include a featured raised area for the executive administration. He agreed that this sounded like a good plan and indicated that he would expedite everyone in the CADD department to make this happen, stat!

Subsequently, I met with the client, and they signed off on my revised programming that included a new security feature for a proposed raised observational platform in the executive area. Everything went off tickety-boo, and we were good to proceed! Sometimes you must wing things as you go. When executive partner Joe Cacarillo heard the good news, he exhaled and said, "*well done*," as he metaphorically wiped the sweat from his brow. I had just saved his company a fortune for a stupid oversight and a potential hit to the firm's stellar reputation at the time.

According to many of my new colleagues, I had *big balls,* and they would frequently mention that I appeared to be getting preferential treatment from the partners and unfettered access to their private office. Most of the time, my female colleagues dismissed me because I was a male and part of the "old boys' club." I responded by telling them that if they wanted to get ahead, nothing prevented them from knocking on their door and walking in. I truly didn't understand what was going on with their reticence.

That is until the day when I soon understood their hesitancy, after attending my first Christmas party at SCR. We had all drawn names from a hat to play Secret Santa, and that was the catalyst that alerted me of their concern. Just a week before the party, I had walked into the shared office of the four partners and given them some surprising news that I was gay. The guys had invited me into their office to join them in a champagne toast to celebrate a recently acquired new client: *Elizabeth Arden* on Fifth Avenue. They were all excited and asked me how I liked all the beautiful (and mostly blonde, blue-eyed) girls that surrounded me on the lower floor, dedicated to the interior design department. Truthfully, I told them that I really could not care less, and I was more into the guys who worked in the printing and copying room, at which point their jaws feel open, and they giggled like a gaggle of school-aged girls. Remarkably, I had their attention, and more importantly, their respect.

When I attended my first SCR Christmas party, I witnessed something particularly egregious and offensive to my nature. I discovered that a few female colleagues seemed intimidated by a couple of male employees at SCR. I had noticed two or three of them had many more Secret Santa gifts compared to everyone else. As expected, we all opened our gifts in front of everyone and tried to guess who the Secret Santa was. In an unanticipated awkward moment, some of my female colleagues received inappropriate clothing, which was clearly embarrassing and humiliating to see. When I looked up at my colleagues' faces, I could see they were not laughing and not even pretending to smile. They quickly threw the tasteless, misogynistic gifts back into the wrapping paper and tucked them aside in embarrassment. My colleagues had no intention of guessing who the inappropriate Secret Santa was, and if looks could freeze the balls off a brass monkey, then the cowardly Secret Santa would be a eunuch.

Out of concern and curiously, I followed one of my female colleagues to the washroom and caught up with her before she went inside. I apologized profusely for having earlier remarked that she had no reason not to knock on the partners' doors to demand more opportunities for advancement; she was remarkably talented and clearly intimidated by unwanted and inappropriate attention from an unidentified colleague. She expressed that I was advancing within the firm more rapidly than the women. I assured her that as a gay man, I certainly had my fair share of intimidation, bullying, and harassment and could only respond with, "I went after everything I earned since I was a child, and at great expense of losing my family ties and security."

Her response was, "I am not prepared to ruffle any feathers."

I responded back with, "How the heck do you expect to learn how to fly and set yourself free from your fears?" And then she disappeared into the Ladies' room.

Once again, my inclination was to somehow protect her, and when she finished and came back out, I told my colleague that I would be honoured to be considered *one of the girls* and that I would watch out for her wellbeing any time, if she needed me! I mentioned that I had been a staunch feminist since the 1970s—a long time before I became a gay activist. More important, I now had a glimpse into the hidden narrative of professional women who were vulnerable to workplace exploitation in the corporate sector. She then put on her coat and headed into the elevator, leaving the despicable experience of the party behind.

I have not experienced anything like this again, thankfully! However, at the time, I had my suspicions about which of my male colleagues may have been the alleged Secret Santa, although the women I worked with never mentioned any specific names to me. It was clear that when certain guys came down to our floor, my colleagues would quickly bury themselves in their drawings or pick up the phone and pretend to be talking with a client, an outside vendor, or some other allied professional. I did not need to hear names. I was a quick study of abnormal behaviours, and I had my suspicions and nothing more. I kept my eyes on the quieter, more reserved gals.

Some of the other outspoken ladies with a backbone could easily handle themselves, and I was not worried for them. And they would eventually become my lunch partners. When we were outside, we frequently stepped into nearby Betsey Johnson's shop for a spark of inspiration and audacity. In fact, we had a recently hired administrative assistant upstairs who only wore Betsey Johnson, and she would talk smack to any guy who appeared lecherous and creepy. She was the most fun of all the employees and put many of the straight boys on notice. If she was just a little larger, I teased her that I would love to snatch that dress off her ass, put it on, and twirl gaily around the office...and there were times when she started to remove her skirt to see if I would follow through.

Ah, the fun memories—I was a full-fledged member of both our unspoken sorority and fraternity. I have always had friends that thought I was just a tad outrageous, and that was my intent: keep everyone squealing for more of the things they dared not do (at least in the open). But eventually everyone succumbs to the rules if they want to get ahead. I merely wanted to stretch the proverbial rubber band of holding things in on appropriate occasions. No harm and no foul!

Meanwhile, I continued working at a feverishly fast pace, receiving other notable projects as senior interior designer, with only the assistance of a dedicated CADD technician to input all my design drawings and mark-ups. My slate of projects included a relatively small advertising project of 50,000 square feet for *Lintas Worldwide*; the *Republic National Bank* (55,000 sq. ft.) in Midtown Manhattan; a small office for Wang Computers; and the *Philip Morris/Kraft Foods Headquarters* (120,000 sq. ft.) in Rye Brook, New York,

Westchester County. The variety of projects pretty much filled my billable timesheets for the two years before my H-1B Visa expired with SCR, and by then I was burnt out from work and the toll of my mounting personal losses, especially with Tony's recent death doing loops in my mind. It was all beginning to take a little too much gas out of my tank.

Frequently, I would take a respite from my work and pull out the New York Times crossword puzzle at my drafting table, which got progressively more challenging throughout the week. Wouldn't you know it, I got caught by one of the partners as I tried to slide it under my tracing paper when he silently appeared at my desk for a work-related chat. His response was, "I like a good crossword myself as a stress relief," and he smiled and continued his daily rounds.

Toward the end of my time at SCR, I started dating random guys out of survivor's guilt. To be brutally candid, I wanted to contract AIDS out of shame and hurt. A part of me desperately wanted to physically die in New York and be buried next to Tony. One of the bars I thought I would target was New York's infamous leather bar, *The Eagle. I was looking for anonymous, unsafe sex, and instead I found* "Dr. Doug" nursing a beer at the end of the bar, and I quickly discovered he was an intern at Beth Israel's psychiatric department in Midtown Manhattan. He was a handsome, preppie-looking guy who just plain looked out of place at the leather bar. And there was no doubt in my mind that he probably thought the same thing about me.

Anyhow, we locked eyes, and before I knew what was happening, we were headed back to his place to the East Village near Astor Place to do a few lines of coke and take it from there. His invitation sounded reckless and was exactly what I was looking for. Unfortunately, or fortunately, depending how you look at it, we did not have sex that night, and he disclosed that he had just been diagnosed with HIV. I thought to myself, well, this is exactly what I signed up. However, when he started talking about how his medical career was just about to take off, he was devastated by the news, and he just wanted to be held tightly in the arms of another man, I melted into his mouth like an ice cube on fire from the heat of his burning, dry lips. I assured him I was his man for the night.

Eventually we fell asleep in each other's arms, with the added assistance of a Valium or two. At some point, we woke up and proceeded to talk further, and then out of the blue, he said, "*I love you, for what it's worth!*" And I understood him to mean that you never know when the time is appropriate, and you should just say it and get over it. It had occurred to me that I had been showing affection to people all my life, and I believed my actions and dedicated intent always indicated to someone that I loved them. But the words "I love you" never came easily, and I realized that I was merely doing what I'd learned at any early age from my parents. It was quite a provocative revelation and insight that Douglas shared with me.

I suppose in retrospect it was a blessing that I'd gone to The Eagle with the intent of just hooking up for anonymous sex the previous night. What I ended up with was so much more interesting, and it took me off guard from my own personal issues. Without question, it was an extraordinary first encounter and a subsequent brief affair with a fascinating and complex man who appeared to have just as many walls up as myself. However, what he challenged us both to do was to break down the stereotypical dad and son gay fetish role-playing that he appeared to be into, and I understood as imperative to him.

He wanted to break down some of his fears and barriers so that we might possibly evolve into an equally balanced relationship. Doug suggested that we needed to be mutually supportive of daddy figures, and that resonated a bit with me, but on a slightly different level. We could both express vulnerability, flexibility, and strength—without the need for domination and submission. And that worked out, for the most part, for me! However, vulnerability was still my Achilles heel that I have continued to work on to this very day.

I was thinking about what Doug had said, that "even daddies need daddies." Both Doug and I had his quote inscribed on the inside of our matching gold bands. I wore mine for some time. Unfortunately, over the years I must have lost it or passed it on to someone else. It makes no never-mind, as it is inscribed fondly in my memory. This simple but profound reminder took my breath away, as I thought of my own father and our estranged relationship outside of my control. Perhaps if he had just lived long enough to see me as a grown man, he could have then let his own guard down and realized just what Doug had so eloquently put to me—even dads need someone to be their dad on occasion; age and societal conventions had little to do with a lonely heart in a shattered man.

Meanwhile, my remaining time at SCR Architects was coming to an end, and about a dozen colleagues organized a wonderful surprise going-away dinner at a Mexican restaurant in the East Village. It was an amazing group of friends and colleagues that I was leaving behind. Just when we were finishing dinner and nursing our last frozen margaritas, I looked up and saw a gentleman standing in a full tuxedo, dressed to the nines. It was my favourite of the four partners, and he told me that he could not go without saying goodbye. He'd had his limo chauffeur wait momentarily as he ran inside to say goodbye to me.

He asked me to stand while all my colleagues clapped. Then he wrapped his arms around me in a huge bear hug and lifted me off the ground, saying, "We're all going to miss you, Michael, and if you ever get back to New York, you always have a job at SCR." He then kissed me on my forehead as if he were the Pope.

Wow, I thought. He sure has come a long way! And just as Joe turned to go, he pulled out a reference letter and handed it to me as he said his final goodbye with a salute. Such a class act! And what a pleasure it was to have worked at SCR.

SCR

1114 First Avenue
New York, New York 10021
212/421-3500
Fax 832-8346

SCR Design
Organization, Inc.

October 12, 1990

To Whom It May Concern:

Michael Plasse-Taylor has been employed as a Senior Interior Designer with our company for the past two years. Due to Immigration policies regarding work visa limits, he must return to Canada at this time. We are truly sorry to see him leave.

Michael's work demonstrates the highest level of professionalism. From pre-design analysis through job completion he has strong design and project management skills which have been appreciated on several of our multi-million dollar accounts. Moreover, his demonstrated keen sense of organization, and ability to establish and work within budget in a timely manner, would make him an asset to any design or facilities organization.

Hence we can, without hesitation, say that Michael would be an asset to any organization.

Very truly yours,

SCR DESIGN ORGANIZATION, INC.

Joseph H. Cacarillo
Executive Vice President

Corporate Interior Designers
Facilities Consultant

SCR Farewell Party

Front (left) Michael with SCR colleagues. **New York going-away party**

Pride in NYC on Doll's rooftop *(overlooking Christopher Street)*

Backrow (Left): Michael, Shane, Jay, Craig, Robert, and Shaun
Front Row Centre: Randy (aka Doll)

West Village Apartment with (Left) roommate Brad (aka Stripe) and I

Closing party at *The Saint*

18
RETURN

DUNLOP FARROW ARCHITECTS, TORONTO, 1992-1993

Around Labour Day holiday weekend of September 3, 1991, it was just a month before my visa was to expire, and I was scheduled to leave my job at SCR and return to Toronto. Out of the blue, I received a call from my estranged eldest sister, Edna, back in Toronto. She mentioned that she had got my number from my brother Jackie, who had recently come for a visit to New York and mentioned to her that he had a great visit. She knew he had come to celebrate his birthday with his new boyfriend Mac and that he had contacted me after all the years of separation from my family. I confirmed that Jackie had indeed reached out to see if he could pay me a visit and I had said, "Of course, please come." And with a little background research on their part, they booked a nearby bed and breakfast on the ground floor suite of a typical New York city brownstone on Hudson and Morton Street, literally a block shy from my apartment. I mentioned to Edna we had got together as planned for dinner and that after so many years apart, it was a little awkward to see him and to meet his new partner. It was as if he had no interest in the circumstances of my life, as he simply wanted to show off that he had a brother living in New York. I felt we should have a long overdue conversation, but he was not interested.

Edna agreed but was hesitant and struggling to find the right words to say. So, I prompted her and asked about the purpose of her unanticipated call. She then felt the courage to respond that she had some tragic news to share regarding our brother John. She quietly informed me that "Johnny" had driven his car at a very accelerated speed into a brick wall and was instantly killed on impact. And she mentioned that it appeared to be no accident. After I extended my heartfelt condolences and sadness to hear of his passing, she said that she believed all indicators pointed toward it being a suicide, despite not leaving any note or any forewarning to family members. According to my sister, he had been separated from his wife and kids and was going through divorce proceedings, which left him sad and feeling depressed. She stressed how much Johnny loved his children more than anything else in the world. The unbearable reality of not being around his kids had broken his spirit to the point of having a clinical diagnosis of acute depression. As a result, his family doctor had placed him on strong antidepressants and sleeping pills, for some bizarre reason, which in combination with his penchant for beer was lethal and resulted in a recent trip to the emergency room for a severe panic attack and heart palpitations.

After managing his symptoms at the hospital, he was clinically discharged after forty-eight hours and immediately thereafter he hopped into his car and sped off. According to the police report, he more than likely intentionally ended his life. According to Edna and the rest of the family, there was no hope in reconciling with his wife, and the pain of losing his kids was just too unbearable. I didn't need to understand all the background details and had a pretty good picture of the condition he was probably in. I was surprized that nobody thought of removing his car keys, knowing of his unstable and medicated mindset.

We were both saddened to think that he had fallen through the cracks and not even the hospital and my surviving family members could have predicted the devastating outcome. She wanted to let me know about the funeral arrangements, and I informed my sister that I would have to check with my employer about compassionate time off to attend the funeral. I proceeded to explain how the awkward timing put me in a little bit of a jam. I mentioned that I was wrapping up a major project for the Penguin Publishers headquarters in Manhattan.

The CEO and his personal assistant were flying in from London to New York on a Concorde in the next couple of days. They had specifically requested to the partners that they wanted to meet with me before their final sign-off of their contractual obligations to SCR. The primary purpose of the very costly visit was to walk through my final interior design installation and point out all the creative custom millwork, furniture, floor patterns, and colour-coded wayfinding with me. They expected explanations of where the notable design features were highlighted and creatively developed to benefit the maximum number of employees. The secondary priority for their visit was to watch me prepare a punch list of outstanding contingencies and deficiencies in concert with them, as representatives of client stakeholders.

And because of these reasons, I explained to my sister that it would be a very costly business expense thrown into the wheel at the very last moment. I really couldn't see how I could cancel their visit to attend the funeral. Moreover, it was highly conceivable that I could potentially put my job and visa sponsorship at serious risk. I told Edna that I wasn't quite sure how to handle things on my end. What exacerbated my anxiety was I didn't want to burden my sister with the fact that I had lost my boyfriend Tony to AIDS a few days earlier. I was barely struggling to keep my head above water when she called with the sad news of my brother.

But God bless Edna's compassionate heart. She responded by saying that she understood my predicament and that it was not necessary for me to risk losing my job and sponsorship. And the crux of the matter is that after being estranged from my family for so long, I really knew nothing about his personal life. She shared Johnny's recent marriage difficulties and separation from his wife and kids, which triggered his rapid spiral down into an unmanageable depression. She concluded she simply wanted me to know about the tragic loss of our brother. I thanked her from the bottom of my heart for the courtesy of reaching out to me and expressed that I hoped we could personally reconnect when I would shortly return to Canada.

Anyhow, two days later, I returned to work as if nothing had happened. As scheduled, I took my visiting CEO and his personal assistant from London to the new *Penguin Publishers* headquarters in SoHo. It was a painfully rigorous and long three-hour walkabout that was all business. When we concluded, I was hoping and praying there was nothing else I had to do with them; I was emotionally drained and wanted to go home and bury my head. Instead of immediately heading back to their hotel, they invited me for lunch at the outside café in front of Citicorp that they explained was within walking distance back to my office on East 61st. Although I wasn't hungry and was reluctant to go, I realized it would be rude of me to decline. So, I marshalled up whatever energy I could muster and told them that lunch would be lovely. And off we went in one crowded back seat of the cab as the two of them reviewed their itinerary for the remainder of the day. I was thankful for the opportunity to zone out.

The moment I sat down and started to catch my breath is when things started to unravel for me, which was my biggest fear in my emotionally fragile state. We had just gotten settled at our table with our drinks and they asked me an innocent personal question about my life as a Canadian working in NYC. They were curious to know how things were working out for me. I was so preoccupied with burying my pain that their personal interest gobsmacked me. Our relationship up to this point had been highly professional and heavy with formality. Knowing they were typically British and generally reserved, I did not anticipate their extended kindness and warmth, causing my fragile emotions to rise to the surface. My hand started to shake so uncontrollably that I spilled hot coffee all over the table and my lap. As I frantically tried to reach for my cloth napkin to clean up my mess, it was like someone else had remotely turned on the water pumps at Niagara Falls. A torrent of tears poured out from my stinging eyes, and I could not get my quick breathing under control; the more I tried, the worse things got, and I felt like I was standing outside my body and witnessing myself falling apart.

The next thing I felt was the executive assistant pulling me out of my chair and pulling me up into the comfort of her arms, where I momentarily collapsed. I was in great fear and anxiety about being fired for this emotional imposition on our multi-million-dollar client. Nothing like this had ever happened to me before. As I tried to control my breathing, I apologized and cried out the details about the two very recent tragic deaths of both my brother and my boyfriend, Tony Esposito, within the past week. My news clearly stunned them, and they seemed miffed that I had not been given any time off to grieve. I told them I hadn't shared my very current misfortune with anyone, and it was not my employer's fault.

Meanwhile, as she held my hand and comforted me, the CEO flagged a cab, opened the door, and the two of them placed me gently into the cab, handing the driver a wad of bills, and dispatched me to my home on Barrow Street. They told me not to worry about my job or anything else and for me to take good care of myself; they were happy and grateful to have been there for me, and their final parting kind words were they absolutely loved the work I had done on behalf of Penguin Publishers. And I fell back into my seat with relief.

When I got back to my apartment, the only thing I recall my roommate Brad saying was that I looked like a mess! And I went off to crash in my room with my adopted chocolate lab Hudson. Much later, toward the end of the day, I received a call from Joe, the vice-president of SCR. He insisted I take a week off with full pay. He mentioned that the visiting London team was very pleased with my work and that his firm received their final blessing and sign-off for payment from a successful completion of my project. He also mentioned that the CEO had asked SCR to "take care of me," and that's when Joe offered his profound condolences and told me not to worry about anything. Two days later, I received a delivery of a large vase of all-white flowers with a condolence card signed by my colleagues at the office.

I felt truly loved and blessed to be working with such generous souls, and I realized just how much they valued me. I felt safe and could finally relieve myself of the grief and shock I had internalized as my private business and responsibility. They taught me a lesson on how they were more than colleagues and that they were my friends who were there for me. Sadly, a few weeks later, while I was still grieving terribly hard, I packed my bags for Toronto to head back for the final application of my Green-Card approval process. But by this point, I was so consumed with pain and tragedy all around *me* in New York, I had no intention of ever returning. The personal loss of my friends and loved ones took a crushing toll on my heart that now outweighed my love and passion for the city.

When I arrived at LaGuardia Airport, I tried to mask my red swollen eyes behind a pair of dark aviator shades. Upon my airport check-in and clearance, I was instructed to remove my shades, and I was asked to explain my red eyes. I think they may have been suspicious that it was from smoking pot, which I never did, or some other sort of substance abuse. Anyhow, as a few errant tears fell down my cheek, I mentioned that I was grieving for my very recent and profound loss of loved ones, and nothing more had to be explained. They allowed me to proceed without any further delay. I suspect they also contacted the inflight personnel of my condition in advance, unbeknownst to myself.

Immediately after I boarded the plane and located my seat in the economy section, I put my shades to cover my cried-out eyes. The flight purser from the first-class section came into my section and tapped me on my shoulder, requesting me to follow her. I was confused but did what was asked of me. When we walked into the first-class section that was virtually empty, she told me to pick any one of the available seats as a courtesy upgrade and that she was there for me and at my service. I felt depleted and my past blessings had all but expired. Instantly, I wondered if I had a guardian angel who was always watching out for me and if it was not simply random "lucky horse-shoes." Her unanticipated kindness gave me pause to reconsider the mystery of higher powers, and once again I summoned my higher angels to show me the mystery of faith in others when I could not find it in myself.

All I knew was I wanted to escape from the hell of unbearable loss and a pain I could not shake. Ever since I lost my dear sister at the age of eighteen, I had been running from the holy spirit within my soul, and up to now I had measured my value in life on my personal accomplishments and personal relationships and not on wealth. As the plane descended into Toronto, I realized how much I had lost about the meaning of life and realized that although I had failed miserably by ignoring my inner voice, the brief flight in the clouds had restored my sense of spiritual purpose and value. Or maybe it was the complimentary wine speaking to me. Either way, I felt hopeful about my future and wherever the road would take me, one step at a time.

My first step was to stay at my good friend's co-op apartment in down-town Toronto. Anthony Ciaravella welcomed me into his home, but I did not want to overstay my welcome and told him I would find my own apart-ment as soon as I could. I simply needed a temporary shelter and a pause to move on with a new life in Toronto. Within a brief period of two weeks, I managed to secure a modest apartment of my own, located on Isabella Street near St. Jamestown and adjacent to the heart of *Toronto's Gay Village*. I had enough savings to get me through six months, and I was certain I could find work within that timeframe. Something in the back of my mind told me not to go overboard with furnishing and designing, so off I went to the local thrift store to see what I could find. I knew I would not stay in this economical apartment for long, but I needed a job and a sense of structure in my life. I had to meet my basic needs and then start to set goals, which meant I had no time to marinate in my past.

Dunlop Farrow Architects at 450 Front Street was situated next to the Globe and Mail and close to the CN Tower, and they had just co-partnered with the *Interior Design Collaborative* for the new building and interior design of the new 650,000 sq. ft. Ontario Provincial Police Headquarters (OPP) in Orillia, Ontario. As per the job advertisement in Canada's Globe and Mail, I applied to the attention of director Michael Borsellino at the Interior Design Collaborative and sent in my resumé. Toward the end of the week, I was contacted by Dunlop Farrow Architects to come in for an interview that Friday, and by the end of the interview, I was hired on the spot as the team's final member. I started the following Monday with a team that was headed by Alana Golding, in concert with three other new interior design hires: Laurie Hatfield, Mary-Jane Ridley, and a third designer whose name eludes me, regrettably.

Alana Golding was a well-experienced and industry-admired team leader on the OPP project and essentially the engine of the Design Collaborative division of Dunlop Farrow Architects. In the first two weeks, as we were acclimating and schematically block zoning the department adjacencies of the project, we were also updating and verifying the program staffing and area requirements, which took us out to various OPP locations throughout the Greater Toronto Area. One of the interesting personal things I discovered was several of the departments assigned to me were in a building that was very familiar to me. 90 Harbour Street was the original address of the Ontario Workmen's Compensation Board and the place where my sister Lois first worked. On occasion, I would drop by to meet her after work, so I was familiar with the historic lobby interior which had now become the main OPP reception and security check point.

Another location I was dispatched to verify the programming for was the OPP/Toronto Coroners Building at 25 Grosvenor Street across from the new YMCA building. I was responsible for the Forensics Department at the new OPP Headquarters in Orillia. It was quite illuminating to discover that in 1977, the OPP was the first police force to introduce laser fingerprint detection to the world. And from what I observed with all the scorch marks on the walls, the experimentation looked just a tad dangerous. Even more interesting on my investigative tour, it appeared that my programming reference did not account for a new morgue in Orillia, and I immediately brought this to the attention of Dunlop Farrow.

Back at the office, I began preliminary schematic layouts of the various departments I was assigned, including public community meeting rooms; a daycare centre; personnel, and human resources that were programmed on the main floor. And on an upper floor in the west wing, I was responsible for the Forensics Department and the Tactical Reinforcement Unit (TRU Team).

Toward the end of the schematic planning there was someone at the Design Collaborative who mentioned they had seen a job posting for a tenure-track position in the Interior Design department at the University of Manitoba, starting in the fall of 1992. I thought, *what the hell, it doesn't hurt to check it out, and so I applied.* At least, if not for any other reason, I would get a free paid trip to Winnipeg, which I had not visited since graduating years earlier, and it would be great to see some of my old beloved professors and friends. It was also a big part of why I pursued my graduate degree at Pratt; I always knew that I wanted the opportunity to teach at some point in my future, after I had gained significant professional practice in the industry. This ethos was indoctrinated into me ever since I was an undergraduate.

Anyhow, much to my unanticipated surprise, I rose to the top of the applicants and was one of two individuals short-listed and invited for individual back-to-back interviews. We were booked into different hotels along Pembina Highway in Winnipeg and not far from the campus. We were strategically timed and chaperoned by individual faculty members on the search committee. Neither applicant had any knowledge of who the other applicant was. The only thing I later found out was that the other applicant was a Cornell graduate who was academically published and had worked at Gensler for a very brief period. I knew from the advertised list of requirements the search committee was looking for a candidate with applied design strength and significant work experience that demonstrated currency in the industry, which happened to be my strength. Moreover, they had past knowledge of the kind of student I was as an undergraduate and had followed my professional accomplishments over the years.

Within a week after returning to Toronto, I received a personal call from Professor Grant Marshall with the surprising news that I had been awarded the position on behalf of the search committee and that the offer would be formally followed up with a letter and contract by mail. He offered me his warmest congratulations and looked forward to seeing me soon. That was how I began my professorial and scholarly career at the University of Manitoba.

19
TENURE-TRACK SACRIFICE
WINNIPEG, MANITOBA, 1995-1997

I was on a one-way airline ticket enroute to Winnipeg, Manitoba, with the aspiration of starting an academic career at my old alma mater. Once again, I checked my worldly possessions into a couple of suitcases. As I sat on the plane and looked out, I reminisced about how I had forgotten my old, navy-blue metal steamer trunk from long ago that housed a few of my school yearbooks and other mementoes. Previously, the trunk had been stored in home of my friend George Yabu's parents on Bleeker Street, and I completely forgot about it. Old memories filled my mind of when I first met George back in the summer of 1977. That was the year he taught me how to drive in his car, which was an old stick-shift Honda that looked like it had seen better days. But it worked and somehow survived my heavy foot on the clutch and the serious grinding of its gears. And yes, I did manage to pass my driver's test on the first try.

Shortly thereafter, George reunited with his old classmate from Ryerson, Glen Pushelburg. And the rest is history for this uber-talented team and partnership of *YabuPushelberg* (YP). By the time I started teaching, they were already internationally renowned as Canada's superstar interior design team, putting Toronto's *Ryerson's School of Interior Design* on the global map. Meanwhile, I had just ended my life in New York while they were establishing a second satellite office in Manhattan's SoHo district.

Back in Winnipeg, Professor *Grant Marshall* was the department head and Professor *Michael Cox* was the recently appointed dean of architecture at the University of Manitoba; we all knew each other very well from my earlier days as a student from the late 1970s.

I was asked to teach a range of upper third- and fourth-year studio design classes, including the thesis practicum during the second semester of fourth year; graphic communications in third year; and *the history of modern design* as a professional elective in fourth year. In addition, I volunteered several extracurricular workshops on programming, conceptual-design thinking, and graphic iterations for my fourth-year students and colleagues who wanted to participate.

The *Interior Design* department had high expectations of me and viewed my addition to the faculty as "a breath of fresh air." And I was excited to rise to the challenges of academia. As part of the interdisciplinary peer-review process for my very first research project on Sign Talk Manitoba; the world's first bilingual/bicultural deaf and hearing daycare, I was surprised in my second year to be nominated for an Rh Institute Foundation Emerging Researcher award. The location of the daycare was in Winnipeg, at 285 Pembina Highway on the periphery of the Osborne Village. My research findings not only impacted the Manitoba planning guidelines for childcare but also became a precedent for a second bilingual/bicultural deaf and hearing daycare in Australia, according to the director (Teresa) of SignTalk Manitoba.

I was comparatively young to the rest of the faculty and a breath of fresh air to the students. I looked to some of my colleagues as role models as I began to teach. Professor Diane Jackman and Professor Ron Veitch had co-authored a book with Mary Dixon on the guide to textiles for interior designers, and their book was mandatory reading in the curriculum.

And then there was Professor Leon Feduniw, whose research focussed on sustainable design and the environmental impact. He was a great inspiration in how he integrated his environmental research into class going back to the late 1970s when I was a student. Everything the faculty took on as scholarly creative work was understood to always connect authentically back to professional best practices in interior design and not merely academic-based theory. Our research had to be rigorously peer reviewed and applied to student learning objectives and outcomes as well as to broader community-based design issues and problem solving. And I knew from the start that my research umbrella would embrace my lifelong mission to bridge the human need for community outreach and a broader range of diversity in design thinking, inclusive of marginalized minorities both inside and outside of the university. I was dedicated to a life of service that focussed on queer youth-at-risk, and it was a part of my DNA.

In addition to community service, I was nominated and served a term as vice-president of the *Professional Interior Designers Institute of Manitoba* (PIDIM) as part of my professional service. While serving in this capacity, I organized Canada's first national AIDS fundraiser involving all the provinces from *Interior Designers of Canada* (IDC) and hosted by *Robert Enright* from the CBC and endorsed by *Prime Minister Jean Chrétien.*

But by far, I was most proud to be a gay activist whom all my students and colleagues respected. In fact, my entire fourth-year class volunteered their extracurricular time to work on my original "Unmasking of Our Interiors" fundraising gala for a local AIDS hospice that was held in a large warehouse donated by my friend Reva Lerner's company, Richlu Manufacturing.

How the two of us originally connected was quite random. When I first moved back to Winnipeg to teach, I did not have a personal social network. However, on one unexpected occasion, I ran into my old classmate *Michelle Mina, who* just happened to be visiting her cousin Penny in Winnipeg. The three of us met up at *Mozart's Cafe* in the Osborne Village to reunite and get caught up. Penny happened to be a budding harpsichordist and through her, I met her good friend Eric Lussier, who was a well-known and highly respected harpsichordist and music director of the *MusikBarock*, along with his partner Shephard and their friend Reva Lerner. We met at a harpsichord recital in St. Boniface.

The five of us, along with a female anesthesiologist from Toronto whose name escapes me, began a dinner-party group, hosting monthly dinner parties that rotated through everyone's homes. My newly adopted family and clique of friends in Winnipeg literally saved me from emotionally disconnecting and isolating myself with my ongoing grief from my recent loss and life in New York. This type of socializing in Winnipeg was all new to me and most appreciated. I loved the intimacy of our group's sexual diversity and our range of ages and socio-economic backgrounds. We were all creative minds with unique areas of interest and professional experience. Everyone at our table was highly fascinating and added a nuance and twist of phrase to everything we discussed over dinner. Everyone had painful issues from the past that everyone could relate to at some level, and for the most part had overcome and survived as a stronger person. We knew we were bonded over our unique personalities and hearts.

At the time, I lived in a large one-bedroom on Roslyn Road that had one large three-piece washroom in the hall and another bedroom ensuite with a shower; it was just perfect! And not too soon after moving in, I met the building owner, Michael, who happened to be gay and periodically invited me as his guest to the opera. Meanwhile, his sister, who I originally had met, ran the day-to-day operations of leasing out the apartments. Not unlike me, Michael was a very private person—a bit of an introvert. He lived in the penthouse directly above me and we shared the same incredible view from our apartment windows and balconies. Mind you, his place was tremendous; he had converted two pent-houses into one and he had a beautiful, custom-installed gas fireplace to make everything warm and comfortable during the long, cold winters.

Both our residences faced across the Assiniboine River and onto the back side of the Manitoba legislature, which was frequently used as a cruising area for gay and closeted guys in their cars. It was an amusing alternative to watching television (which I rarely had the time or inclination to see). The top of the legislative architectural dome was appointed with a gilded bronze statue of the Roman god Mercury. The sculpture was colloquially referred to as "the golden boy" and was viewed at eye level from my balcony. Most Canadians recognized this symbolic gateway and landmark to the prairies, and it was the perfect-picture window.

I could not ask for a better view and source of inspiration. In an odd kind of way, I felt my good fortune and luck had indeed favoured me as a golden boy, holding up a torch for myself. I'd always thought of myself as being blessed with luck, and in Winnipeg, I felt the spiritual energy of the golden boy as a beacon and reminder. It was inspirational and humbling to look out my window to see this every day. My apartment view was a wonderful surprise and a reminder from the universe to let me know that my advocacy mattered in Winnipeg. It was almost like I was a mediator between the spirit world for my friends and lovers lost to AIDS and the mortal world of my gay activism that sparked while working at the University of Manitoba. I was alone but never lonely, with a foot in both the physical and spiritual world.

Over time, I developed a deepening friendship with professor and chair Grant Marshall. We would frequently lunch together at work, and on occasion I would get invited to his home for dinners prepared by his uber-gifted wife, Marilyn (Marnie) Young. Marnie and Grant Marshall had originally met decades before, backstage at the Royal Winnipeg Ballet where she had been a principal dancer. Marnie was a mature woman, and her facial bone structure and elegant features never faded with the passage of time. Her profile had not lost her classic ballerina's form and she remained effortless, poised, and elegant! She stood with quiet confidence in the shadow of Grant's enormous talent and his long list of creative and artistic accomplishments. But her light shone bright nonetheless, and I always found Marnie to be an effervescent and terrific host. I never had a chance to thank her for just being a tremendous partner and anchor in Grant's life.

At the university, I would join Professor Grant Marshall along with the talented Professor Winston Leathers, who were both artistically talented and devoted to the students; particularly at the annual summer sketch camp where they supervised and instructed watercolour painting. It was an honour to be invited along as a colleague! Every single student and graduate who attended summer sketch camp was blessed with a once-in-a-lifetime gift to be taught watercolours by the masters.

As a colleague, I was embarrassed by my comparative lack of professional expertise, and I would often go off on my own to experiment and play in the paint. I couldn't compete with these men! Holy smokes! They were both established artists who loved to share their passion for art and watercolours, and I have never come across this kind of faculty talent at any other university I have subsequently been associated with in Canada or the United States.

And trust me, when I later served on the board of visitors for the Council for Interior Design Accreditation (CIDA) I visited many of the top-ranked programs throughout the United States, and none of the faculty I met could hold a candle to these masters. Professors like them were rare and highly valued in the face of a plethora of theoretical scholars without an ounce of personal talent.

In my experience, students were the best metric for uncovering and separating mediocre professors from true pedagogical ground-shifters and shakers; they craved authenticity and significant in-field experience and could only get it from outside industry experts or faculty with the latest advancements in interior design practice and professional development. I often preached from my classroom pulpit: "Do not rely on your professors for your individual thinking and repository of knowledge that is your individual responsibility and choice."

I would encourage them to go look elsewhere for inspiration, telling them to travel, play and explore their personal lives. Or read a trashy book and throw a few darts and see what they hit. More important, learn the rules and don't be afraid to break free from them. In my experience, so many schools (to this day) prescribe their myopic views on good design based on opaque rules and past conventions...to which I say, "Blah, blah, blah!" There are far too many sheep and not enough good shepherds and leaders in our industry.

Students have got to figure out what they are paying for in their post-secondary education. As the archetypal romantic poet Dylan Thomas would say, "Do not go gentle into that good night." And as a proud queer activist, I would frequently suggest that my students be audacious and throw a little shade on those tired conventions, saying, "Kick up your heels, girls, and fight back," referencing the greatly beloved Miss Marsha from the Stonewall riots.

In my opinion, interior designers must be careful not to let their guard down, as many allied professionals, educational leaders, and non-professionals are apt to label you a generic "designer," which is egregious and personally insulting to the men and women who have fought for the provincial *interior designer titles acts,* restricting the practice of interior design to those who have met stringent educational requirements and testing. Interior designers must not be assimilated into the milieu and swamp of anyone and everyone with a dream and a shingle who can advertise as a "designer."

I was a proud member of *the Association of Registered Interior Designers of Ontario* (ARIDO) and the *Professional Interior Design Institute* (PIDIM) that supported the pedagogical and professional research necessary for the creation of our act that gave equal footing and legal protection to those qualified to use the term "Interior Designer." The Interior Design title act was now recognized across Canada and by many industries and educational leaders across the United States and the world. This is another legacy and benchmark not discussed with any frequency in schools of interior design, regrettably. I am fearful that our Canadian legacy is being lost as everything becomes increasingly globalized and homogenized. I worry that the younger generation of professionals will not know the legacy of our Canadian history.

As leaders in post-secondary education are increasingly imported from around the world, Canadian schools with accredited programs in Interior

Design have become at great risk of losing their unique cultural heritage and historical footprint in the building of our profession. It appears to me that Canadian universities are willing to let this happen without much fore-thought of any negative impact this may have on Canada's new generation of interior design leaders, shapers, and shakers. We are a highly lucrative profession that was built on the diverse backsides of many women and men who moved our cherished profession forward while frequently being dismissed as irrelevant, or at best peripheral to architects. I say shame on them and shame on schools that promote the ethos that architecture reigns supreme. To that I would have to say a big, unequivocal, "Not on my watch!"

I am happy to be from an era when there was a real atelier approach to applied theoretical knowledge and global problem-solving underpinned a solid acumen of new materials and industrial construction techniques that led to exquisitely crafted conceptual ideas of furnishings, fixtures and equip-ment that no longer relied on historical precedents as if they were sacro-sanct. Moving forward to the rebellious and anti-establishment 1970s era, I saw interior design students at the University of Manitoba rebel against the confines of an international modern design order that over time diminished vernacular context and the stories of unique cultural differences.

Ergo, the era of postmodern thinking and design advanced a brief period of resetting and rethinking of new goals for industry leaders and allied professions with emerging trends in the world of design. Programming the seeds of placemaking and well-being has always been integral to the funda-mental core of interior design. Old rules and principles like "form should follow function" or "less is more" were now being rightfully replaced with "less is a bore" and beginning to honour what interior designers and decora-tors have known throughout history.

Creating a place (placemaking) is a historical component of interior design and decorating, and it has been an amusing ride to see scholars and other allied professionals in the built environment catch up. This may have been a revelation to scholars, but it was basic common practice to every-day people. We need to applaud all those "dolly decorators" who knew this on an intuitive and creative level. The unsung decorators, such as Budd Sugarman and Robert Dirstein in Toronto, often acted as high-paid consul-tants to Toronto's largest architectural firms who were outside their league of expertise and remain so to this day. Yet, some interior design schools shamelessly dismiss decorators as allied professionals to this day.

Looking back to my professorial role at the University of Manitoba, I see how blessed I was to be surrounded by faculty who possessed a Bachelor of Interior Design as their common underpinning, and many possessed a master's or a doctoral degree in inter-disciplinary areas. It was a critical staffing model that originated under the founding department head, Professor Joan Harland. In my opinion, she set the bar that distinguished graduates from the University of Manitoba's Interior Design department as a model of academic excellence unparalleled in North America.

During my three years as a tenure-track professor, I developed a very close mentorship with a handful of gifted students who demonstrated a lot of creative talent. Today, many of my students have become leaders, like Anna Szczepaniak at *Forrec Design* and Judy Cheung, who went on to do a master's in architecture at the University of British Columbia and moved on to work for Norman Foster's architectural office in London.

I could not be prouder to have played a mentoring role in many students' lives. And to this day, I remain in contact with many graduates on social media. I was fond of so many and was their biggest cheerleader, and not to just the top students. I always had a soft spot for the underdogs, and I would do my best to give them the additional one-on-one time that they needed. I never forgot the many years I felt like an underdog, and I recognized potential when they couldn't see it for themselves! I watched out for these diamonds in the rough.

Just one final personal memory of Professor Grant Marshall that cemented our love and mutual admiration as colleagues. Grant asked me to meet him in his office to go out for lunch at the faculty dining room in Pembina Hall. He wanted to discuss our planning of an upcoming trip to New York for our fourth-year class, which we used as a motivational carrot for students in the lower years. When I arrived at his office the door was open, but he must have momentarily stepped out. His office had two doors: one led to the public corridor of the fine arts building and the other led directly into the faculty administrative office and copier room, where I assumed he had gone.

As there were no cell phones in that prehistoric era, I needed to make a quick call to someone regarding the research and design project that I was doing on behalf of SignTalk Manitoba. Anyhow, I knew Grant would be fine with me using his desk phone, so I rolled around to the back of his desk and sat in his chair. I must have been quite relaxed because I had one leg up resting on the corner of his desk and I was in the middle of a conversation when Grant re-entered from the corridor after returning from the washroom.

As he stood in the door buck (metal doorframe) and entrance to his office, he did his best dramatic spot-on Bette Davis imitation from *All About Eve*, which was my absolute favourite movie classic of all time. Ignoring the fact that I was on the phone, he said: "Eve Harrington, I see what you are up to, you little upstart!" and he tossed his head back like Margo Channing, minus the hair! I had to instantly end the call, as we both fell into a fit of snotty-ass snorts and giggles. And then we deployed our fat lard asses across the campus to lunch at Pembina Hall.

Grant always accepted and supported my open and unabashed gayness as part of my in-your-face persona. He was a true and unapologetic gentleman and much ahead of his time. And as a point of fact, Canadians were generally far more progressive and open-minded than our American neighbours to the south when it came to queer diversity and living free of shame or reprisal. We were fiercely proud as an official French/English bilingual country, and we advanced our unique Canadian values for sexual and gender equality under our federal *Bill of Rights* to protect human rights, enacted by Parliament in 1960.

My memory of the two of us will always be my most cherished, and I have only ever shared it with one or two people since that time. His spontaneous imitation as Bette Davis captured the man I knew and held dear in my heart; nobody fucked around with Grant and how he chose to head his department with unbridled flair, style, and dignity for every human life. I truly adored this mentor and friend of mine. I understood who he was, and he embraced who I was; we both had the utmost respect and love for each other. There will truly never be another friend like Grant Marshall, or as fine a gentleman. He was a most beloved human being.

After three years of a promising future at the University of Manitoba, I considered resigning for personal reasons of feeling isolated and lonely in Winnipeg. I was burned out, and the denial and heartbreak of my recent past had caught up with me. Winnipeg gave me sanctuary and security, but it was not enough to sustain me moving forward for the long term. It had never been my intention to live there long-term, and I needed to cut my losses before I got further entangled in something more permanent. I had taken a calculated risk and given it my best shot. But I was ready to move on.

I needed to re-immerse myself back in Toronto. It was the only place in Canada that I ever considered home, and the closest thing I could relate to that came anywhere near the exuberance of New York. I was armed with teaching experience, research, and scholarly creative work under my belt and was anticipating a fresh start. Over the years, there had been a few accredited programs in interior design at various universities, colleges, and private schools in Ontario, and I already had another job offer waiting at the *International Academy of Design*. I trusted my instincts and was not afraid of taking risks. I would make a major move just one more time ... to the place where I was born and felt most at home in Canada—Toronto.

I had given my absolute best to my colleagues and students at the University of Manitoba. In fact, I stayed intensely focussed on teaching to escape the guilt of surviving AIDS and the countless loss of dearly departed peers and loved ones. Some of my acquaintances at the university expressed concern over my lack of interest in meeting a partner to share my life in Winnipeg. And I figured that they had no understanding of the urgency I felt in spearheading a national AIDS fundraiser from my vice-presidential platform with the *Professional Interior Design Institute of Manitoba* (PIDIM) and as an active member of Interior Designers of Canada (IDC).

The *Unmasking of Our Interiors* gala had evolved as an emotional outlet for me to share the impact of my untenable loss as a long-time survivor of the scourge of AIDS. I was walking around as though I were highly functional, and I needed time to remove the emotional mask that I hid behind so I could freely enjoy the prairie sun on my face once again. I was a lonely man with a broken heart and a shredded soul.

I started teaching with a genuine, heartfelt smile at the University of Manitoba. I quickly came to my senses as I began to "unmask my feelings" and accept the fact that I had been living in complete and utter denial of the impact of my profound loss. In my mind, the only way I could reluctantly let go of my past was to find a way to acknowledge my loss by honouring my deceased buddies whom I helplessly watched as they withered and perished. I attempted to leave their memories behind, and it was burdensome. I felt compelled to do something to mark their lives and honour their memory. And Winnipeg provided a brilliant opportunity for me to achieve this goal.

Maximizing my platform as vice-president of PIDIM, I knew that Manitoba would be the host province for the annual general meeting (AGM) of our provincial organizations from across Canada. As I started to discuss the merit of using this opportunity for a design gala with a socially responsive message, I realized that like myself, many folks wore a mask or persona to hide behind for one reason or another, and I thought this would be a great opportunity for our professional affiliations to "unmask" our ethical obligation for community service in a fun way that would utilize the creative design talent from across Canada. Within two weeks of intensive planning and coordination, I had sent out the AGM invitation with a request for each provincial representative and other membership from *IDC* to donate a unique, custom-designed "mask for auction." The proceeds would be donated to support the recent opening of an AIDS hospice in Winnipeg.

Before I knew it, everyone in Winnipeg was asking how they could help. As previously mentioned, my dear friend Reva Lerner donated the use of one of her warehouses for the event space; my friend Cheryl and her family's florist donated centrepieces for each table and feature arrangements spread throughout the warehouse (and the portable washrooms). In addition, Cheryl's family donated the catering of food and beverages for the gala. We had volunteers who coordinated and organized the entertainment, including talented musicians; fashion runway models who were dressed courtesy of *Club Monaco*; and bare-chested, buffed men who drummed up excitement and modelled the masks for auction. There were plenty of toiletries and beauty products donated by *Holt Renfrew*, and advertising revenue generated by local businesses covered the cost of the souvenir program and printing costs.

It invigorated my soul when I saw all my fourth-year students volunteer to assist with the venue car park and chaperone the guests inside the manual cage elevator up to the gala floor. Volunteers worked behind the bar and acted as washroom attendants, providing complimentary perfumes and colognes, shoe-shine, and moisturizers for the guests. In the event planning and lead-up, the acclaimed journalist *Robert Enright* from the CBC interviewed me about the event and volunteered to emcee the event.

Truth be told, everyone in Winnipeg and from across Canada "unmasked their hearts" with great kindness and support for a national fundraiser that was very dear to my heart. It all came together seamlessly, and I thank God for the spiritual privilege and professional platform to make a loving difference. My destiny and purpose were revealed in my valuable short time in Winnipeg, and I felt truly blessed by everything that transpired on a personal and scholarly level. It was a long overdue gift toward my healing, and my experience at the University of Manitoba remains one of the greatest joys in my life.

Service to our provincial organization

THE UNIVERSITY OF MANITOBA   Winnipeg, Manitoba, Canada R3T 2N2   FACULTY OF ARCHITECTURE
Department of Interior Design
(204) 474-9386

June 24, 1994

To Whom It May Concern:

Re: Professor Michael Plasse-Taylor

I have known Professor Plasse-Taylor for 13 years. He was a student here and graduated in 1981. Michael was a brilliant design student.

When the Faculty of Architecture advertised for a full-time tenure track position to begin in 1992, Professor Plasse-Taylor applied for the position. He was the successful candidate out of over twenty applicants. In his two years with us he has proven to be an excellent and hard-working teacher. His assignments have been in Graphic Communication, Theory of Design, Programming, Studios II, III and the Senior Project -- which is the graduand's comprehensive term-long design problem. Michael excelled in all of the aforementioned subjects. His student evaluations are exemplary.

Besides his heavy schedule, he sat on many Faculty and Departmental committees and performed extra duties such as running a week long rural sketch camp and organizing an out-of-country field trip.

Professor Plasse-Taylor also undertook a successful research project on bilingual, bicultural deaf and hearing daycare facilities during his first year here.

Michael is out-going, personable and is a "team player". I recommend him highly.

Sincerely,

C. Grant Marshall
Professor and Head

CGM/sc

Reference from Professor Marshall and department head

Unmasking **program souvenir**

Plasse-Taylor's unmasking of our interiors

A warehouse design gala & mask auction social on Saturday, Oct. 22, 90 Annabella Street, Winnipeg.

A benefit for AIDS with profit proceeds donated to The AIDS Shelter Coalition of Manitoba.

Endorsed by: The Professional Interior Design Institute of Manitoba, The Interior Designers of Canada and Prime Minister Jean Chretien.

The warehouse gala social will be emceed by Robert Enright. Doors open at 9:00 p.m. to the classical harpsichord duet performed by Eric Lussier and Penny Margolis. As a tribute to persons who are living with AIDS, and acknowledgement for persons we remember, Winnipeg's Dominance of Glamour and Le Lavendou will produce a conceptual fashion show and hair design tribute, with stage runway, lights, and sound system coordinated and directed by Christie Wigston. A parade of masks with models outfitted by Club Monaco will lead into Terry Wachniak's auction of masks designed by interior designers from across Canada.

We are thrilled to have Canadian renowned artist Esther Warkov exhibit her current three dimensional drawings at this gala, and a feature door prize mask designed my Manitoba Artist Di Thornicroft will be awarded to some lucky individual who has purchased a premium ticket at $100.00.

There will be plenty of visual surprises, fashionable people, DJ music, food and a cash bar to complement the social/interactive experience. We would love for everyone to come and make this unique AIDS fundraiser a success. We hope that after this first event, it will alternat from province to prov ince and city to city eaci year, underscored by th support and endorse ment of the Interior De signers of Canada.

Advance ticket pui chase available from Ticket Master and ASCM Tax receipts availabl upon request. Parkin; and entrance from th parking lot at the Richl Sportswear building.

"I am greatly encoui aged and appreciative t have a national profes sional organization sucl as The Interior Design ers of Canada uniting t increase awareness an funding to assist person: on disability and livin; with AIDS. It is througl our strength and cour age in numbers that w can continue to show support to our family o Canadian brothers anc sisters living with AIDS and I am proud to have this event initiated in the center of Canada - Win nipeg, Manitoba." · Michael Plasse-Taylor, project coordinator and artistic director.

The Right Choice For '94

THE ELI HERSCOVITCH ORCHESTRA

CALL ELI HERSCOVITCH AT 489-5267

Local review of Unmasking of Our Interiors

Michael Plasse-Taylor
Gala Co-ordinator & Artistic Director

Life is truly a precious gift from god and far too meaningless when not lived with honesty, passion and love. In the year of the family we need to address and recognize all culturally defined family minorities that are built on love and respect.

As a culturally recognized gay-positive interior designer, educator, and community volunteer, it gives me enormous pleasure to be blessed with an opportunity that brings together my professional colleagues and friends in a joint venture that can make a difference. Today we raise our collective consciousness, love and fund raising profits to benefit Manitoba's extended family of brothers and sisters living with AIDS. This is the right thing for families!

A paramount component of this project concept is my wish and mandate that all profits from "PLASSE-TAYLOR'S UNMASKING OF OUR INTERIORS" be donated to the AIDS Shelter Coalition of Manitoba, and that all gala profits will be respectfully earmarked, exclusively, for the financial needs of persons living with AIDS in Manitoba.

Michael Plasse-Taylor PIDIM, IDC, BID, MSc
Vice-President
PROFESSIONAL INTERIOR DESIGN INSTITUTE OF MANITOBA

Margaret Stinson
Interior Designers of Canada

On behalf of our members from coast to coast, I bring greetings from the INTERIOR DESIGNERS OF CANADA. Our Board of Directors has come to Winnipeg this weekend for the IDC Annual General Meeting and our Board meetings. We are thrilled to be the guests of the Professional Interior Designers Institute of Manitoba at this important benefit gala for the AIDS Shelter Coalition of Manitoba.

I congratulate Michael Plasse-Taylor and his colleagues on their creativity and energy in producing UNMASKING OF OUR INTERIORS. I hope that this imaginative event will be the first of a series of benefits to be organized by interior designers across Canada. This Winnipeg event will help to provide housing for those suffering from AIDS, a goal that the national interior design community supports wholeheartedly.

Margaret Stinson PIDIM / IDC
President
INTERIOR DESIGNERS OF CANADA

Artistic Director Professor Plasse-Taylor

SIGN TALK CHILDREN'S CENTRE

2nd Floor, 285 Pembina Hwy, Winnipeg, MB R3L 2E1
Phone: 475 - 8914 (TTY)   475 - 8906 (Voice)   FAX: 475 - 9980

January 20, 1995

Michael Plasse-Taylor
Department of Interior Design
Faculty of Architecture
University of Manitoba

Dear Michael:

Now that Sign Talk Children's Centre is open and operational in its new space, we have time to reflect on the processes that brought us to this point. On behalf of the Board of Directors of Sign Talk Children's Centre, I would like to take this opportunity to thank you for your significant contribution to the Deaf community through your creativity and sensitivity in your work on the creation of a new Sign Talk Centre. Your research outlining environmental design considerations in a bilingual, bicultural environment for Deaf and hearing children will have lasting significance - both for the local Deaf community and for Deaf communities throughout North America. In addition, the Manitoba Daycare Office and the Manitoba Housing Authority have copies of the research, so it will benefit others through their systems.

Throughout your involvement you respected Deaf community processes even though this meant many more meetings (including numerous 'town hall meetings') than might have occurred had you been doing this work in your own culture. This was true both in the research and design phases. Work in a different culture and language requires sensitivity, patience and a willingness to struggle through ambiguity. You showed these qualities, and the quality of work produces is testimony to your willingness to follow that path. At points we faced tight time lines and work needed to happen quickly. You were flexible and willing to accommodate us. We appreciated your professionalism and your willingness to volunteer your time to this worthy project.

Winnipeg's Deaf community is proud of their new children's centre. The space, the flow, the visually open environment contribute to a real sense of a 'Deaf' centre. While budgetary/fundraising constraints limited us in our ability to transform all the design features into physical reality, your clear foundational work on how space ought to operate in a bilingual, bicultural environment survived any and all of our restraints. Thank you for your design. One of the coloured glass windows in the new centre acknowledges your work and, as we say in American Sign Language, keeps your name 'shining' for future generations of Sign Talk kids and their families. We look forward to any future association with you that may occur.

In addition, please extend to the University of Manitoba our thanks for suggesting you as a resource to us.

Sincerely,

C. Demianyk

Carol Demianyk
Chair,
Sign Talk Children's Centre Board of Directors

cc. Dr. Dana Stewart, Department Head, Department of Interior Design
     Mr. Michael Cox, Dean, Faculty of Architecture

Pro-bono *research and interior design*

20
ACADEMY OF DESIGN
TORONTO, ONTARIO, 1997-1998

When I arrived back in Toronto after resigning from the University of Manitoba, I was welcomed with an immediate job offer from my friend Joyce O'Keefe at the *International Academy of Design*. We were originally introduced through a mutual friend and allied colleague of mine back in New York City. Maria worked as a furniture dealer when I'd worked for SCR in Manhattan. Initially, I met her on a consultation for systems furniture and seating for the LINTAS WORLDWIDE advertising project I had been working on. Over many visits to Maria's showroom, I had come to know her as a gregarious and kind person. She had a lovely, soft-sales approach as a representative for her company that was in the A&D (Architects & Designer) building on East 58th Street, between Lexington and Third Avenue. Just before I left Manhattan for my final return to Canada, Maria invited me for a farewell lunch and an opportunity to thank each other for our professional relationship that had evolved into a friendship. I can't recall if Maria was a Canadian expat (and possibly a Manitoba graduate), but she did have a Toronto connection with her very dear friend who she insisted I meet.

Joyce O'Keefe had her own professional practice in Toronto. Maria insisted that Joyce set up a date to meet me upon my return. She thought we might hit it off, and we did. Joyce and I went on many lunches and jaunts around the city when I worked at the *Design Collaborative* at *Dunlop Farrow Architects*. About a year later, around the same time that I accepted my teaching position in Manitoba, Joyce accepted an administrative position as chair for the Interior Design program at the International Academy of Design.

Joyce and I had remained in touch throughout my time in Manitoba, and in my final last days I called her in Toronto and informed her that I was resigning and coming back. Without wasting a second, she interrupted me with an immediate request, "Oh, please come work for me at the International Academy of Design! We'll have fun, and we could use someone with your academic qualifications and fabulous work experience!" I agreed to join Joyce's team as a part-time instructor upon my return from my post at the University of Manitoba.

Part-time employment was perfect, as it would allow me the freedom to take on a consulting private practice for myself. In addition to teaching, one of my first tasks at my new job was to help Joyce prepare the International Academy of Design for a review and display of the student work, in anticipation of an accreditation visit from what was then known as FIDER (the Foundation for Interior Design Education & Research accreditation), prior to CIDA (the Council for Interior Design Accreditation). I believe it was the first time the academy had ever applied for accreditation, and it was Joyce who had made this all happen.

The FIDER Accreditation Board at the time awarded the academy a six-year accreditation, and I continued to assist Joyce to strengthen the areas of recommended improvement from the FIDER site team of volunteers. This was quite remarkable at the time, as it was the first private school in Ontario to receive interior design accreditation outside our public universities and colleges. As part of my ongoing professional service, I joined FIDER and became a visiting site visitor following my training in 1996. This allowed me access to first-hand knowledge about a variety of interior design programs across North America.

In addition to teaching several studio-based courses at various levels, I quickly established my own private consulting practice, focussing on retail and hospitality, which started to take off by word of mouth. One of my first private clients was *Alexa's Home Furnishings*, which garnered my client a citation from the *Historical Preservation Society* in Markham, Ontario. Another project of historical relevance was an *arts and crafts* interior restoration project for an old buddy of mine, Jim Foley, who had just retired from his medical career at Toronto's *Sunnybrook Hospital.* For this special-interest project, I consulted with the immensely talented and creative skills of Principal Mary Jane Ridley at Ridley/Roy Design as well as Gwen Krieger from *Blue Hat Studio.* I had known both women as professional colleagues for decades, going back to our earlier days as classmates at the University of Manitoba.

Another project I completed about the same time was a high-end design concept for *Atelier Leonidas,* located out along the Danforth just east of the Don Valley ravine. The proprietor, Leo, had worked many years at the upmarket Harry Rosen and Holt Renfrew stores on Bloor Street and knew the type of client he wanted to cater to at his own shop. The interior had to reflect the refined taste of his upscale clients, and although it was a fast-tracked turn-around, it was a heck of a fun project with an open-ended budget. The project was filled with floor-to-ceiling exquisite custom millwork and wall panelling, wood floors with Persian area carpets, and original atmospheric paintings and sculpture. It was a small project that was wonderfully detailed and executed in the design and the renovation. After some careful negotiations with the tailor next door, I busted a hole in the wall and created an archway into the adjacent shop, facilitating immediate access to alterations. I was sorry to see his business go tits-up after a couple of years, due to lack of high-end traffic in Greektown. And Leo eventually moved his business back into the swanky neighbourhood of Yorkville.

Meanwhile, my private consulting was moving along, with a variety of contrasting clients and budgets simultaneously. At one point, I was consulting on the interior design for the prestigious *Canadian Embassy* in New York City. I would finish a meeting with the architectural firm, then run home and change out of my jacket and tie, and then slide into a casual shirt and blue jeans appropriate for another prospective client, *the Toronto Hemp Company* that was located on Yonge just south of Bloor Street. And my day was still not over. I would then have to rush home and prepare for my evening classes that I was teaching at the academy. It was a lot to juggle, but I was young, entrepreneurial, and ambitious. It was all very exciting and unpredictable! And it kept me on my toes and kept my waistline trim! The only gym I had time for was my client, Jim.

Eventually, I had to forfeit much of my professional consulting, as Joyce grew more and more dependent on me to take on several classes in both the day and evening. At the same time, she wanted me to assume more of an unofficial leadership role in the broader curriculum development. One of my favourite curricula developments was a complete overhaul of the Fundamentals of Design course. My new proposal sounded refreshing and exciting to Joyce, and she asked me to test it out at the start of the semester. The theoretical underpinnings of the new principles and elements of design were integrated into a series of experiential explorations throughout the course. And the final course assignment was a visual demonstration of the student's theoretical understanding of individual research, analysis, and design, applied to a randomly selected landmark building in the Greater Toronto Area. The design precedent was inspired by the 1934 New York Gala Beaux-arts Ball at the Waldorf-Astoria Hotel. The event celebrated the absurd and ephemeral creativity in wearing architectural hats and costumes as fodder for social interactions and amusement.

The Toronto *Skyscraper Hat Project* included a variety of buildings throughout the urban fabric and timeline of Toronto: from the nearby historic Royal York Hotel which began construction in 1927 and was built by the Canadian Pacific Railway. It dominated the Toronto skyline until 1967 with the arrival of the Toronto Dominion Bank Towers, built in the International Style, by Mies Van Der Rhoe. Then the timeline proceeded into post-modernism, exemplified by Mississauga City Hall, which opened in 1987, and was designed by architects Edward Jones and Michael Kirkland. Another noteworthy landmark structure that became a part of the Skyscraper Hat Project was the world-famous CN Tower. All these buildings were a part of the lottery for students to randomly select from a hat.

Once a building was selected, the students were required to do a preliminary site visit and provide evidential proof of their in-situ site observations and documentation of the existing as-built conditions, noting evidence of key design elements and principles. In addition, students were expected to annotate public wayfinding, traffic patterns, and behavioral responses by the end-users. The preliminary findings had to be communicated by photographs noted with alpha/numeric data, critical to the structure, end-user interplay, ephemeral activities, and visual aesthetics. It sounds like a lot of work, but the students grasped the theory and applied themselves to the task at hand with passion and determination.

The next project phase required the students to do several iterative design concepts and sketches to transform the original design with an added element of something whimsical or ephemeral. The students were required to go back to the original findings and revise the preliminary analysis of the elements and principles of design according to the new conceptual inter-pretation. The construction and engineering of the presentation model/hat was the last phase. Students were required to build a replica model of the building that would sit on top of a six-inch pedestal with a cut-out and inset for their head as a portable architectural hat. Around the perimeter of the base, the students were required to integrate a series of "Plasse-Taylor theory plates" that integrated their analysis of key elements and principles of design. And as directly stated, the presentation of the model/hats could be as high as necessary; "the higher the hat, the closer to a heavenly mark!"

The last day of class presentation was a term-end celebration for my class. As part of the structural integrity, the students were required to go out of the building and onto the corner at Bay and Wellesley Street. They were required to walk around the block in a single-line parade, which brought ephemeral joy and happiness to everyone! The students stopped traffic with their outrageous parade of hats and made curious people randomly ask, "Who are you and where are you from?" After the parade, the students returned to class for a final individual presentation of their work.

And although I can recall many spectacularly models, there was one pre-sentation that resonated with me and is emblazed in my design conscious-ness, even though I have forgotten the student's name! Anyhow, she was somewhat of a shy student who always sat alone at the back of the class; she tended to stay aloof and removed from the other students. For the design lottery, she had picked Toronto's historic *Royal York Hotel*, which was a neo-classic hybrid of styles for a twenty-eight-storey building. It was aesthetically complex and challenging, with all the architectural and ornamental details, but she said she was up for the challenge.

On the day of her class presentation, she showed up with her husband, who was dressed like a limo chauffeur. She stood behind him in her stiletto heels, wearing a very short black sleeveless and form-fitting dress, like the girls and classic background dancers in Robert Palmer's video "*Addicted to Love.*" She entered the room carrying a magnum of champagne. Without uttering a word from her crimson-red-painted lips, she sat the bottle on my desk and her husband proceeded to pop the cork and poured champagne into two flutes, handing one to myself and the other to his wife. At this point, she started her presentation with a raised toast to the *Royal York Hotel* and proceeded to place her large model/hat on her head, saying, "Let's talk about the toast of the town."

The entire presentation was executed like a well-oiled performance piece. And I started to realize that I was looking at beautiful shades of bread she had toasted for the façade; everything from white to beige to medium- and dark-brown tones were creatively fashioned into environmentally friendly construction materials. To create structural integrity, she allowed the bread to go stale before toasting and constructing the model. Creative thinking outside the box was a project requirement, and that was precisely what I got from her.

Definity she was thinking outside the box, and I was highly impressed with her concern and creative application of sustainable materials that could easily be broken down and organically decomposed. She had hand-painted all the oxidized green copper metal on the building with water-based paints. And the scholarly analysis around the podium was highly analytical and graphically stunning. It was the first and only time that I'd ever awarded an A+ in a *Fundamentals of Design* course in my academic career. And she well-deserved it. My only regret is that I did not save any pictures from my wonderful Fundamentals of Design class at the academy!

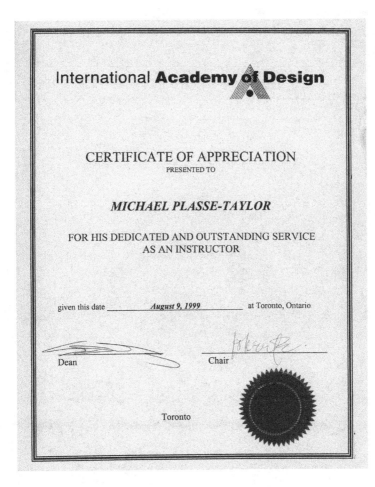

International **Academy of Design**

CERTIFICATE OF APPRECIATION
PRESENTED TO

MICHAEL PLASSE-TAYLOR

FOR HIS DEDICATED AND OUTSTANDING SERVICE
AS AN INSTRUCTOR

given this date _____ *August 9, 1999* _____ at Toronto, Ontario

Dean   Chair

Toronto

21
RYERSON UNIVERSITY
1999-2019

My connection to the currently renamed Toronto Metropolitan University (2022) started at Ryerson University's *School of Interior Design* in the summer of 1997 when I sent my curriculum vita off to the department chair, Professor Lorna Kelly. I patiently waited for a response, and it wasn't until the late fall of 1998 when I heard back. Professor Kelly invited me to come in for a "chat." At the time, she was impressed that I had a graduate degree in interior design and that I was a site visitor for what was then known as the Foundation for Interior Design Accreditation Board (FIDER). Although she did not have a tenure-track position available, she asked if I would consider teaching a fourth-year design seminar class. I responded in the affirmative, "Of course, I would be thrilled to help you out!" And that's how I originally got my foot in the front door at Ryerson.

The seminar class I inherited had been running for a couple of years and required minimal tweaking. What intrigued me from a pedagogical perspective was how the Ryerson student would respond to me as a first-time instructor, especially during the final semester. Would the class be open to my personality and perspective on design matters? It felt a little strange not knowing anything about the background level of knowledge they had acquired during the past four years. And I normally had some prior awareness of the class individuals. It seemed like getting to know each student posed a daunting challenge, initially.

In addition to my normal icebreaker where I provided relevant professional and academic background experience, pertinent to Ryerson's School of Interior Design, I extended an outside class invitation and scheduled private twenty-minute informal "get-to-know-you" sessions for each one of my students. I suggested they might enjoy an outsider's view on their personal aspirations and challenges and in return. I was hungry to see what made them tick as potential new entrants into my beloved industry.

Initially, I could see from a handful of the students, who rolled their eyes into the back of their sockets, that my invitation appeared like another assignment/burden, and it occurred to me that some of them were already out the door, psychologically. However, I kindly assured them the interviews were totally voluntary and confidential. There would be no mark assigned and no penalty for anyone who decided it wasn't for them. I promised the class that I would not keep any record of our private chats, but there *was* a caveat to the preparation for the appointment. Students who wanted to meet with me had to come prepared and respond to three specific open-ended questions, structured to maximize our time and focus.

1.   Tell me about your past or current passion and hobbies outside of school.

2.   As a senior student looking back, what do you believe are the academic strengths and weaknesses of the program (if any) at Ryerson?

3.   Share some of your dreams about your future, which may or may not have anything to do with interior design.

Shannon Kim was one of the most memorable students in my *seminar* class and well beyond the maturity level of her classmates. She was a formidable and exuberant presence, and I admired her courage immensely. On the last day of class, she sought me outside in the corridor to specifically invite me to view her thesis at the year-end show scheduled the following week. I was honoured and touched by her kind invitation, and I promised her that I would surely attend on one of three days that she mentioned. Early in the term, we had bonded in our preliminary introductions during our scheduled private meeting at my office.

At the time, Shannon had confided in me that she had been working with a law-enforcement agency prior to starting at Ryerson. She had no intention of "opening a can of worms," but she wanted to share how she and a number of Asian students mistrusted some of the students and faculty who did not respect them as equals and only "tolerated" them, simply because they looked different and spoke English as a second language. Without mentioning any specific names, she shared how she and a few of her friends felt marginalized throughout the four years and how she wished the faculty would emphasise to the student's acceptance of diversity and more multicultural approaches to collaborative learning.

When I asked her why she was motivated to bring this up with me as an outsider, she told me that she felt safe to share this one area of concern with someone who she believed understood discrimination as an openly gay professional in interior design. She found it very refreshing to have a professor who was open about his identity as a queer activist and an advocate for other minorities, such as herself. And she mentioned, "It would have been great to have had you as one of our full-time studio professors."

Shannon shared the truth of her personal experience at Ryerson, and her advocacy for her Asian classmates touched my heart. Her awareness of diversity issues could rival the knowledge of most of my professional and academic colleagues. Her authentic passion for others, coupled with her brilliant personality, was disarming! She captured my attention as a remarkable human being, and I told her that I believed she would one day make a profound difference in other people's lives.

As we ended our chat, I expressed how I looked forward to seeing her work on display at the year-end show. The only titillating clue she mentioned about her thesis was her intention to present her findings through a non-conventional use of several computers to communicate a multi-sensory, interactive experience, while pretty much all her classmates were presenting conventional manual drawings and renderings mounted on conventional panel-mounted boards, augmented by a sample board.

Anyhow, when I mentioned my intentional visit to Ryerson's year-end show to my colleague Joyce (from the academy), the two of us decided to go together. However, we opted out of the gala party scheduled on the opening

Thursday night, in favour of the following Saturday morning when it would be quiet and less hectic. We knew it would be the best opportunity to take a quiet, nuanced account of the student's preparation to enter the workforce. We both knew the International Academy of Design was gaining traction, as several of our graduates were finding entry-level employment in prominent firms such as YabuPushelberg; II BY IV Design, Gensler; and HOK. And we wanted to see how Ryerson students contrasted and excelled in comparison.

The International Academy of Design did not hold our year-end show on the school premises as Ryerson had. We convened our year-end show at the Design Exchange (DX) in Toronto's original stock exchange building. Our expensive gala was highly publicized in the media and netted an extraordinary turnout, followed by a huge uptick in applications to the academy. Of course, we were a privately funded school with significantly higher tuition costs, operational expenses, and corporate profit.

Many industry professionals were brought on board to both Ryerson and the academy, including Principal Eleanor Brydone from *Rice Brydone* and Marion Marshall from *Marshall Cummings*, who were some of the very first female trailblazers in a male-dominated industry who had a professional footprint in Toronto. They forged a path for younger generations of females, and their impact cannot be minimalized. Under the academic leadership of Ryerson's *Lorna Kelly* and the academy's Joyce O'Keefe, they became pivotal role models to scores of younger women, encouraging them not to play second fiddle and to aim for leadership roles.

However, when it came to a significant minority of professionally qualified gay men like me, who forged a path for a diverse range of male students both gay and straight, there is no question that the International Academy took the lead in advancing teaching opportunities for qualified instructors from the queer community. Clearly, role models and representation of sexual and cultural diversity was not prevalent when I was a student and professionally coming up in the ranks. And it is remarkable how little progress has been made in academia, considering how many gay men and lesbians have been practicing in the field for as far back as I can remember. In my opinion, there was and remains to this day a lack of respect and welcoming into the academic fold. However, I will say the opposite can be said of the students and younger generation. Unlike a few of my colleagues, Ryerson students lapped up every welcomed lick of queer diversity like a refreshing Dairy Queen on a hot summer day.

When I had earlier applied for the chair position when Professor Kelly retired, I was rejected by the search committee and offered a tenure-track position instead, which I graciously accepted. Ryerson's School of Interior Design certainly had a stellar reputation. No question about it. The program enjoyed being the only game in town for several decades. But things were changing, and other *Council for Interior Design Accreditation* (CIDA) accredited programs were sprouting and gaining in popularity. It was no longer a guarantee that our graduates would be the first to be hired. The workforce knew that diversity of learning, training, and visibility mattered in the industry.

I can't tell you how many times industry professionals contacted me over the years to vet applicants and graduates when I first began teaching at Ryerson. I was a very qualified straightshooter who did not pussyfoot around when it came to references. I knew the type of character and integrity the industry valued and was looking for. My professional history and reputation were well documented and known in many circles. More important, I had a clarity and delivery that belied my Canadian pretentiously polite identity. I was often described as a native New Yorker with my sometimes-brutal frankness that I came by naturally. It was one of the things I found most admirable about New Yorkers. You always knew where you stood, immediately.

I would share my wisdom with the class, and on occasion, I would need to meet with a select few who would have a pattern of either being late or not showing up for weeks at a time. Without the courtesy of touching base or providing a reasonable explanation, I was forthright in explaining that they were wasting everyone's valuable and limited one-on-one time in the studio.

My response to this type of student was, "I am not being paid to be your private tutor. Go back and review your responsibilities as delineated on Ryerson's website and in the school's handbook and course outline. If you need to be registered with the student access centre, you should not be waiting until the night before an assignment is due." I thought to myself, how in God's name did these students expect someone to ever hire them and pay them for selfish indifference to their individual responsibility and obligations? It was mind boggling to comprehend how some of them made it to the upper school level.

Interior design companies were not only scouting out the creative and technical best, but they were also looking favourably for applicants who possessed individual character and integrity that reflected the population's diversity. They homed in on how well an individual would work in team environments with a sense of humility and a willingness to grow. Nobody wanted a student who presented as uber-narcissistic and an inflated sense of self. Without fail, such persons went to the bottom of my list of recommended applicants in a no-nonsense decisive manner. I would inform the employers that I would preferably recommend an average student with great potential over a top-grade student who was an ass and clearly in desperate need of a personality adjustment, as we had enough of those folk in the industry already! And most of my professional contacts would invariably whole-heartedly agree. Marks were generally irrelevant unless the student was pursuing graduate studies.

Students were enrolled in a professional degree program, and this is where the rubber met the road. In the first couple of years at Ryerson, I found many of my colleagues to be a little out of touch with the professional world. I certainly didn't want to ruffle any feathers and chose to bide my time; I had never quite experienced such a politically charged department as I had at Ryerson. There was a lot of innuendo, gossip, and various alliances that felt at times like quicksand under my feet. And I found it hard to discern one pile of crap from the next. But I soon found my metaphoric hip waders and walked through it all with a plugged nose.

There were a few remarkable colleagues early on in my career who avoided the swamp of destructive gossip and shepherded me through the early stages of my career. During my first two years, I coordinated the first-year design studio with Professor Andrew Vasilevich and Arlene Dougall, who were always collegial and took time to answer questions. Likewise, my esteemed colleague Professor Bill Vine provided complete confidence in me and was never critical. They were exceptionally gracious, welcoming, and best of all, stink-free!

In my first year, I took on the role of course coordinator for graphic communication and remained in that position for close to twenty years. I built our reputation in the community for training interior designers who could sketch well and understood the theoretical underpinnings of perspective construction and design development. I must say how deeply hurt I felt when l was unceremoniously removed from this role in my last few remaining couple of years prior to my retirement. And I saw an immediate sharp decline in the students' manual sketching, as they increasingly got unchecked and tried to pass off their doodling as sketching.

Our local industry started to recognize the impact on their professional end, where more and more graduates could not communicate without being tethered to a laptop. And countless time was now spent on verbally explaining information that wasn't communicated in an effective alpha/numeric/graphic design sketch. What was once considered a strength of our graduates was apparently becoming a weakness, according to my industry colleagues and contacts. As usual, it took a while for me to suck it up and accept a changing of the guard, but eventually my bruised ego capitulated, and I had to let it go. Which, oddly enough, tied into my prior interest and research on multiple intelligences as it related to student learning.

One of my ongoing scholarly research umbrellas and theoretical applications to studio teaching was in "Multiple Intelligences" (MI) and the impact on student learning. It was clear to me that people who were quick to categorize and label others as left or right brain thinkers, seemed to be a bit naïve and ignorant to a range of learners who did not fall neatly into the two binary options of being a left- or right-brain thinker. The theoretical underpinning of multiple intelligences was researched and published in Howard Gardner's *Theory of Multiple Intelligences* (MI), and explored seven key areas of intelligence as identified by him:

1. Verbal Linguistic
2. Logical/Mathematical
3. Spatial
4. Musical/Rhythmic
5. Body/Kinesthetic
6. Naturalist
7. Interpersonal

Armed with this knowledge, I created a multi-disciplinary charrette to test the impact of MI on learning outcomes. In another building on campus, multi-disciplinary students who volunteered to participate were randomly placed into various groups to explore and apply the theory of MI with the purpose of identifying and presenting their key findings at the week-end charrette. The teams had to creatively problem-solve an existing design challenge on the campus determined by the group. My framework included a value-added learning enrichment process by including faculty observers and outside guests, who were pre-introduced to the role of Multiple Intelligences. They would simply be there to monitor and document the various strategies and collaboration of the groups and would only inject themselves on day two when they had an opportunity to provide critical feedback on their observations after the presentations were completed by the students. The outside guests had a specific role to provide input on how the student findings might help fill a gap between education and professional practice.

The *McConnell* research grant I was awarded covered the charrette expenses to advertise, recruit, and host this event at Ryerson University. The findings were peer assessed by an external panel of judges, including Architect *Sheila Penny* (Toronto School Board), *Dr. Rheta Rosen* (Director of Ryerson's Teaching and Learning Office), *George Sanders* (world-renowned Canadian watercolour artist and designer), and *Eleanor Brydone* (Principal Rice/Brydone).

There were two sample groups of multi-disciplinary volunteer students who were from a range of disciplines at Ryerson, including: the School of Nursing; Early Childhood Education; Architecture; and Interior Design. The first student volunteer group was designated *field-based problem solvers;* N=200 participants. The second group of volunteer student participants acted as student *peer assessors and process journal documenters;* N=75 participants. Meanwhile, based on the results tabulated from student surveys, it was interesting to see how many of the participants from interior design studio started the charrette with an assumption that their strongest intelligence was clearly spatial, and through the process came out on the other end with a completely different perspective and self-awareness.

In 2001, my research findings were selected to be peer-reviewed at the 2001 *Interior Design Educators Council (IDEC)*. The annual event rotated its location every year. This event and peer assessment of my experimental research was hosted by the *American Intercontinental University* in Atlanta.

Based on the survey results from my peers, the research and application to interior design thinking was well received, and I was encouraged by their comments to test it exclusively on interior design students.

Upon their recommendation, I would use Multiple Intelligences as a design charrette to kick-start third- and fourth-year design studios. And as a personal case study for my students, I used myself to illustrate the application to the MI, through the validation that musicality was my dominant intelligence and how I interpreted rhythmic cadences to visual language, concept development, and design development. It helped me abstract organic shapes and man-made geometry into two- and three-dimensional spatial development. I had spent my entire life in music including choirs, bands, and musicals.

Multiple Intelligences was a creative approach and an intellectual tool for expanding learning differences and how to communicate more expansively about the built environment. I would use examples of my professional work to show how I stitched my affinity and love of music into my interior design process. As I tried to convey to students, nothing is truly random, and nothing just pops into your head if you take time to do a deep dive into your life experiences. Science + Art + Self-Awareness = my personal algorithm for MI, and I shared this simple equation freely with my students.

Self-awareness was a construct that I embraced with the fact that I was a quintessential gay activist and proud to represent an alternative point of view to my students. I could freely tap dance and act my way through any situation with an abundance of flair and drama, much to the distaste and chagrin of one or two of my conservatively straight and homophobic male colleagues!

Case in point: on one of my teaching assessments, a colleague commented that I gestured too dramatically in class for his liking. What a myopic dick, I thought! My response to him was, "You try living in New York for a decade and then refrain from gestural mannerisms!" I found it all rather queer, myself. Admittedly, there were times when I had to take off my stilettoes and become "Professor Plasse-Terror" when I was called to battle over homophobia! Thank you very much to the credit of Miss Marsha P. Johnson. It was moronic Neanderthals like him who were lingering far too long in the School of Interior Design and motivated me to pursue my other umbrella area for scholarly research and creative applications for integrating queer diversity into the program.

As an educator and queer activist, it was important that I introduced my students to LGBTQ+ visibility through community outreach projects that identified unique client profiles for the students. They learned it was okay to look and act differently as part of a universal queer minority that transcended all cultures, races, societal norms, and beliefs. Ryerson's student diversity encouraged me to talk about how it was not only okay to look and act differently from the majority, but it was also our professional and moral obligation to see our differences as a strength.

My students were introduced to the concept of pro bono design opportunities and community service to marginalized communities who couldn't afford to advocate for themselves, underscoring issues of poverty, accessibility, gender diversity, ethnicity, race, and cultural restraints. It was important to me that my interior design students had some real-life community service and supervision before they graduated. In my opinion, that was the gold standard of a true and honourable professional. And for young designers interviewing for a job, you might consider a good response to the common last question by an interviewer which is normally "is there anything else you would like to know about our company?" You should be prepared for that one, as it will leave a lasting impression if you answer it with some forethought. My advice is you might want to consider asking how the firm responds to community outreach and public service.

My pedagogical imperative was to destigmatize vulnerable students from marginalized communities through experiential learning and in-situ field research within our local community. I advanced "community service" as a small part of the course mandate, whether it involved: volunteering at food drives; community-based fundraisers; pride events; or other queer initiatives in the Church Street community outside the front door of Ryerson's School of Interior Design. Placemaking memories for my students was a part of my philosophical paradigm and complimented the hands-on studio learning, inside and "out."

Many of my Ryerson graduates will recall my Toronto-based, queer-friendly roster of clients and curriculum studio-based projects, such as: *Buddies in Bad Time Theatre*; *People with AIDS* (PWA); *the AIDS Committee of Toronto* (ACT); *Michelle Du Barry and The Great Imposters*;

the *Toronto-Trans Community Project* (with the fabulous Enza Anderson), and *Parents and Friends of Lesbians and Gays* (PFLAG). External industry experts were happy to mentor my students throughout the term and not merely show up unprepared for the final presentations. Iterative student design development and ongoing mentoring were essential in my studios; I was always humbled and very grateful to my industry colleagues for their extensive time in volunteering from start to finish. And it didn't hurt that many of my professional volunteers were amongst the first who offered my students employment to boot!

Further, I offered highly creative for-profit projects such as the fictionalized *Superman Can Publishers* and *the world-renowned Canadian Mac Cosmetics,* which targeted the interest of young working adults and students. And finally, there was *the Downtown Animal Hospital* in the heart of the Gay Village, whereby anyone who did not love a pet was no friend of mine. To not consider the therapeutic role of pets in planning, programming, and designing for wellbeing continues to be immoral in my book. Even my dentist brings in an emotional support animal to help calm the clients and mitigate the requirement for pain management.

I would never have survived my tenure at Ryerson's School of Interior Design if it had not been for the close support of Dee-Dee, along and the friendship of two other colleagues, Professor Samantha Sannella and Dr. Lorella Di Cintio. It seemed I was forever threatening to resign from a lack of administrative support. However, Arlene would always manage to straighten out my one remaining fried nerve and insist the students and the industry needed me to hang in there for as long as I possibly could. No surprise, I was a bit of a drama queen at times but it sure was a great cultural tool that allowed me to throw off shade and press on. No one really took my threats seriously. Least of all myself.

My beloved colleague *Professor Samantha Sannella and I collaborated on the main third-year design studio in both semesters of the school year.* In a funny sort of way, we considered ourselves not just friends but surrogate siblings; she had unexpectedly lost her brother Michael, and I had lost my sister Janet. When the two of us met, we knew we were the missing puzzle pieces in our personal lives, and we spent a lot of time outside the school. We equally matched our passion and pure unadulterated joy for the students. We worked their asses off, to be frank; we knew how demanding our industry was. We spent countless hours discussing and researching how best to prepare our students so they could execute a high level of conceptual thinking and creative design development. And to our surprise, many students exceeded our scope of work and appreciated the clarity of our expectations.

But it wasn't all about the hard work—we always made time to ensure the students had a good time and a few laughs at our expense along the way. There was one occasion on Halloween when "Sam" had the brilliant idea for us to show up for class in drag; she would pretend to be Professor Michael, and I would pretend to be Professor Sam. Let's just say that a few of our colleagues recoiled in horror when they saw us, but we paid them no nevermind. We marched into our third-year class in full character and began our opening remarks and lecture in full drag, as if it were not Halloween.

When our class was over, I hobbled back to my office in Sam's high heels and chaffed ankles, in anticipation of an outstanding appointment with a fourth-year foreign exchange student regarding his preliminary thesis development. Immediately after arriving back, I kicked off Sam's open-back heels; my feet burned and ached as I sat at the window desk. I needed a few seconds to quickly review my recent grading and notes about the student's recent thesis proposal. My focus was so intense that I momentarily forgot how ridiculous I looked dressed in my farcical Halloween drag and red wig. Sweat was starting to drip down my face from the heat of the wig, and before I had a chance to remove it, I heard a soft *knock-knock* on the door. Without turning, I said, "Come on in" as I pulled up a guest chair to my counter where I had his graded thesis report opened as a reference.

The foreign exchange student sat down next to me and appeared even more painfully shy than he normally was in class. His English comprehension was rudimentary, so I proceeded to articulate the strengths and significant weaknesses that had culminated in a borderline passing grade for his effort. I turned to him and looked for some sort of a response before moving on with suggestions for improvement. He didn't say a word and simply capitulated with an affirming nod from his head. No words. After a prolonged moment with no "verbal" response to my feedback, I said, "You've got to take this constructive feedback more seriously, young man!"

And at that precise moment, I caught a shocking glimpse of myself in the reflection of the window! Oh crap! He must have regretted ever registering with me as his thesis advisor. I am sure he thought Canadian professors were remarkably weird and strange. I am sure he had no concept it was about Halloween, and I speculated he was about to book the next possible flight back to Taiwan.

Fortunately, I was interrupted by Samantha's greeting: "Hey Michael, are you ready for a girl's lunch date?"

"Are you kidding me, dressed in this crap?" I replied. The confused and terrified student looked at his watch and mumbled his unconvincing thanks for the feedback. He literally ran out the door. Meanwhile, I pulled Sam into my office and shut the door behind her. I told her what had just happened after I caught my hideous reflection in the glass window and realized that I had not explained to the exchange student why I was dressed this way. Sam broke out in hysterical laughter! She plopped into one of my guest chairs with tears of laughter forming in the corners of her eyes. At that point, I snatched that dollar-store wig off my head, dropped it into her lap, and walked out the door to change at the nearby washroom.

Later in the semester, as we were approaching Christmas, I figured it was now time for me to exact a little revenge on Sam's Halloween drag extravaganza caper. I told her it would be fun for me to dress up like Santa and she could come as Mrs. Claus. Our class could easily be transformed into "Santa's Workshop." I would install a miniature artificially lit tree and a few other holiday decorations. I suggested that while I was doing the final lecture, she could serve our students hot chocolate with mini marshmallows and home-baked cookies.

This time, however, I was not going to be outdone by Sam. She showed up looking like a traditional Mrs. Claus, wearing an old grey wig, gold spectacles, and a white-ruffled apron. On the other hand, I showed up looking like a modern, well-groomed, and physically fit Santa Claus. I walked into the class wearing a vibrant red pair of designer painter pants, a form-fitting long-sleeve red undershirt, black suspenders, and shiny black construction boots. My face sprouted a two-day beard, and my head was topped off with a stylish Santa toque.

Samantha looked at me and said, "Oh thanks! You made me look like an old granny, while you look like you just stepped off the cover of a GQ magazine!" Merry Christmas, Sam! And now it was my time for a good laugh as she pouted and served the students their treats.

We were a united team of colleagues in our ongoing effort to bring periodic surprises to our class; it was essential for us to create great placemaking memories that were not normally a part of the school's typical studio experience! We freely argued different perspectives to encourage diversity of thinking and snuffed out even a whiff of prescriptive responses to design thinking and problem-solving. We worked hard as hell to make learning fun and underscored a serious boatload of project expectation with strategic moments of levity. No one complained about the workload and frequently surpassed what we asked of them. Eventually, good old Professor Sam had other exciting plans and goals for her future. I knew well in advance of her impending departure, as she had asked me for a professional reference to submit along with her application for the position of president of the *Design Exchange* (DX). I reassured her that she had the job in the bag and within a few short weeks, she was awarded the position. She may have only lasted a few short years at Ryerson, but her impact on her students and me was phenomenal. We would continue to meet regularly for lunch and share our latest adventures and work highlights.

On June 21, 2005, Sam hosted a huge design gala on my behalf as a fundraiser to support *Casey House*, which provided compassionate and palliative support for people living with HIV/AIDS. My project, *Sew Who Cares,* began as a research initiative for educational enrichment and community service that I had worked on for the past six months. Earlier in March, my scholarly research and creative work (SRC) was informally peer reviewed by the local queer community and endorsed by *Casey House.*

President Samantha embraced my project and offered to help coordinate, finance, and curate every detail of the gala, including a display of donated quilts for auction that I had solicited and secured from various members of the Toronto's Gay Village. In addition, Sam provided live music; party favours; alcohol; food; entertainment, and so much more! I will always be grateful to her. We were clearly each other's biggest cheerleader! Like the previous undertaking of my Unmasking of Our Interiors at the University of Manitoba, the community outreach was robustly supported and lauded as a meaningful contribution to others less fortunate.

In terms of scholarly peer review, I submitted my pedagogical research findings to the University of Toronto, and I was approved to present two distinct, community-based research projects at their Healthy Queer Conference, sponsored by *the Ontario Institute of Studies in Education* (OISE) on June 6, 2008. The two Toronto-based design case studies were based on *PWA* (People with AIDS) and *Buddies in Bad Times Theatre (the largest black-box theatre in North America dedicated exclusively to queer culture).*

Both projects were presented after the keynote speaker inside the large auditorium. The keynote speaker was the proudly out, gay Canadian politician and advocate for human rights Mr. George Smitherman, who worked in the Legislative Assembly and represented the riding of Toronto Centre. It was an honour to follow his introduction and it was of great significance to my advocacy of queer rights and integration of queer diversity into the curriculum at Ryerson's School of Interior Design.

As best as I know, no previous faculty from *Ryerson's School of Interior Design* had ever participated in queer diversity research, nor presented at conferences like the *Healthy Queer Conference* at the University of Toronto nor at the annual Interior Design Educator's Council (IDEC) conference. And although I had invited colleagues to come support me, I was met with anaemic apologies that they were "too busy and could not make it." It didn't feel good as I had frequently attended presentations of their research when I was invited.

In retrospect, my twenty years at Ryerson University were some of the most challenging and best years of my life. Everything I did was in the best interest of preparing my students for the world outside. My final chapter at Ryerson barely captures the totality of what I learned and gained in my personal and academic growth that was rooted in human values and ethical design. I had managed to stitch my past into a harmonious whole, retaining a sense of pride and dignity. My message for any of my struggling gay youth/adult-at-risk who wanted to carve out a future in interior design was, "Be audacious and find your way forward on your own terms. You were born with natural instincts that are unique to yourself and you must do whatever it takes to realize your dreams of a better tomorrow." I cautioned them to close their ears to the naysayers and to be fearless. I thought they needed to march their ass gayly forward, holding their God-given head up high! I knew from experience they could find a way to do it! From personal experience, I assured them that their dreams would be manifested, providing they stay focussed and self-disciplined.

Now that I am in the position of a gay elder who has amassed a lifetime of queer and straight allies, I can tell you that there were plenty of marginalized folks who did not get a fair kick at the can along the course of my personal and professional journey. Many suffered and even died. And not only from AIDS-related causes, but through societal brutality and homophobia that silenced their voices.

Fortunately, my dear friend Bill Novak and his partner Norman, who I met years earlier when I was a student as Pratt Institute, were the exception. They made a surprise visit to Toronto during my last year teaching at Ryerson. Bill and Norman were intellectuals and principled men with good values. In a sea of gay men looking out for themselves, they always stood out and did not succumb to homophobia at a time when there was no such thing as legal gay marriage. Bill and Norman were ahead of the curve as unprotected gay men with no legal rights. Bill had adopted Norman as his legal son back in the year 2000. By that time, they had left New York and retired to Bucks County in Pennsylvania, which did not recognize their domestic partnership. This was ground-breaking at the time and was the only option. Gay marriage didn't happen until decades after the adoption, and when it did, the local judge agreed to vacate the adoption in front of thirty of their friends.

A recent documentary film that specifically featured Bill and Norman's story premiered at the Toronto Film festival around 2018-2019, and it happened to be the first time I saw Bill and Norman outside of New York. During their Toronto visit, they were conveniently housed at the Courtyard Marriot, right outside my back door at Alexander and Yonge Street. After their premier, Bill told Norman that I lived somewhere close by on Alexander. As they strolled around, they randomly stopped a stranger and neighbour who happened to live in my building. When he asked him if he knew of Michael Plasse-Taylor, he said, "Of course, he actually lives in my building," and he escorted them to my front door. The next thing I knew, my doorbell rang, and when I looked through the peephole, I just about crapped my pants! Bill and Norman were standing outside my door! It had been at least twenty years since I'd last seen them back in New York before they retired to Bucks County.

I immediately invited them both in, hoping that they would at least have time for a quick coffee in their busy promotions during their weekend visit. Our brief get-together was spontaneous, and a joyous surprise. It was a miracle that a random resident let them in our secured building, escorted

314

them up the elevator, and then ushered them right to my apartment door. Talk about co-operative living. I had some pretty kind neighbours and friends at City Park who went out of their way, and I was thankful for the serendipitous timing. Everyone seemed to be in the right place at the right time, without advance warning and preparation.

I hadn't seen Bill for decades and he looked recognizable but seriously aged and walking with a cane. When Bill and Norm talked, I discovered they were both making plans to go into the same nursing home very soon, and it kind of took me breath away. I am not overly religious and probably not the best example of a Christian, but I knew God had a hand in this chance meeting at my apartment; we all implicitly understood that it was probably the last time we would see each other staring into each other's eyes as a portal to our very souls. Then in a flash, our visit was over. We kissed and lightly hugged goodbye for the last time. They were headed back to the hotel to pack their bags and return home to beautiful Buck's County.

I am alive today and feel blessed to share our collective queer history through a personal narrative that I trust will resonate to younger generations. Contributions by gays and lesbians in our professional interior design organizations is a legacy that must not be forgotten and glossed over. Interior design was one of the safest professions to implicitly recognize and support queer diversity. Many of us are a testament to the record of our body of knowledge that we have carefully co-crafted over the years. *I am hoping that my effort* to forge a more queer-friendly inclusive path in design leadership through teaching will be built upon by ongoing educators from within our community.

Our professional history will not be thoroughly documented and taught without the nuance of those who fought with courage and personal risk for diversity and inclusion. I know I have done my very best to initiate and integrate diversity into interior design academics in all three of the post-secondary settings I was blessed to be a part of in Canada. And I can tell you quite frankly it felt very lonely at times, but it was all well worth seeing the positive impact that I had on marginalized students.

However, I know from travelling on work-related matters and committees that there are many minorities who continue to work in locations where it is unsafe to live their authentic truth. I hope I have illuminated a precedence for activism that can open a wider path of diversity and visibility. It is who we are as Canadians and what we value at home and abroad. And I hope in some small way that beyond my students and graduates, our industry leaders will find some wisdom in my personal narrative and consider, with a wink and a nod of approval, to embrace someone who needs an opportunity and a mentor. A smile and a little love can go a long way, wouldn't you agree?

Parents and Friends of Lesbians and Gays (PFLAG) RSID class and industry mentors

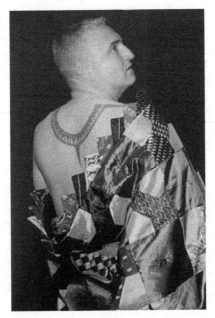

Sew Who Cares? Design exchange fundraiser for Casey House.
June 21, 2005. Ryerson University. Professor Plasse-Taylor

ROUNDTABLE ON QUEER DIVERSITY & FINAL PROJECT PRESENTATIONS

STUDENTS, GUESTS, DX PRESIDENT & MICHELLE DU BARRY

PWA AND QUEER GUESTS IN STUDENTEXCHANGE

QUEER DESIGN & EXCHANGE OF IDEAS

STUDENT INTERIOR DESIGNER: CHRISTIANNE CELOTTI

Michelle Du Barry and The Great Imposters Queer Diversity Project
Ryerson School of Interior Design/Professor Plasse-Taylor

MICHAEL PLASSE-TAYLOR

Presentation Abstracts
(Listed in order of presentation)

Buddies In Bad Times Project (10:30 am - OISE Auditorium)
Michael Plasse-Taylor
Ryerson University

The Buddies In Bad Times Project explores, integrates and affirms queer culture and gender diversity into The School of Interior Design's curriculum at Ryerson University, Toronto. The final studio-based project will explore the role of queer gender identity as it relates to North America's largest and oldest community-based queer theatre venue. The goal will be to explore how queer culture and gender diversity awareness and knowledge translates into design application? How will student awareness and design knowledge be applied to a cultural a community queer venue that supports society members primarily identifying as Gay, Lesbian, Bisexual, or Transgender (GLBT)? Teaching and learning strategies will include a range of experiences, such as: collaborative and individual case study research, self-directed individual or group field-trips to queer venues or cultural events, GLBT Canadian literature research, Local GLBT community icons, interviews, verbal discourse. Students will research local Canadian GLBT heroes and supporters relative to queer culture in Canadian history and identify design intervention areas for innovative and creative design programming and development. Students will explore unique social spaces, sensory experiences, community land marking, way finding features, and integration of community heroes and benefactors into art, sculpture, and branding. The project concludes with a presentation to faculty, peers, industry professionals and invited queer community stakeholders from "Buddies".

EPILOGUE
Associate Professor Emeritus
2019-Present

Like the Japanese art of Kintsugi that mends broken pieces with gold, I have learned over the years to methodically restore my heart and soul from a broken past. Instead of discarding the shards, I have been blessed with an opportunity to reassemble all the pieces into a new whole, using forgiveness as the golden glue to emphasize the beauty of all my imperfections, cracks, and fissures. No question, it has been a spiritually painstaking process, but I believe in my soul that if I can do it, then other people who feel broken and unworthy can find a modicum of inspiration in my story. Over the years, I have shared my wisdom with struggling friends and students at risk, utilizing the *principles* and *elements* of design that I have stored in my toolbox of communication over the years.

A healthy interior for myself has manifested my wellbeing as a priority after years of denial and neglect. It's taken a while to figure that it was okay to stop and look back without guilt and shame over some of the brutal choices I have had to make in my life, along with the family and friends that have fallen by the wayside. Intrinsically, I knew that I had a sense of place and purpose greater than what I could have ever imagined for myself, which is one of the reasons why I deviated from my professional practice after several years of personal success and transitioned into educating the next generation, underpinned with decades of activism and community service. And that's a big deal. It took me a hell of a lot of years to look in the mirror and not see a mask reflected.

All the personal sacrifices I have made in my life have led to my courage to remove the service smile I hid behind whenever I went out into the world. And now I find myself naturally smiling at the most random things whenever I go out. I am truly grateful for my challenging childhood, as it crystalized my character and strength from a young age when I was more resilient and could run without fear of the unknown.

When I was much younger, I leveraged my mistakes and failures that led to countless opportunities and experiences that have moved me forward. My stubbornness and steely focus on education and passion for interior design was the only passport and stamp of approval I needed. At the time, my empathy and activism for marginalized queer youth was the motivational bedrock of my early life. However, over the years, the range of nuance has exponentially embraced a broader, multi-generational epidemic of disenfranchised and persecuted minorities under the queer umbrella of non-binary folks, races, religion, and diversity of age. And I continue to use my personal platform whenever I can.

Regardless of my past personal loss of romantic partners, I did give romance one last shot on Valentine's Day back in 1998. I had met a beautiful man in *Starbucks* during a winter storm, and for whatever reason, God only knows, he pursued me, and I caved at the notion that he wanted a relationship with me. "Sparky" and I gave the relationship our best, but I struggled to let down my guard and trust again. And so, we ended our relationship after three short years, after I started to teach at Ryerson. By that point, I knew I was utterly depleted, and I knew that I needed time to fall in love with myself first. I decided to metaphorically marry myself, with a promise to heal and love myself for the remainder of my life. And so far, this life strategy has brought me peace and a newfound sense of self-respect.

The freedom and insight that comes with reaching a mature age is the world's best secret, if you are lucky enough to survive. I would have to take umbrage and disagree with the screen legend and gay icon *Bette Davis* that "getting old ain't for sissies!" I say it sure the hell is, and the bigger the sissy the better! Enough of toxic masculinity—it serves no purpose. There is nothing tougher than unmasking a fierce sissy!

I can end this memoir with the knowledge that I have outlived most everyone I have known and loved. And I will always admire and respect the fearless *sissy-boy* mantle that I was assigned in my childhood. Sissies are heroes; they serve as a metaphoric slap in the face of male toxicity. To that I say "sissy on" to all my friends! I hope we continue to cross paths and raise eyebrows along the journey, fighting for equality and advancing possibilities for the disenfranchised in the world. You are not alone at any age or stage in your life. But you've got to fight for the privilege of a better life. This is what I know with conviction: opportunities will not be handed to you unless you actively seek them out.

I am truly blessed to have earned the respect of many colleagues and countless students who have enriched my life. They have become a part of my adopted family over the years. And to this day and through the gift of social media, I can continue to mentor and inspire the next generation to do great things that better the world we all share.

Although my nascent retirement goal was to step back for one year from social media and limit any contact with professional acquaintances, colleagues, and past student to create a *tabula rasa*, I am happy I met that goal and I look forward to reconnecting to my future. Moving well into my second year of retirement, I feel completely refreshed, with my old sense of levity and spunk. We will see how long that works out. If history is a past indicator, I should not only be fine but even freer to express myself. As a senior citizen, I can openly do and say outrageous things, and younger folks will just write it off as speculated senility. I am honoured to follow in the footsteps of all the senior crazies before me; they have my utmost respect!

Recently, I explored one of the sources of enjoyment from my youth, and that was singing! In my delusion, I imagined that I could still use my voice in a pleasing lyrical way and carry a tune. After all, I was once recognized as a decent singer throughout my teenage years in the choir and in all the past performances of my high school musicals. So, I thought to myself, let's dust off that old album of past hits and give the old singing-with-gusto a go, much to the chagrin of my neighbour Bob, who I swear could hear the ultrasonic chirps of a bat in the dark! Oh well! I will not be restrained by his commentary of my choice of musicals and opera, but it does make me chuckle. I have paid a lifelong price to sing with unbridled joy, and so be it! Let's see what else can be manifested after I publish this memoir. I hope and pray that my creative passion takes on unexpected and welcomed new opportunities.

I recognize that I am my own best company, but I must admit I do not live alone. In fact, I cohabit with three fur babies who give me reason to shovel crap with a smile each day. There is *Missy*, my gentle boxer dog who is loyal and loving as she continues to wind down into her golden years. Then there's *Rib*, my senior tuxedo cat, who still thinks he runs the household and follows me around talking cat-smack at me. And finally, there is my crazy wild child and first generation (F1) Savannah *Kit*, who inspires me to stay a bit feral and unpredictable. Everything considered, they complement my complex personality and a life that is in harmony with the world; this is my latest iteration and concept of a beloved family.

Clearly, I am not the best example of a Christian, and I certainly have been no angel to others in my lifetime. However, if Jesus Christ said, "I am the way, the truth and the light," and the spirit of God is within all of us as I had learned as a young child, then I will continue to have faith in myself and ignore the judgement of others. And for the price of a coffee and a crumble-ass donut from my satellite office at the window counter at Tim Horton's, I will gladly hock my memoir and signature to anyone willing to shell out a loonie or two! I mean, let's get serious, girls, a pension can only take a gay widower so far!

I am telling you straight-up, as best that I can, that it wasn't always easy marching gaily forward as a homeless and transient adolescent decades ago. Clearly, I don't welcome that same fate in my humble "golden years." My nascent retirement and beloved ghettoized queer community that I cherish is currently plagued by an influx of strung-out addicts and homophobes on the prowl. There has been a recent resurgence of hatred and inhumanity directed once again at queers and other marginalized minorities. As the new condo towers go up, so does the local crime. The neighbourhood is a complete contradiction and contrast in lifestyles and the only thing guaranteed about my future is that my taxes will surely increase and demise. Even the gay politicians have packed up their big Liberal girl panties and moved out of the hood.

However, I remain grounded as a fierce guardian to my gay roots and the gritty-grey streets that I grew up on. If I can forge a modest path from the Dark Ages of my past, then I hope my wisdom can serve as a lesson for other vulnerable youth-at-risk. Things will get better for the new generations of marginalized and disenfranchised youth. And as far as I can see, the ongoing fight for equality and visibility may always be a local and global issue, but today we have considerably more public awareness and support not afforded in my generation. Some of us queer elders are still on active duty and not giving up.

To put it more bluntly in Professor Plasse-Terror terminology, if you don't like the circumstances of where you live, then pack your hot rollers, stamp your own passport, and say adieu to a better life elsewhere. And then haul ass, kids! There are wonderful people/mentors and places in the world with welcoming arms to give you a respite and the wings that you have earned to soar above it all. I suggest my kindred souls take a moment to reframe their self-worth and rightful place in the world. Have a little courage and take a risk! Sometimes, it takes time to recognize that you are the gatekeeper of your precious life, as I have learned from personal experience. However, there is one outstanding question lurking at the end of my memoir. Who else cares about the ***UNMASKING OF OUR INTERIORS?***

Kintsugi

Looking ahead to a creative retirement

APPENDIX
Maternal Family Genealogy

RELATIONSHIP	NAME	DATE OF BIRTH	DATE OF DEATH	CAUSE OF DEATH
Maternal Great- Grandfather	**Fred** Pratt	June 5 1880	October 9 1977	Natural Cause
Maternal Great- Grandmother	**Esther** Watson	January 17 1887	August 31 1978	Natural Cause
Maternal Grandmother	**Lucina** Kirk/ Pratt	March 31 1904 Married June 15 1903	January 3 1999	Natural Cause
Buried at Woodland Cemetery in London, Ontario				
Maternal Great-Aunt	**Violet** Pratt	February 10 1910	April 1 1918	Influenza *Buried in the USA*
Maternal Great-Aunt	**Ruth** Pratt	February 14 1915	April 1 1918	Influenza *Buried in the USA*
Maternal Great-Uncle	**Edward** Pratt	April 13 1918	February 4 1986	Natural Cause
Buried at Woodland Cemetery in London, Ontario				
Maternal Uncle	**Keith** Pratt	October 14 1930	Unknown	Unknown
Maternal Aunt	**Mary** Pratt	Unknown	Unknown	Unknown
Fraternal Uncle	**Kenny** Kirk	Unknown	Unknown	Unknown

RELATIONSHIP	NAME	DATE OF BIRTH	DATE OF DEATH	CAUSE OF DEATH
MOTHER	Edna Fissenden Taylor/ Kirk	August 9 1925	May 12 2000	Alzheimer's

Mother Buried at Meadowvale Cemetery in Brampton, Ontario

Maternal *Half-Sister*	**Edna** Krychenko Brennan/Taylor	December 6 1942		
Maternal *Half-Brother*	**Kenneth** Taylor	March 9 1944		
Maternal *Half-Sister*	**Lois** Livingston Webber/Taylor	February 25 1946		
Robert (*Bobby*) *Half-Brother*	**Robert** Taylor	1947	1947	Infant Jaundice
Maternal *Half-Brother*	**Dale** Taylor *Raised by Grandparents*	1948		
Maternal *Half-Brother*	**John** Taylor	December 23 1949	1990	Suicide Car Crash
Full Sister	**Rosemary** Graessel (Plasse)Taylor	January 29 1950		
Full Sister	**Janet** Lucina (Plasse)Taylor	May 3 1953	December 23 1973	Suspicious TBD
SELF	**Michael Thomas** Plasse-Taylor	May 31 1954		
Full Brother	**Jackie** Joseph (Plasse)Taylor	June 16 1955		

Maternal *Half-Brother*	**Ricky** Taylor	July 12 1959		
Maternal *Half-Brother*	**Greg** Fissenden Taylor	June 21 1964	*Resident of Florida*	
Stepbrother	**Paul Fissenden**	**Unknown**	*Resident of the United States*	

FATHER LUCIEN PLASSE
Paternal Family/Partial Genealogy

RELATIONSHIP	NAME	DATE OF BIRTH	DATE OF DEATH	CAUSE OF DEATH
Grandmother	**Angela** Plasse	May 26 1892	1924	Unknown
Aunt	**Marie-Louise** Plasse	Unknown	Unknown	Unknown
Father	**Lucien** Plasse	1921	1973	Stroke
Buried in Saint Rose DeLima of Chicopee Cemetery Chicopee Hampden County Massachusetts, USA				
Uncle	**Alpherie** Plasse	October 15 1912	1985	Natural Cause

CPSIA information can be obtained
at www.ICGtesting.com
Printed in the USA
LVHW081353010722
722551LV00018B/1032